Four Great Decipherments of Ancient Times

- ➤ Ancient Egyptian: finally deciphered in 1822 with the help of the Rosetta
- ➤ Cuneiform: deciphered in the mid-19 Rawlinson.
- ➤ Linear B: deciphered by Michael Ventr
- ➤ Maya Glyphs: cracking the code is an on-going process.
- ➤ Ancient scripts that have yet to be convincingly deciphered include Linear A from Crete, the Indus Valley Script, and Rongo-Rongo from Easter Island.

The Seven Wonders of the Ancient World

- ➤ The Great Pyramid at Giza
- ➤ The Pharos Lighthouse at Alexandria
- ➤ The Hanging Gardens of Babylon
- ➤ The Mausoleum at Halicarnassus
- ➤ The Colossus of Rhodes
- ➤ The Temple of Artemis at Ephesus
- ➤ Statue of Zeus at Olympia

alpha
books

Twenty-Five Great Archeological Sites and Discoveries

(A mere selection and in no particular order.)

- ➤ Sumerian Royal Death Pits of Ur, Iraq.
- ➤ Otzi the Iceman, Italian Alps.
- ➤ Machu Picchu, Peru—a lost Incan royal estate.
- ➤ Tomb of Tutankhamun, Egypt—intact tomb of a pharaoh.
- ➤ Tomb of the Maya ruler Pacal, Mexico.
- ➤ Royal Moche Tombs of Sipan, Peru.
- ➤ L'Anse aux Meadow, Newfoundland—a New World Viking settlement.
- ➤ Pompeii and Herculaneum, Italy—Roman cities preserved in volcanic ash.
- ➤ Lascaux Cave, France—art from the Ice Age.
- ➤ Knossos, Crete—the ancient Minoan capital.
- ➤ The Great Zimbabwe, Zimbabwe—a magnificent African city built in stone.
- ➤ Terracotta Army, China—ceramic guardians of China's first emperor.
- ➤ Sutton Hoo, England—the inland burial of an Anglo-Saxon ship.
- ➤ Dead Sea Scrolls—early Biblical manuscripts.
- ➤ The Nubian Pyramids, Sudan.
- ➤ Easter Island, Pacific—big stone heads on a tiny remote island.
- ➤ Angkor Wat, Cambodia—temples in the jungle.
- ➤ Ozette, Washington—village preserved by mudslide.
- ➤ The Cheops "solar boat," Egypt—buried at the base of the Great Pyramid.
- ➤ Macedonian Royal Tombs, Macedonia—may be the tomb of Phillip II.
- ➤ Mesa Verde, Colorado—Anasazi cliff dwellings.
- ➤ Mohenjodaro, Pakistan—ancient sophisticated city of the Harappans.
- ➤ Stonehenge, England—enigmatic stone circle.
- ➤ Cleopatra's Sunken Palace, Alexandria, Egypt.

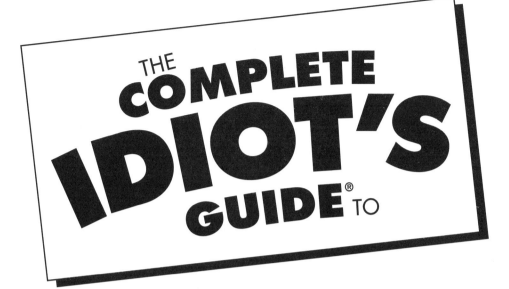

THE COMPLETE IDIOT'S GUIDE® TO

Lost Civilizations

by Donald P. Ryan, Ph.D.

alpha books

A Division of Macmillan General Reference
A Pearson Education Macmillan Company
1633 Broadway, New York, NY 10019

Macmillan General Reference books may be purchased for business or sales promotional use. For information please write: Special Markets Department, Macmillan Publishing USA, 1633 Broadway, New York, NY 10019.

International Standard Book Number: 0-02862954-X
Library of Congress Catalog Card Number: 97-80967

01 00 99   8 7 6 5 4 3 2 1

Interpretation of the printing code: the rightmost number of the first series of numbers is the year of the book's printing; the rightmost number of the second series of numbers is the number of the book's printing. For example, a printing code of 99-1 shows that the first printing occurred in 1999.

Printed in the United States of America

Alpha Development Team

Publisher
Kathy Nebenhaus

Editorial Director
Gary M. Krebs

Managing Editor
Bob Shuman

Marketing Brand Manager
Felice Primeau

Acqisitions Editor
Jessica Faust

Development Editors
Phil Kitchel
Amy Zavatto

Assistant Editor
Georgette Blau

Production Team

Development Editor
Mary Russell

Production Editor
Tammy Ahrens

Copy Editor
John Jones

Cover Designer
Mike Freeland

Photo Editor
Richard H. Fox

Illustrator
Jody P. Schaeffer

Book Designers
Scott Cook and Amy Adams of DesignLab

Indexer
Tim Wright

Layout/Proofreading
Angela Calvert
Mary Hunt
Julie Trippetti

Contents at a Glance

Contents

xiii

Foreword

The detective work that reveals our hidden past is called archaeology—the public is fascinated by it. Each week there seems to be a television documentary or special that features Egyptian tombs or lost Mayan cities. The public's interest seems unflagging. There is just something about our past that attracts us. Having been an archaeologist for 25 years, I know why it interests me, and as a teacher I know what interests students. Archaeology is our chance to learn something new and surprising about our past—something that we never even imagined existed—and to be amazed at the sophistication of civilizations now lost.

Of course, what we really want is a time machine, but for now, at least, physics denies us that, and we are left with what Hollywood has to offer—or archaeology. Our hominid ancestors have been on this planet for some four million years. About 5,000 years ago, the first civilizations arose in the wake of the invention of agriculture. A lot has happened in the 250 generations since. Parts of the story are known, but much also remains hidden beneath the surface in ruins that await discovery. And there *is* still more to discover, as each new press release shows us.

Often we hear extravagant claims—mummies that walk, lost continents that have slipped beneath the oceans, alien airports in Peru. How in the world can the ordinary person tell sense from nonsense and fact from fiction? Students always ask, "But, how do you *know* that's true?"

Don Ryan's book provides us with some of the answers. Not only does he introduce us to amazing past civilizations that really did exist and debunk some of the myths about those that didn't, he also shows us the "how" of modern professional archaeology. In these pages you can learn the methods archaeologists use to find out about the past—how they date ancient finds, how they figure out ancient lifeways from the trash left behind, and much more. You can learn how we actually determine what things are true about the past, and distinguish fact from fiction. After all, human history on this planet is amazing enough all by itself; it doesn't need embellishment with fanciful or outrageous stories to hold our interest.

Don Ryan, Ph.D., scholar and explorer, brings nearly two decades of experience as an archaeologist to these pages. He has worked in Egypt's Valley of the Kings among the world's most famous ruins. He has discovered and explored ancient tombs. He has walked among the gigantic Moai of Easter Island and has dug in ancient sites on the Canary Islands. This is both a personal story of his work on past civilizations as well as a light-hearted account of his profession—peppered with anecdotes—that shows he is a serious archaeologist who doesn't take himself too seriously. A rare breed.

It seems there's not an airline trip or dinner party where someone doesn't say to me: "Oh, I always wanted to be an archaeologist." Did you ever wonder what it would be like? Now, between these covers, you can find out for sure.

—Richard E. Reanier, Ph.D.

Richard E. Reanier, Ph.D., has been a professional archaeologist for 25 years, with experience in North America, Europe, and the Pacific. His research focuses on the archaeology of the Arctic and the peopling of the New World. With more than 80 publications to his name, he is best known for helping lead the research team that discovered evidence of ancient Paleoindians living above the Arctic Circle in Alaska at the close of the last Ice Age. His recent research includes a project on Easter Island in the South Pacific and a study of the prehistory of an Eskimo village. He is president of his own archaeological consulting firm, and has research affiliations with the University of Alaska Fairbanks and the State University of New York at Brockport.

Introduction

Welcome to the fascinating world of exploring the human past! Humans of one sort or another have been running around this planet for perhaps two million years, yet we know relatively little about what they were doing. Writing has only been around for about 5,000 years, and even then, we can't always read it, understand it, or even believe it! Being the curious creatures that we are, many people are interested in our long, exciting career as a species: a story that has to be carefully extracted from surviving clues by scientists serving as detectives.

In this book, we're going to do a little survey of how we go about trying to discover what went on before the present day. Obviously it's a huge subject, with each area of the world having it's own exciting ancient history. In the process, we'll find that past humans were as smart, creative, and resourceful as they are today.

With a book of this size, I can only provide a mere taste: just enough to whet your appetite. In the first two parts, we'll make a quick survey of how we go about studying ancient civilizations: what survives from the past, how we dig it up, and what it can tell us. After that, we'll be taking a little trip around the world to look at just a few of the many thousands of archaeological sites to be found on this planet: lost cities, ancient shipwrecks, drawings in caves, tombs and mummies, and much much more. And we'll learn a little history in the process.

In the last part, we'll spend a few chapters dealing with some controversial subjects such as lost continents, mummy curses, Old World visitors to the New World prior to Columbus, and the delicate subjects of who actually owns the remains of the past and whether or not archaeologists have any business digging up dead people. Finally, I'll share some insights about what it takes to become a professional archaeologist and give some tips about how you might be able to participate in this field.

Other authors would each write this book differently. My own background is in Egyptology, so you'll hear a few examples drawn from that field. I also really like ancient languages and scripts, which are fun to learn and fascinating to decipher. I'm quite interested in ancient seafaring as well. Come to think of it, I'm interested in most of this stuff, and the more I learn about it, the more intriguing it becomes! In the back of the book, Appendices B and C will provide some recommendations for additional reading and some other resources to explore the subject further.

By the Way...

Throughout the book you'll find little boxes. These contain explanations, elaborations, or additional little facts.

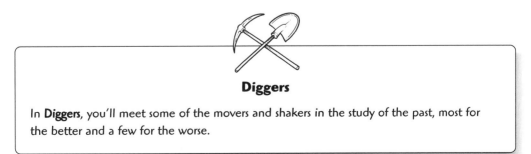

Diggers

In **Diggers**, you'll meet some of the movers and shakers in the study of the past, most for the better and a few for the worse.

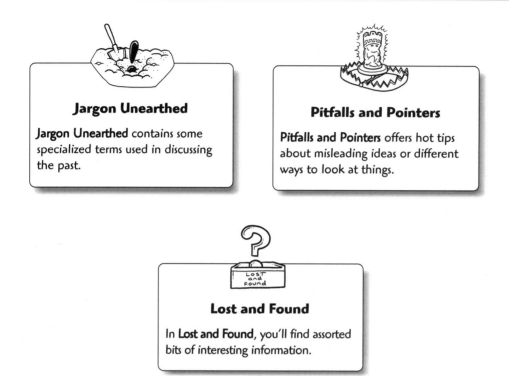

Jargon Unearthed

Jargon Unearthed contains some specialized terms used in discussing the past.

Pitfalls and Pointers

Pitfalls and Pointers offers hot tips about misleading ideas or different ways to look at things.

Lost and Found

In **Lost and Found**, you'll find assorted bits of interesting information.

Acknowledgments

Many thanks are extended to Sherry Ryan and my little assistant Samuel; Gary Krebs, Mary Russell, John Jones, Angela Schuster, and the other fine people involved in the editing and production of this book; Mr. and Mrs. M. D. Schwartz; my various archaeological cohorts including Dr. Rick Reanier, Dr. Eric Nelson, Professor Brian Holmes, Dr. Daris Swindler, and Dr. Mark Papworth; Madeleine Lynn, Sharon Nelson, and Kenneth Feder, and two flea-bitten noisy felines, Betsy and Stripe.

About the Technical Editor

Angela M. H. Schuster, a senior editor for *Archaeology* magazine, is editor-in-chief of *The Explorers Journal* (the quarterly of The Explorers Club) and a science correspondent for the Milanese daily *Corriere della Sera*. She is also a contributor to *The Oxford Companion to Archaeology*, published by Oxford University Press.

Part 1
Tools for Discovering the Past

If we're going to take a look at lost civilizations, we need to know something about archaeology. In this first section, I want to introduce you to a few of the fundamentals in order to lay a foundation for looking at the discoveries of archaeology in further depth. What are we looking for? How do we find it? How do we tell how old it is? It's not just about shovels and trowels, either. A lot of it is about ideas and explanations. We'll also take a brief look at how archaeology began so we can get an idea of the past behind the study of the past.

Chapter 1

Archaeology: Establishing a Foundation

I've got the greatest job in the world. I get to travel to exotic places, meet fascinating people, solve ancient mysteries, and dig in the dirt. I've discovered lost tombs and uncovered old Egyptian mummies. Nice work if you can get it, right?

Superficially, archaeology might look like just a lot of fun and adventure, but it's actually a very sophisticated and scientific field of study. In this first chapter, I'll introduce you to a few of archaeology's fundamentals, and lay a foundation for looking at its tools, techniques, and discoveries in further depth. We will begin by defining archaeology, and then I'll explain the framework of time and some terms that we can use to discuss the subject. Finally, we'll look at perhaps the biggest question of them all: Why should you care?

Archaeology and Yesterday's Garbage

Simply stated, archaeology is the study of the human past. I tend to look at the past as a big black hole: The deeper into it you go, the harder it is to see. Surprisingly, despite all of the digging that has been done over the last couple of hundred years, we still know relatively little about what actually went on in earlier times. Writing has only been around for about 5,000 years, and even when we have written documents, we frequently can't understand them fully, or they give us only limited insights into a greater picture.

Often, our best source of information is actually yesterday's garbage. It is not, however, sufficient merely to discover, count, describe, and display potsherds and other debris.

Jargon Unearthed

Archaeology is the study of the human past. It attempts to reconstruct and explain past human behavior primarily by the careful analysis of surviving material remains.

As archaeologists, we ultimately want to explain the past. Archaeology provides us with a flashlight to shed a little light into that big black hole.

What can garbage tell us? Here's a sample:

➤ Pieces of broken pots can often tell us who made them, when, and how they were used.

➤ The remains of someone's dinner can give us an idea about diet and what sort of food resources were available to create that meal.

➤ Discarded, broken or lost tools can provide us with some technological insights.

➤ Writing, whether it's an old newspaper or some crude scratchings on a rock, allows us to ponder the thoughts and culture of ancient people.

Lost and Found

In 1972, archaeologist William Rathje of the University of Arizona initiated the Garbage Project. Using trash cans and landfills for data, the Project has excavated and sorted through tons of refuse in an attempt to arrive at conclusions about modern human behavior, especially product consumption.

In the United States, archaeology is usually considered a sub-discipline of anthropology, a field which also includes cultural anthropology, physical anthropology, and linguistics. (In other countries, archaeology is often viewed as a subject all its own.) Unlike cultural anthropology, which studies living people, archaeology deals with the people of the past. And since we can't directly interview or observe our subjects, we have to study their bones and the surviving debris of their behavior and environment—everything from the remains of an old Egyptian lunch to the graffiti left on the wall outside an ancient Roman pub. On the other hand, archaeologists are interested in the same thing that anthropologists study: human behavior.

Modern crime scene detectives are essentially archaeologists, although they work in a relatively recent time frame. Their interest in documenting and explaining physical evidence overlaps with archaeology, but with more specific goals: to catch the bad guy. While we're on the subject, you don't have to be dealing with stuff that's thousands of years old to be an archaeologist. Some scholars, known as historical archaeologists, specialize in examining the remains of such things as America's colonial history or the unrecorded details of the Industrial Age.

With the goal of learning about the human past, archaeologists borrow from any and all fields of study that can assist us in our difficult task. From geology, for example, we have taken the idea of reading layers, or *strata*, in the earth and have learned to examine dirt to unlock the history of an archaeological site. Biologists have shown us how to identify and interpret bones, and we have learned how to conserve artifacts through a knowledge of chemistry. Specialists in ancient languages help us peer into the minds of the dead and trace the migrations of ancient peoples.

Archaeology: What It Ain't

Many people have erroneous ideas about what archaeology is. Let's dispel some of the myths right now. First of all, it doesn't have anything to do with dinosaurs. That field is known as *paleontology*, or the study of fossils. Paleontologists and archaeologists do, however, have a few things in common. They both wander around outdoors with trowels and shovels and dig bones out of the earth, and they both lurk around museums, libraries, and universities. Paleontologists, though, are concerned with all of the Earth's life-forms, going back as far as the origin of life itself. In the big scheme of things, humans, who are the subject of archaeology, are real latecomers.

The Dinosaur Age was kaput tens of millions of years before humans came around. However, ancient hunters did meet a lot of now-extinct and often scary animals, such as woolly mammoths and giant cave bears, which are of interest to paleontologists. The various evolutionary scenarios and early "ape-men" are the domain of the physical anthropologists, who study the physical aspects of the human creature and our primate ancestors and relatives.

Jargon Unearthed

Anthropology is the study of humans, and is often divided into four sub-disciplines. *Cultural anthropology* studies the cultural aspects of living peoples. *Archaeology* addresses the human past. *Physical anthropology* is the study of the physical nature of human beings, including primates and human evolution. *Linguistics* is the study of human languages.

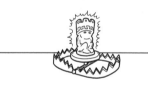

Pitfalls and Pointers

Do you want to know more about some of the creatures that were around when humans weren't? I highly recommend *The Complete Idiot's Guide to Dinosaurs* by Jay Stevenson, Ph.D, and George McGee, Ph.D.

So, despite the fun notion, seen in many an old Hollywood movie, of hairy, club-wielding cave-folk living a terrifying coexistence with Triceratops and his old nemesis Tyrannosaurus rex, it didn't happen—dinosaurs were gone when humans appeared. What's more, archaeologists tend to confine themselves to the last 100,000 years or so, when anatomically modern humans began to populate most habitable places on the earth and become the dominant species of our planet.

Speaking of Hollywood...

The general public's notion of archaeology has been largely shaped by a series of entertaining adventure films featuring a character known as Indiana Jones. So successful are these movies that the swashbuckling Jones has become to many people a frame of reference for what archaeologists do. Sorry to break the news, but as fun as it is to watch the dashing professor being chased by evil thugs, archaeology is usually not quite like this. In fact, from a scholarly point of view, Jones is more of a tomb robber than a real archaeologist. More on this later.

Yes, many archaeologists travel to exotic lands and excavate sites thousands of years old. But digging up stuff is just a fraction of the work we do. The average archaeologist spends infinitely more time in the laboratory measuring potsherds and arrowheads than avoiding volleys of poison arrows in the Amazon or narrowly escaping ancient booby traps.

Diggers

Indiana Jones is perhaps America's best-known archaeologist, even though he doesn't really exist. Jones is the creation of producers George Lucas and Phillip Kaufman, along with director Steven Spielberg, who were inspired by the cliff-hanging tales featured in old movie matinee serials. The first film featuring Indiana Jones was the hugely successful *Raiders of the Lost Ark* (1981). Two sequels, *Indiana Jones and the Temple of Doom* (1984) and *Indiana Jones and the Last Crusade* (1989) were likewise successful. A television series, *Young Indiana Jones*, aired between 1992 and 1994 and featured the youthful adventures of the globe-trotting archaeologist.

Pitfalls and Pointers

There are a few people out there who claim to be the living inspiration for the fictional Indiana Jones character. Don't count on it. His creators in the film business made him up. Indiana was the name of George Lucas's dog, and the character's last name was originally Smith.

Most archaeology is just plain hard work, but that doesn't make it any less fascinating. Of course, there *are* still unexplored ancient cities in the desert and lost tombs in Egypt. But there are also tiny clues in dirt and debris that are often even more valuable to our understanding than the discovery of the intact tomb of the golden prince. And here's the big difference between guys like me and Indiana Jones: Jones is a fake, a wonderful fictional product of the imaginations of his cinematic creators. My fellow archaeologists and I, however, are real—as are our discoveries—and that's what makes true archaeology all the more fascinating.

The Indiana Jones thing is funny, however. Journalists now frequently compare any and all archaeologists to the character. A reporter might call an archaeologist from southeast New York, for example, "the Indiana

Jones of Poughkeepsie." I know some archaeologists who are annoyed by the distorted fantasy image of their profession. Then there are others who play off the attention-grabbing icon, wearing a Jones-like hat and spinning tales of wild derring-do.

It's About Time

Since we are dealing with the past, and "the past" is a concept of time, there are a few things we should consider about the nature of time, including some inevitable terminology. We will avoid that mind-boggling area of inquiry known as the philosophy of time, which, if studied correctly, might cause you to become dizzy, feel disoriented, or perhaps question your own existence. In this book, we'll just assume that time works the way we were generally taught to believe.

Just for laughs, though, I'll throw this one at you: If the past has already occurred, the future is yet to be, and the present is a momentless dividing line between the past and the future, then where do we exist in time…right…now? And, if that is so, then the only thing we can study is the past, right? Which means we should all be archaeologists.

Temporal paradoxes aside, to discuss the past, we need to organize time, and we need to organize it in a way we can all agree on. Calendars of one sort or another have been around for ages. Many early people had a good knowledge of astronomy, studied lunar cycles, and even incorporated solar measurements into their monuments. Many of these early calendars were amazingly accurate. Ancient calendar designers had to be careful, though, since an error of one day or even a fraction thereof could cause a great distortion of the system in just a few years.

The calendar used universally today was developed in A.D. 525, when a monk named Dionysius Exiguus (known as "Little Dennis" to us English speakers) was asked by Pope St. John I to reform the calendar then in use. The new calendar would begin its annual count from what they considered the most significant event in human history, the birth of Jesus. So the "zero" point was the birth of Jesus, and the count continues to this day. Thus, for example, the year 1999 is considered to be one thousand nine hundred and ninety-nine years since the birth of Jesus.

Lost and Found

Why would ancient people need calendars? For the same reasons we need them today: anticipation and planning. Farmers need to know when to plant and harvest crops, hunters and gatherers need to know when their favorite animals and plants are abundant, and it's useful to know when winter is coming.

Apocalypse When?

This is all very nice and convenient, except that there is strong historical evidence that Jesus was born four if not seven years earlier than year zero. This really doesn't matter, however, since the calendar still provides us with a useful framework for discussing time.

Of course, if you are someone who, for apocalyptic or other reasons, is overly concerned with the coming of the new millennium, or the year 2000, you might be concerned. If Jesus was born four years prior to year zero, the millennial thing already happened, back in 1997! But don't blame Jesus; it was Li'l Dennis who restructured the calendar. It's also amusing to note that although the dates were Christianized, the names of the months still retain their old pagan Roman flavor. July and August, for example, are named for Julius Caesar and the emperor Augustus.

More Confusing Calendrics

Thanks again to Dionysius Exiguus, we have another calendar conundrum. There was no "year zero" on either side of Jesus' birthday, so the counting began with year one. The first century from the birth of Jesus then includes years 1–100 A.D., and the second century A.D. includes years 101 through 200. This can be confusing, since it seems to make sense that the year 1950, for example, should be in the nineteenth century, and not in the twentieth. Nope. The nineteenth century includes the years 1801 until 1900.

Now some of you might not be happy with the year 1900 thrown in that last statement, but if we are counting ten years in a decade, then the last year of a century will end in a zero. This, of course, is another part of the fallacy of the so-called new millennium celebrations, which technically should occur on January 1, 2001, since the year 2000 is really the last year of the twentieth century.

Pitfalls and Pointers

Don't let logic keep you from going to all the good parties on December 31st, 1999. You can use your knowledge of the true date of the millennium to impress or irritate people.

Time Terms to Reckon With

Now that we've got the calendar straightened out, it's time to look at the terms we use to discuss points in time and how they relate to each other.

➤ B.C., "Before Christ," refers to the number of years before the birth of Jesus.

➤ A.D. Many people think that because B.C. means "Before Christ," then A.D. must mean "After Death." Not so. First of all, if that were the case, you'd have to add about thirty-three years to your actual date to account for the tenure of Jesus' life on earth and then come up with a special term for dealing with those years. And, from a theological point of view, Jesus was only dead for a couple of days before being resurrected anyway.

Fortunately, we don't have to worry about all that: A.D. is actually an abbreviation for two Latin words, *anno Domini*, which mean "Year of Our Lord." From the perspective of a Christian calendar-constructor, every year since the birth of Jesus would be a Year of Our Lord.

Now there are some folks out there who don't care for the theological bias of these terms. Perhaps they don't share Christian beliefs or simply feel that religion should not be imposed on such a universal apparatus as a calendar. To address those concerns, there is an alternative pair of terms that essentially mean the same things. The terms recognize that our current Christian calendar is entrenched and in common use and is not going away, but the theological implications are neutralized:

➤ B.C.E., or "Before the Common Era," means the same as B.C.

➤ C.E., or "Common Era," is the equivalent of A.D.

The term "Common" refers to the calendar dates that we all use in common, regardless of their religious origin. The B.C./B.C.E. and A.D./C.E. distinction is mostly known in academic circles, where it is unevenly applied. It's often a matter of personal choice and occasionally it is an editorial policy, but B.C.E and C.E. are being used more frequently, so it's best to recognize and understand them for what they are. The important thing is to have a system that everyone can understand.

How Long Ago?

Another useful way of noting a point in time is with a B.P., or "Before Present," date. Essentially, B.P. means "years ago." So if this is the year A.D. 2000, and I'm talking about 10 years B.P., I'm referring to the calendar year A.D. 1990. Or, to make matters slightly more complicated, if this is the year A.D. 2000, and I'm talking about 2500 B.P., I'm referring to the year 500 B.C.

Why would anyone want to do this? As you'll see when we discuss dating techniques in a future chapter, in some methods, like radiocarbon dating, the age of an object is assessed from the time of the laboratory procedure. A date produced in the laboratory ten years from now would be different (by ten years) from a date provided today.

'Round About Then

One last term of time you'll see often is *circa*, which is abbreviated with a simple "c" or "ca." Circa means "about that time." It is useful for rounding off dates for a general discussion or for referring to dates we can't pin down exactly.

Pitfalls and Pointers

Here's an old riddle for you: What's wrong with a Roman coin that's stamped with the inscription 32 B.C.? If it's not obvious, reread the previous section.

Lost and Found

Apart from the Christian or common calendar, there are others, also with religious foundations, in use today. The Jewish calendar begins with a creation date that converts to 3761 B.C., so most of the common year 1998 would be the year 5758 by that calendar. The Jewish year, though, begins and ends on different dates than those of the common calendar.

History Before History

History can be defined in a number of different ways. In its broadest sense, it can mean everything that humans have ever done. By that definition, feeding your cat this morning made history, and it's up to the historians to decide whether or not it's worth noting. (Determining what's significant and what isn't, of course, is a whole other can of worms.) Using that definition, *pre*-history should mean a time before there were humans.

Another definition is that history is a record of human activities—for example, a history of Rome or a history of the conquest of Mexico. Scholars who call themselves "historians" typically deal with written or other documents to produce their studies of the past.

Our use of the words "history" and "prehistory" as archaeologists is a bit different, and usually refers to the time before and after written records, or histories, are available. In Egypt, for example, writing appears around 3100 B.C., and the time before that is considered prehistory in Egypt. On the other hand, writing didn't appear in the Hawaiian Islands until after the Europeans stopped by in A.D. 1778, so by this definition the historical period there begins relatively recently.

There are many archaeologists who deal with ancient preliterate cultures, and they have the option to call themselves prehistorians. Those who operate in Egypt, for example, do fine work examining the evidence of humans living in the Nile Valley during the thousands of years leading up to the time of civilization when writing first appears there. Their work is essential to understanding how Egypt's culturally complex society arose. Ask them to read some hieroglyphs and most wouldn't know where to start. But give them a trowel and turn them loose, and they'll come up with information that won't appear in any ancient text.

Lost and Found

The Islamic calendar begins with the date the prophet Mohammed fled from Mecca to Medina, an event known as the Hegira. This took place in A.D. 622. In the Islamic calendar, therefore, 1998 would be 1419.

Two Questions for the Professor

So why should you care about all this old stuff, anyway? What's the point? Those are fair questions to ask about anything you might study. Why bother with the study of archaeology and lost civilizations when we've got a mortgage to pay, children to raise, and concerns about world peace and the environment? Shouldn't we be looking forward rather than backward?

I can understand why some people are more concerned about personal survival in the present than about mounting an expedition to some far-flung corner of the globe to dig into someone else's old business. In fact, as we shall see in the next chapter, archaeology evolved as the non-essential product of a leisure society.

To be perfectly realistic, if every archaeologist disappeared off the face of the earth tomorrow, the world would still spin and life would generally go on as usual (though maybe their mothers would miss them). On the other hand, human beings are innately curious creatures. And the ancient world has the potential to address some fundamentally intriguing questions: Who are we as humans? What have we been doing, and why? How come they buried King Tut with all of that expensive stuff?

The Secret of Life

I like to startle my young students by telling them that I'm about to share with them a profound secret that will utterly shatter their world view and reveal to them the value of archaeology, history, and similar pursuits. They get all excited and prepare for their dose of great wisdom, and then I tell them the profound secret: "The world did not begin the day you were born!"

Most of the students are disappointed with my "revelation," but in actuality, many of us assume that our toys and conveniences were always here. Wrong! Archaeology can help us understand how we got to be where we are and why we are the way we are today. It can sometimes even give us a clue about where we are going.

Lessons of History

A knowledge of the past is also a hallmark of an educated individual. Abstractly, it adds a certain indefinable quality to our lives. If you sell pencils, for example, knowing the history of writing could prove both personally satisfying and professionally savvy and entertaining as you interact with your clients. Less importantly, perhaps, it makes great cocktail party fodder. Try this ice-breaker: "How about them Sumerians, eh?"

From a practical standpoint, once in a while archaeology produces some data that is of immediate value to modern society. The study of ancient irrigation practices has allowed parts of the Negev desert to bloom in the Middle East. Rediscovered agricultural techniques have increased sweet potato production in the Andes. Evidence of natural disasters in the past can provide us with warnings for the future. And if we are wise, we might actually be able to learn from the various human successes and follies perpetrated over the millennia.

The Least You Need to Know

➤ Archaeology is the study of the human past.

➤ "The past" is a term of time, and we need a framework for understanding how events in time relate to each other. In archaeology we often use relative terms like B.C., B.C.E., A.D., and C.E.

➤ Prehistory is a time in a given culture prior to the advent of writing.

➤ The value of archaeology is both abstract and practical, from personal enrichment to finding solutions to real problems.

Chapter 2

Looking Back

In This Chapter

➤ Early thinking about the past

➤ The origins of "history"

➤ How ancient texts influenced European views about the past

➤ How archaeology developed from a collectors' hobby to a modern science

---

No matter what you might study, knowing something about the history of the subject is always worthwhile. The history of archaeology is no exception—it's full of interesting people and their ideas, adventures, and discoveries. In this chapter, I'll give you just a taste of some of the highlights. There'll be more stories in future chapters.

The Old Digging Up the Old

Possessing natural curiosity, or out of sheer necessity, humans have probably always had some sort of interest in their past. Even the most technologically simple groups pass down their myths and legends, their practical knowledge, and their genealogy from one generation to another. Lacking scientific notions, curiosity might be satisfied by reverting to folklore as explanation.

In Europe just a few hundred years ago, for example, prehistoric arrowheads could be explained as "fairy darts," and large Stone Age hand axes found in the ground were sometimes thought to be the product of lightning bolts. In some places, buried pots were believed to grow spontaneously in the ground, and fossils could be perceived as accidents or "sports of nature."

Although the formal study of the human past as an academic discipline is relatively new, there are some interesting examples of early archaeological activities by some of the "ancient" people themselves. The Babylonian king Nabonidus (r. 555–539 B.C.) is one of the earliest known excavators. Nabonidus dug up old temple foundations and collected artifacts in his quest to learn the proper way to restore ruined monuments.

Lost and Found

At the great Sphinx at Giza, Egypt, a stone tablet between the massive statue's giant paws tells the story about how a future king, Thutmosis IV (r. 1401–1391 B.C.), was notified in a dream that he should excavate and restore the sphinx, which was then over a thousand years old and buried up to its neck in sand.

The classical Greeks had ideas about their past based on such things as the legends of Homer and their cultural mythology, and occasionally they dug things up or retrieved relics. Real examples of archaeology per se, though, were infrequent.

The Romans were great collectors and were interested in old things primarily as artistic objects to be collected and displayed. They traveled widely, as did the Greeks, and acquired antiquities from many different lands. There are more standing Egyptian obelisks in Rome than anywhere else in the world, including Egypt. Although digging took place, there was no real scientific interest in the digging or the artifacts. They had other ways, however, of contributing to our knowledge of the past.

Who Invented History?

Writing is only about 5,000 years old, and even so, a lot of the early writing doesn't tell us much about individual events or historical processes. Of the thousands of clay tablets bearing ancient texts from Mesopotamia, for example, the vast majority are economic, legal, or occasionally literary documents. Egyptian texts tell us quite a bit about their culture, but the pattern of events is mostly constructed from temples, tombs, and other surviving monuments to the elite. Not surprisingly, most of them tend to be flattering testimonies to their builders or owners. Actual historic narratives from the earliest times are rare.

A Greek named Herodotus is often called "the father of history." His multi-volume work, known cleverly as *The Histories*, is an account of history as he knew it, including not only events in the Greek world, but also in places such as Egypt, Persia, and lands in between. Although some scholars are critical of his apparent exaggerations or weak information sources, Herodotus does present a history whose details are regularly quoted as factual today.

Other Greeks followed his example, as did the Romans. The Roman historian Livy, for example, wrote a history of Rome that covered events hundreds of years before his time. One of his successors, Suetonius, could be considered an early tabloid journalist, recording the often salacious lifestyles and deeds of the Roman emperors in his oft-quoted *Lives of the Caesars*.

Although any document has to be studied in light of its motives and potential for accuracy, ancient writers of history such as Herodotus and Livy provide us with a framework for the study of their times. Unfortunately, this doesn't help us in those areas—such as North America and many other parts of the ancient world—where writing didn't take off.

Diggers

Herodotus (ca. 485–425 B.C.), a Greek from Halicarnassus, is known as "the father of history." Herodotus attempted to gather and write the history of his region and other places, including Egypt, which he claimed to have visited himself. A number of his comments about Egypt seem so far off, though, that some modern scholars have suggested he never went there, but relied on hearsay from other travelers. On the other hand, the pyramids were already 2,000 years old in his day, and perhaps his guides were themselves uninformed or information was lost in the translation. Either way, Herodotus has provided a useful, detailed starting point, and has given us some great stories.

Modern Archaeology: The View from the West

Although archaeology is now practiced in virtually all countries, it essentially developed in the Western or European world over the last several hundred years to become what it is today. And though there has been an interest in the past in various parts of the globe at different times, it was the social, cultural, economic, and geographical climate in the Western world over the last thousand years that led to the gradual development of what became modern archaeology.

The Bible Tells Me So

Before archaeology could develop, there had to be a need. For the majority of people in the Western World, with their common Judeo-Christian belief system, there was no need to delve into the details of the human past or the age of the Earth, because the Bible served to explain the origins and history of both.

Jargon Unearthed

Many of the geographical terms in use today were contrived by Europeans. From that standpoint, "the West" was Europe and "the East" was Asia, with the Middle or Near East in between. Thus we have the Occident (the West), the Orient (the East), and terms such as the New World (the Americas), as opposed to the Old World (Europe and the continents of which it was aware: Africa and Asia).

Lost and Found

For many centuries, the Bible provided the explanation for the early history of the Earth and its occupants. The opening lines of the first book, Genesis, set the stage for creationist belief: "In the beginning, God created the heavens and the Earth." The original Hebrew, however, can also be translated as "when God created," which has a lot of different time possibilities. A wealth of insight can be provided by studying the Bible and many other great books in their original languages.

Using Biblical information and theological ideas, Irish archbishop James Ussher (1581–1656) in 1654 calculated the date of the creation of the Earth to the year 4004 B.C. This was for a long time the accepted date from which to calculate the age of our planet. Although scientists today might add a few billion years to the age of the Earth, we should be careful not to scoff at the archbishop, who arrived at a reasonable conclusion given the beliefs and tools of his time: the Bible and a fundamental belief therein.

The occasional discovery of fossils or petrified bones of unknown creatures deep in the ground provided no obstacle to a Biblical interpretation. The story of Noah and the Great Deluge could explain how the creatures became interred in sediments during a global flood.

As for the remains of unknown animals, some believed living representatives of the giants' bones could be found in places as yet unexplored by Europeans, such as the African interior or the New World. American President Thomas Jefferson, who collected fossils, asked the explorers Lewis and Clark to keep their eyes open for animals such as mastodons and giant ground sloths on their expedition across the North American continent.

The opening lines of Genesis as they appear in the Hebrew text.(From Hebrew Old Testament, *London: British and Foreign Bible Society)*

בְּרֵאשִׁית בָּרָא אֱלֹהִים אֵת הַשָּׁמַיִם וְאֵת הָאָרֶץ: וְהָאָרֶץ
הָיְתָה תֹהוּ וָבֹהוּ וְחֹשֶׁךְ עַל־פְּנֵי תְהוֹם וְרוּחַ אֱלֹהִים מְרַחֶפֶת
עַל־פְּנֵי הַמָּיִם: וַיֹּאמֶר אֱלֹהִים יְהִי אוֹר וַיְהִי־אוֹר: וַיַּרְא
אֱלֹהִים אֶת־הָאוֹר כִּי־טוֹב וַיַּבְדֵּל אֱלֹהִים בֵּין הָאוֹר וּבֵין
הַחֹשֶׁךְ: וַיִּקְרָא אֱלֹהִים ׀ לָאוֹר יוֹם וְלַחֹשֶׁךְ קָרָא לָיְלָה וַיְהִי־
עֶרֶב וַיְהִי־בֹקֶר יוֹם אֶחָד:

Between folklore, the Bible, and the works of the Classical historians of the Greek and Roman world, there was little need to speculate otherwise about much of the past. European pilgrims visiting Egypt on the way to the Holy Land might explain the pyramids by referring to the comments of Herodotus, or perhaps speculate that they were the storehouses of grain in the Biblical story of Joseph, or that they were built by Hebrew slave labor.

Antiquarians and Collectors

During the European Renaissance and thereafter, it became increasingly popular for educated, wealthy individuals to tour around the continent and admire the ancient monuments. Aristocrats would form private collections of such things as ancient Roman statuary or Greek vases. Leisured "antiquarians" would study the ancient monuments—of Britain, for example—and concoct various ideas to explain their origins and purposes. Further interest and speculation were inspired as the continents and oceans were explored and made known to the West.

Private and public museums also became popular, developing from random assortments of natural and artificial "curiosities" to well-organized collections based on themes. One of the classic examples of an early museum, or "cabinet of curiosity," was that of the Ole Worm. A 1655 drawing of the Danish museum shows a hodgepodge of interesting and delightful items, including sea shells, a stuffed polar bear, crocodile, bows and arrows, antlers, a lobster, Inuit clothing, a walrus skull, and a kayak.

Jargon Unearthed

Antiquaries, or *antiquarians,* are those individuals who collect or study antiquities. The term usually applies to people with an interest in artifacts prior to the era of modern archaeology.

Ole Worm's cabinet of curiosities. (From 'Ole Worm, 1655,' Musei Wormiani Historia)

Free-for-All!

The growing interest in acquiring antiquities during the late 1700s and first half of the 1800s often resembled more of a free-for-all than anything scientific. In Egypt, the

Turkish pasha would routinely issue permits allowing a foreigner to come in and remove essentially whatever was wanted. Intense nationalistic rivalries developed as people competed for the choicest bits of the past to send back to the home country. Things would often get nasty, with occasional acts of violence and sabotage.

Giovanni Belzoni is one of the best-known of these early antiquities-grabbers in Egypt. An Italian carnival performer who immigrated to England, Belzoni arrived in Egypt in 1815 and became an expert in tomb-finding and the removal of large stone objects. He is often harshly criticized by modern scholars for his apparently reckless behavior. In his book, Belzoni describes using a battering ram to open a tomb, accidentally dropping an obelisk into the Nile, and crawling through rooms full of mummies: quite typical behavior for his day.

Belzoni, however, was more than just a treasure hunter. Unlike his competitors, he made drawings and plans of many of his discoveries, anticipating appropriate archaeological procedure by decades. It wasn't until 1858 that a formal government agency was established to regulate the activities of excavators in Egypt.

Diggers

Giovanni Battista Belzoni (1778–1823) was born in Padua, Italy, but left for England, where he made a living as a carnival performer with a strong-man act. He visited Egypt in 1815 and began to collect large antiquities for England. He is the first excavator known to dig in the famous Valley of the Kings, where he discovered several important tombs and was successful in opening one of the giant pyramids at Giza. Although many of his antics remain controversial, he was generally better than others of his day. He died of dysentery in 1823 while in West Africa searching for the source of the Niger River.

The case of Lord Elgin and the Elgin marbles is notorious. Elgin was the British ambassador to Constantinople and took upon himself the task of acquiring some of the most choice of Classical Greek antiques for his home country. Beginning in 1801, Elgin initiated the removal of much of the surviving sculpture from the Parthenon, the majestic temple on the Acropolis of Athens which serves as the very symbol of Greece. The work was not performed carefully, and the act of removing the sculptures from this precious monument generated outrage which continues to this day. The "Elgin Marbles," as they are called, remain on exhibit in the British Museum.

The Museums of Europe are full of antiquities imported from all over the world, many of which were acquired during the free-wheeling days of antiquity collecting. Although one might bemoan the fact that they were yanked, often indiscriminately, from their homelands, the majority were probably legally acquired, in a world whose ideas of property and nationalism were much different than those of the present. (See the discussion in Chapter 23 for more on this subject.)

Giovanni Belzoni: plunderer or pioneer?

Order Descends

As ancient scripts such as the Egyptian hieroglyphs and the cuneiform of Mesopotamia were translated, more careful expeditions were mounted in the 1800s to study the monuments and ancient civilizations whose texts could now be read. Eventually a concern for antiquities grew out of the abuses mentioned above, and means for controlling the rampant pillage of monuments and antiquities were established.

Vast excavations were conducted, particularly in Europe and the Middle East, with a lot of the recovered goods ending up in museums. Archaeologists like Heinrich Schliemann and Austen Henry Layard explored the ancient lands of Greece and Mesopotamia, while others such as John Lloyd Stevens tramped through the jungles of Central

Pitfalls and Pointers

The well-known treasure hunting antics of the 19th century are by no means over. Apart from professional treasure seekers who secure permission to do their work, grave robbers and pot-hunters continue to ply their illegal trade in many places where antiquities remain sufficiently unprotected (see Chapter 23).

America looking for lost cities. (We'll meet them in later chapters.) Archaeology was still largely a matter of treasure hunting, but the hunt was becoming more disciplined.

Three Ages

A milestone of sorts in archaeology as an organized field of study was the museum work of Christian Thomsen (1788–1865). As a curator of antiquities at the Danish National Museum in Copenhagen, Thomsen examined the museum's collection of antiquities and arranged them in a systematic way to reflect their age and material. Thomsen sorted them as artifacts belonging to three successive ages: the Stone Age, the Bronze Age, and the Iron Age. The idea, as published in the museum's guidebook of 1836, was based on some rather old notions (discussed in Chapter 9) about the technological progress of humanity that were generally confirmed by later excavators.

This three-age framework set up a technologically ordered system by which artifacts could be arranged in time. Thomsen's contribution was soon followed up by others, and the basic terms are still used today in several parts of the world, although with a great deal more refinement. Especially in Europe and elsewhere in the "Old World," the Three Age System is alive and well. The classic Stone, Bronze and Iron ages are often subdivided into smaller fractions, for example, the Middle-Late Bronze Age or Iron Age II, used in Syro-Palestinian archaeology. We'll run into a few other terms later that fill out the picture a little bit. The term "Neolithic," or "New Stone Age," for one, was created to describe a period of time before the Bronze Age when ancient cultures were practicing agriculture rather than merely hunting and gathering.

New Views of an Old Earth

In the mid-nineteenth century, a number of discoveries in Europe led some scholars to speculate that humans might have been around longer than previously thought. Deeply buried human bones and sometimes stone tools were found in association with the remains of extinct animals. Advances in geological knowledge, too, suggested a great time depth for the existence of the Earth, as the rates of erosion and other natural processes were calculated to account for the various land features.

While geology and the study of fossils were suggesting that the Earth was quite ancient, the theory of evolution proposed by Charles Darwin provided a new means for explaining the diversity of life, the development of new species over time, and the role of survival and extinction. In 1859, Darwin's *Origin of Species* was published, with much controversy to follow. It today provides the foundation for the notions of biological evolution accepted by most scientists. With a postulated age of the Earth far older than a few millennia, the world of the past was vastly expanded for its students.

Pitfalls and Pointers

Many religious people, including some scientists, have little trouble reconciling Darwinian evolution and Biblical creationism. Some look at the Bible and science as apples and oranges, each explaining what the other cannot. The Bible, for example, might explain the purpose of humans on Earth, while science might explain the means God used to create them.

Digging Correctly

While the study of the past was becoming gradually more sophisticated and profound, the actual techniques for excavating and documenting sites and artifacts were nowhere clearly defined. The quality of digging ranged from abysmally destructive to admirably competent. Two excavators in particular greatly influenced the development of the proper method of conducting a dig.

Augustus Henry Lane Fox Pitt-Rivers (1827–1900) is often recognized for bringing a systematic and well-organized approach to the world of archaeological excavations. As a British army officer, he worked with military precision and set a fine example for careful digging and accurate recording. And he published excellent reports of the sites he explored, many of which were on his own property, in the late 1800s.

Englishman William Matthew Flinders Petrie continued in the mold of Pitt-Rivers with his excavations in Egypt and Palestine. His book *Methods and Aims in Archaeology* (1904) spelled out the need to be careful and gave direct practical instruction on how to conduct proper archaeological work for the turn-of-the-century archaeologist.

Both Pitt-Rivers and Petrie have been credited with being the founders of systematic and scientific archaeology. It took a while for things to catch on, but eventually they did.

Diggers

William Matthew Flinders Petrie (1853–1942) was an English archaeologist who first went to Egypt in 1880 to study the pyramids, thus beginning a long career reported in his book *Seventy Years in Archaeology*. Petrie conducted numerous excavations throughout the years and published prolifically. He is best known for promoting scientific archaeology, and many young archaeologists were trained by him in good digging methods. Although he was a respectable and dignified scholar at home, his field camps were notorious for their poor food, meager accommodations, and generally sparse conditions. He spent his latter years digging in Palestine.

Having given Petrie and Pitt-Rivers their well-deserved credit, I should now introduce perhaps the world's first genuine scientific archaeologist, who preceded our two English friends by a hundred years. It is none other than Thomas Jefferson (1743–1826), the amazing scholar and gentleman who would become the third president of the United States.

Jefferson, who had a wide range of scientific interests, was curious about the mounds found on his Virginia property, which some had suggested were constructed by a mysterious group of "Moundbuilders" unrelated to the present native population. He explored this idea in 1784 with an organized, systematic excavation of a mound, in which he carefully noted the strata and their contents and arrived at the conclusion that the burials were of local origin. He published the results, too, but never became an archaeological specialist, having an otherwise busy life.

Pitfalls and Pointers

It's easy to make fun of people like Archbishop Ussher and others who came before us. But before we sit and harshly judge them, we should try to understand the standards of their time and then assess how they fit in. Who knows? The archaeologists of 200 years from now might think the scholars of today are pretty ignorant, too.

Jargon Unearthed

The *scientific method* involves formulating an idea (a "hypothesis") to explain a given phenomenon and then using deduction to test the validity of the idea.

Into the Twentieth Century

During the first half of the twentieth century, most archaeologists began to adopt scientific methods as expeditions from many countries excavated in many parts of the world. In doing so, specific and regional chronologies were developed that would form the framework for our knowledge of the past on a global scale. The development of archaeological techniques followed the development of technology. With the invention of the airplane, for example, aerial photography to locate and record ancient sites became possible. Archaeologists regularly adapted and applied new advances in biology, chemistry, physics, and other fields to the study of the past.

In the late 1950s, two graduate students at the University of Michigan, Lewis Binford and Mark Papworth, became increasingly critical of the status quo in archaeology. They thought it was getting too sterile, with its endless cataloguing of sites and artifacts. With a good deal of thought and creativity, and the insights of a few of their professors, the two laid the foundation for a theoretical revolution in archaeology, which became known as "The New Archaeology."

The study of the human past would never be the same. The New Archaeology emphasized understanding and explaining the past rather than merely describing it. Since human culture was their primary interest, an anthropological perspective was heavily promoted. Quantitative techniques such as statistics were used, as was an approach that emphasized the scientific method, which involves forming and then testing hypotheses to explain what you observe. Binford became the system's principal advocate, and the rest is history, so to speak.

Today, archaeology has branched out in all different directions. Specialists and super-specialists abound, including historians of archaeology, archaeological philosophers, theorists, and dozens of others who address very specific topics. There are those who explore such current topics as social issues, feminist perspectives, and ecological questions as viewed through the remains of the past. New or improved scientific techniques abound, and more can be anticipated in the future.

The Least You Need to Know

➤ Although there are occasional examples of early people interested in the past, archaeology didn't develop into a serious study until relatively recently.

➤ Folklore, the Bible, and the writings of the Greeks and Romans served as ready explanations of the past up to the nineteenth century.

➤ The recognition of the antiquity of humans, the development of a system for organizing artifacts in time, and Darwinian evolution pushed archaeology into a new realm during the nineteenth century.

➤ During the 1800s and beyond, the reckless free-style collection of antiquities was gradually replaced by careful means of excavating, recording, and preserving archaeological remains.

➤ Modern archaeology attempts to explain the past rather than to merely describe it, and takes advantage of the advances made in many fields.

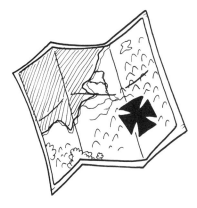

Chapter 3

The Search Is On

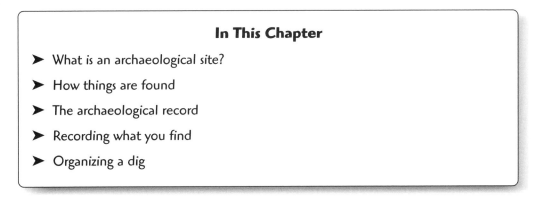

In This Chapter

➤ What is an archaeological site?

➤ How things are found

➤ The archaeological record

➤ Recording what you find

➤ Organizing a dig

If we want to explore lost civilizations, we need to be able to find what's left of them. For a lot of the obvious stuff, no shovel is required—it's just a matter of opening your eyes. The great pyramids of Egypt, for example, are so massive you can see them from miles away. Or consider the Great Wall of China. It's so big you can see it from outer space. Or Stonehenge, plain as day on Salisbury Plain. Yes, they are big and easy. But there are a lot of other things out there, too, that aren't so easy to see: whole cities hidden in the jungle under thick vegetation, or huge ships on the ocean floor under thousands of feet of water. And it's not all big stuff. Clues and answers to the puzzles of the past come in all sizes, and it's often the little stuff that's the most informative. Read on.

What's a Site?

First of all, what's an *archaeological site*? Can a single object in a remote location constitute a site? Could an arrowhead falling accidentally from the pocket of a hunter crossing a mountain pass be considered a site? Or does there need to be two or more remains? I would say that anywhere that artifacts or other traces of past human activity are found counts as an archaeological site.

A lot of things can be discovered by looking for little clues sticking out of the ground. A scatter of stone chips or a few fire-cracked rocks might suggest evidence of an ancient campsite. Some pottery here and there might be the clue to the buried city nearby. A local farmer might prove a wealth of information. Archaeologists might also look in likely spots, places favorable to live. Spots close to fresh water or places that might be sheltered or easily defended could reveal old places of habitation.

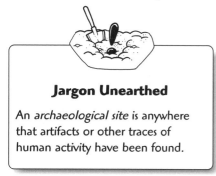

Jargon Unearthed

An *archaeological site* is anywhere that artifacts or other traces of human activity have been found.

Many things are found accidentally, too. More than one donkey's hoof has stumbled into a small hole to reveal a magnificent discovery below. Miners, builders, and even hikers stumble across things regularly. The famous cedar boat found at the base of the Great Pyramid in Egypt was discovered by road workers who encountered some large limestone slabs, and mountain climbers found the 5,000-year-old body, clothes, and hunting equipment of Ötzi, the celebrated Iceman. (You can read more about him in Chapter 14.)

Taking a Look

I do a lot of homework before I go out looking for sites. I consult maps, the notes of previous explorers, and old photographs. If possible, I look up what the ancient people themselves had to say about a particular area. In many ways, this preliminary search is almost as much fun as the actual excavation. Finding the right information can take me to archives and libraries full of fascinating stuff. (Of course, it's often easy to get sidetracked by all of the little things I find on the way.) Finally, armed with the clues at hand, I go out into the field and look around.

Pitfalls and Pointers

Technology and fancy gadgets don't always rule. I rediscovered a lost Egyptian tomb by first gathering information and then scrutinizing the terrain for telltale signs. I uncovered the long-lost tomb in less than half an hour by using a broom to sweep the debris from the bedrock to reveal an ancient excavation.

Up in the Air: Aerial Photography

Trekking around doing a survey on foot is often effective, but sometimes an overview of the terrain is useful. Things look a lot different from the air than they do on land. Photographs taken from airplanes are often very revealing. The pictures can be taken not only from directly above, but from the side, or *obliquely*, where different lighting can sometimes highlight surface variations. Hot air balloons and even kites mounted with cameras have been used in a similar fashion.

In addition to letting you see more than you can from ground level, aerial pictures might reveal clues to underground structures by the uneven growth of crops or other plants, or a freshly plowed field might show unnatural patterns in soil color. Sometimes using infrared photography, which records thermal differences, lets us see what the naked eye cannot. Satellites, too, have been used with good result, as have images taken from the space shuttle.

Under the Ground: Remote Sensing

A number of devices can be used to peer at things under the ground without digging anything up using techniques called *remote sensing*. Remote sensing techniques are those used to study archaeological sites without actually being there, using techniques like aerial photos, satellite images, and ground-penetrating radar. Perhaps the simplest and best-known remote-sensing device is that favorite of the beachcomber, the metal detector, which uses magnets to detect metal under the surface.

The sophisticated stuff is much more complicated and expensive; it typically involves penetrating the ground with a form of sound wave or electromagnetic energy and then recording the differences encountered. Since waves travel at different speeds depending on the materials they encounter, subsurface archaeological features such as buried walls, building foundations, or tombs will produce signals different from soil that has been left undisturbed. By recording the differences in these signals, archaeologists can often determine the boundaries of a site, and the locations of buried deposits. We'll talk about a few more methods when we get into the subject of underwater archaeology.

Jargon Unearthed

Remote-sensing techniques are those used to locate and study buried archaeological material that leave the sub-surface remains undisturbed.

Taking a Sample

Once the dimensions or boundaries of a site have been determined, an archaeologist might decide that a site is too huge to investigate thoroughly, since "huge" usually means outrageously expensive. Faced with these problems, the archaeologist might choose to take a sample of the site in order to get an idea of what might be hidden beneath the ground. There are at least two main approaches to this: random and non-random sampling.

Random Sampling

Random sampling usually involves superimposing numbered grid squares of a selected size—let's say ten meters square—on a map of the site or the area to be explored. Randomly selected numbers are then used to determine which squares will be explored. The random numbers can be picked out of a hat or generated by a computer.

I'm no great fan of this method, for two reasons. First, it's theoretically possible to use random sampling and completely miss the hidden archaeological remains. Second, the choices people made to use this or that place in the past wasn't always random. The benefit, though, is that data can be used to produce statistical results from which archaeologists try to make generalizations. And as a bonus, this kind of sampling might force you to look where you wouldn't ordinarily look.

Jargon Unearthed

Sampling techniques allow archaeologists to explore a site or an area of interest without digging up the whole thing. In *random sampling*, areas to be sampled are randomly selected, and statistical formulas can be applied to the data. With *non-random sampling*, archaeologists sample an area of the site they feel might be most productive.

Non-random Sampling

Non-random sampling, too, can start out with the grid over the map, or it can be less formal. The basis for choosing where to dig could be intuitive, or one might perhaps choose to investigate every other or every third grid square.

For the actual sampling, the archaeologists might examine the surface of the given area or dig a test pit. This is essentially a small hole, sometimes one meter square, and is sometimes called a "telephone booth" because of its shape. This lets us see if anything is there and gives us an idea of the layers in the ground. Or we might simply turn up a shovel or two of dirt, pound a probe through the soil to detect hard objects, or use an auger and examine the contents churned up when it is removed.

Jargon Unearthed

The physical remains of the past are referred to in general as the *archaeological record*.

Let's Look at a Site

Often, a combination of all of the above techniques does the best job. Here's a real-life example. A few years ago, I was involved in an excavation at a very large archaeological site in the Middle East, a place mentioned in several ancient texts. The site was huge and was dominated by a large hill which was mostly composed of the piled-up debris of thousands of years of human occupation. The problem was how to choose the most productive places to dig, and here is how some of the choices were made.

First, some obvious spots were explored. The tops of a couple of stone columns peeking out of a hillside indicated something below. They turned out to be old Greek columns reused to support a Crusader-period chapel later converted into a mosque. An area with a nice view on top of the hill was a likely looking spot, and revealed an ancient bath-house bordello.

The old excavations of previous archaeologists were re-explored and a giant auger was used in likely locations in an attempt to find the old seaport. Finally, large areas with no particularly compelling attraction were sampled by using random numbers to determine where to dig large 10-meter-square excavations. The results have been impressive, and this big-budget expedition has continued to produce wonderful information and plenty of surprises.

The Archaeological Record: What Survives

The physical remains of the past are referred to in general as the *archaeological record*. And the record varies considerably, depending on what sort of activities took place and what the conditions for preserving the remains are like. The cold slap of reality is that not everything that ever happened in the past made it into the archaeological record, and a lot of what did didn't last for long. Let's look at two hypothetical examples.

Suppose a couple of our distant ancestors are sitting around a campfire cooking a few fish. The conversation turns from the age-old pastime of lying about the giant trout that got away to questions about the nature of reality, the origins of the universe, and whether or not there really exists a good ten-cent cigar. Such a conversation might be intellectually profound and perhaps even eventually result in a worldview that has a widespread effect on other people. But what physical evidence is left of this event? Perhaps the hearth and some fish bones from their tasty meal, and absolutely nothing of the more provocative event, the conversation.

Another example: Our ancient friends had a heck of a birthday party. They brought in some tables for the occasion and a huge cake topped with the appropriate number of candles. The guests danced in wild abandon on the tabletops and sang loudly with the raucous music. In the wee hours of the morning, the party broke up after a drunken brawl. Thousands of years later, the archaeologists find a few puddles of surviving melted wax from the birthday candles next to the hardened small squares of soil where the table legs were forcibly pressed into the ground. Nothing left of the paper party favors, the wild dancing, the off-key singing, the buffet items, and so forth.

The lesson? Not everything survives, and some of the best bits that do survive are difficult, if not impossible, to interpret. A lot of what survives is dependent upon what we call the *environment of deposition*. The dry desert climate in southern Egypt might splendidly preserve wood and other organic remains in the dry heat. Most of the stuff in King Tut's tomb was in excellent condition when it was opened 3,000 years later. On the other hand,

Pitfalls and Pointers

Much of our knowledge of Egypt comes from temples and tombs—monuments built to last for eternity—while more domestic remains have vanished. This has inspired the idea that the Egyptians were obsessed with religion and death. Imagine what a weird idea people might have about America if future archaeologists excavated only cemeteries and churches, or for that matter, ski shops and caddyshacks.

Jargon Unearthed

The *environment of deposition* is the location and physical conditions in which remains of human behavior are deposited. The environment of deposition can heavily influence what survives from the past and what does not.

complete preserved woolly mammoths—and frozen people too—have been found in icy northern areas. Different soil conditions can result in different degrees of preservation of materials. For example, the chemical nature of peat bogs in places like England and Denmark have allowed for amazing preservation of human bodies and artifacts.

The Destructive Art of Digging

The sad fact is that each time you put a shovel in the ground, you alter a site. In this sense, archaeology is an intense responsibility. By digging, you are essentially destroying the site, so it's up to you to make sure that everything is properly noted and recorded as you found it. The ideal archaeological excavation is well-organized, meticulous, and neat. Sometimes archaeologists will not completely excavate a site, thus saving a portion for future archaeologists whose ideas and tools might allow them to make different kinds of discoveries.

A meticulously excavated archaeological site is a happy archaeological site. The late and truly great archaeologist Doug Esse (pictured here) knew that this was so.

Everything in Its Place

Archaeologists must document as much as possible. Most begin with a map. Surveying is an important skill for recording the overall area to be examined, followed by small-scale mapping to note everything in its place. The term *in situ* refers to things as they are found, in place; and keeping notes, photographs, and a detailed description of everything *in situ*, before it is disturbed, is essential.

There are at least three things to consider for every object found, and they're somewhat similar to the questions journalists ask. We call this information "context."

Context:

➤ Where was the object found? Was it six feet under the ground or three inches to the left of something else? A very specific location is necessary. The term for this is *provenience*.

➤ In what was it found? Was it sandy soil, tar, or a jar full of mud?

➤ With what was it found? What things were found nearby? Was the gold bowl found next to the skeleton? Were there three more just like it in the little room where the futon fragments were found? Or was it completely by itself? A group of objects found together is called an "assemblage."

The importance of this kind of information can't be overemphasized. This data allows the artifacts to "speak to us," so to speak. Most museums have plenty of objects whose provenience and in-situ context is unknown. Some are donations or purchases, and although the artifacts are often still of great interest, their lack of context has muted much of their story. Many people in America have arrowheads or other native artifacts found in fields or elsewhere. They make nice little curios, but the story that chipped stone might have told, had it been recovered scientifically, could have been even more fascinating.

That's why many archaeologists don't like dealers of antiquities. The objects they sell are often of unknown or uncertain provenience. Selling such undocumented objects also tends to encourage those who might go out and loot archaeological sites for profit. Needless to say, these sort of "collectors" are not engaging in the painstaking, detailed work necessary to preserve the archaeological record. (See Chapter 23 for more on this subject.)

This is a serious problem, with untold thousands of ancient graves and other sites looted. And that's why Indiana Jones is not a good archaeologist. He acts like a treasure hunter, hoping to find or collect specific things. He doesn't bother to record the greater context of what he finds, and his only interest seems to be to grab the object and get away before the booby traps, snakes, and bad guys do him in.

Jargon Unearthed

In situ is the term used to refer to artifacts in their original location, just as they are found by the archaeologist. *Context* refers to the complete situation in which artifacts are found (where, with what, and in what).

Jargon Unearthed

The specific location where an object is found is called its *provenience*. A variation of this same word is *provenance*. A group of objects found together is called an *assemblage*.

Diggers

Flinders Petrie was darn serious about the responsibilities of the archaeologist when he wrote the following: "Recording is the absolute dividing line between plundering and scientific work....The unpardonable crime in archaeology is destroying evidence which can never be recovered; and every discovery does destroy evidence unless it is intelligently recorded."

—Methods and Aims in Archaeology (1904)

Don't Hurt Me!

Thankfully, there are increasingly non-destructive methods in use. Some of the remote-sensing techniques mentioned above can give us a good idea about sites without wrecking the place. Burials are especially sensitive objects of study, as more and more people exert their rights not to have their relatives exhumed. (Again, see Chapter 23 for more on this subject.)

In Tuscany, Italy, land of the Etruscans, archaeologists have been able to explore cave-like Etruscan tombs by drilling holes and inserting tiny cameras. The tomb is left basically undisturbed, and the archaeologist can decide whether or not there is any extra-special reason to spend the time and expense of trying to dig the thing up and deal with its contents.

It's Expedition Time!

So, you want to conduct a little archaeological work, eh? First of all, it's not just owning a shovel and buying a plane ticket to some exotic land. Nope. Typically there are qualifications to meet and laws and other hoops to jump through. Most professional archaeologists would prefer that you were well trained or apprenticed before you try anything on your own. (See Chapter 26 for more about opportunities and careers in archaeology.)

Making Plans

Once you've passed those hurdles, you've got to have a plan: an idea about what you are going to do and why. Maybe a site was found accidentally during a construction project, or maybe a construction project is planned and the law says that the area must be examined for "cultural resources" before work can take place. Maybe there's a special location or group of people you would like to explore.

Diggers

The eminent and well-organized archaeologist Sir Mortimer Wheeler wants you to keep things in line: "An ill-considered excavation is liable to develop into a chaos of pits and trenches, difficult to supervise and record...It is an axiom that an untidy excavation is a bad one...The guiding principles are not difficult: they are 'Have a plan,' a carefully thought-out scheme, and execute it in an orderly fashion."

—Sir Mortimer Wheeler, *Archaeology from the Earth*, 1956, Harmondsworth: Penguin p. 80.

Many archaeologists today have special research designs. They often pick and choose where they work based on their interest in some question that archaeology might be able to illuminate. If you were interested, for instance, in the origins of agriculture in the Near East, you might choose to explore a series of sites that might shed light on the big question. Of course, your documentation must be rigorous, so that it can also be useful to other people with different interests.

Getting Permits

Okay, so now you've got an idea about what you want to do. Most every place has its own rules and regulations. In America, there might be local, state, or federal regulations that govern who can do what and where. And if your site is on private land, you need to get permission for that, too. Sometimes getting the permission is the hardest part of the dig.

While some countries are glad to have anyone qualified come on over and do some work, others maintain fickle and Byzantine bureaucracies whose attitudes can change from day to day. I've heard horror stories where archaeologists have put together big expeditions, obtained big money, and had permits approved, only to be told to go home upon arrival. International and nationalistic politics can mess things up, so that one day you are in, the next O-U-T. It seems to get harder and harder every year.

Many countries take the responsibility of maintaining their antiquities very seriously. In Egypt, for example, the Supreme Council of Antiquities is made up of scholars whose job it is to care for

Pitfalls and Pointers

The mix of personalities on an expedition can make or break the project. Trust me, a bad combination of team members can take the fun out of the work and have a negative effect upon productivity. For some of the qualities of a good archaeologist or archaeological volunteer, see Chapter 26.

Egypt's thousands of monuments and sites. The Israel Antiquities Authority governs the wealth of sites in Israel. Both countries are, in fact, huge archaeological sites.

Assembling a Team

Let's assume you've got a plan and permission to dig. Now it's time for some serious logistics. You need to pick some good people if you can't manage the project alone, and you usually can't. Fortunately, there are plenty of specialists out there to lend a hand. Some really big digs will have specialists to deal with very specific fields, which can include:

➤ animal bones

➤ human remains

➤ pottery

➤ plant remains

➤ architecture

➤ artifact conservation

➤ mapping

➤ photography

And often they're not the people who move the dirt. Students or volunteers might be enlisted to do the actual digging under supervision. And all of these people need to be housed, fed, and kept healthy and happy. Getting out to the site might require vehicles, and all of the tools for the work have to be rounded up.

Some things you might want to have when you're digging.

TOOLS FOR EXCAVATION		
Shovels	String	Knapsack
Hoes	Line Levels	First Aid Kit
Trowels	Tape Measures	Work Gloves
Hand Picks	Plumb Bob	Knee Pads
Whisk Brooms	Compass	Hat
Brushes	Theodolite	Dust Mask
Dental Probes	Pens and Pencils	Bug Repellent
Dust Pans	Field Notebooks	Canteen
Buckets	Plastic Bags	Strong Back and Happy Face
Sifting Screens	Labels	Snacks to share with the
Wheel Barrow	Camera	Director.

Paying the Bills

By now, you may conclude that all of this can cost a lot of money. It certainly can. I have seen digs involving a couple of people on a local site costing under $100, but some big projects cost over $100,000 year after year. In some countries, it's really inexpensive to operate, and getting there is the principal expense. In other places, everything is expensive, especially if you have to pay a lot of salaries.

In the old days, many museums would sponsor digs to obtain objects. Private individuals would also become involved either to bolster their own collections or to contribute to their favorite museums. Today, however, money from wealthy individuals is the exception rather than the norm. Most archaeologists in the U.S., at least, compete for grants. Given the competition and the limited amount of money available, many projects do not get funded, and some work, therefore, doesn't get done. And on top of that, many countries today keep most if not all of everything that's found, so if finding and keeping objects is your motivation, you might be out of luck.

The Least You Need to Know

➤ An archaeological site is anywhere that artifacts or other traces of human activity have been found.

➤ There are many ways archaeological sites have been found, both intentionally and accidentally. Tools include remote sensing and aerial photography.

➤ Digging is often a destructive activity, and it's essential that archaeologists record as much as possible.

➤ Archaeological expeditions are often complicated and require a lot of planning.

Chapter 4

The Lowdown on Dating

In This Chapter

➤ Relative dating with strata and style

➤ Carbon-14 and other remarkable radioactive dating methods

➤ Using tree rings to figure out the age of wood

➤ Other clever means of telling how old something is

Archaeological dating? Dinner and a movie? Not quite. If we are studying the past, and we want to put everything into its place in time, we need to have ways of determining how old things are. This is not always easy, though, and there are a variety of techniques that can be used to date individual pieces of evidence or even an entire site.

Relative Dating: Nothing to Do with Your First Cousin

One category of dating techniques is called relative dating. Relative dates don't tell us exactly how old something is, but can tell us that one thing is older or younger than something else. The primary methods of relative dating include:

➤ stratigraphy

➤ style

➤ certain chemical analyses

Let's take a closer look.

Stratigraphy: Stack 'Em Up!

Geologists have shared with us the notion of *stratigraphy*, the study of layers in the earth. Stratigraphy is based on the law of superposition. Simply stated, this law says that as various layers, or *strata,* are formed and accumulate, the older ones are usually found on the bottom. The same principle can be applied to undisturbed archaeological sites. If we find a layer of dirt full of stone tools, and a layer above it with a bunch of pottery, and a wrecked Mayan temple on top of that, we can conclude that the pottery is younger than the tools and older than the temple. Simple, eh? Not always.

Jargon Unearthed

Stratigraphy is the study of layers, or *strata* (singular *stratum*), in the earth.

Lost and Found

How deep? An old debate among archaeologists is whether to dig in consistent levels (for example, 10 centimeters deep at a time) or in natural levels, even though a particular stratum might be meters thick. Each case calls for its own decision, and some archaeologists dig one or both ways depending on the circumstances.

Watch Out for Worms

With natural geological layers, what you see is usually pretty straightforward: Rock layers tend to stay in the order they were deposited. But with humans involved, we can't be so confident. Later people, for example, might dig a well through an older layer of human debris and introduce young stuff into the old, and toss old stuff out of the hole to mix with the young. There are also a number of natural processes that can disrupt the layers.

Burrowing animals can throw old artifacts in with the new, and even the activity of earthworms can move things out of their original contexts. And even artifacts caught in the roots of toppled trees have been known to produce cases of "reverse stratigraphy." Hopefully, the archaeologist can detect these various mixings up and set things straight. Some big digs even employ archaeological "stratigraphers," whose job it is to sort out the various layers in the earth and how they all relate.

Stratigraphy

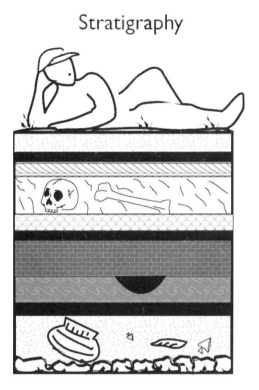

Studying the layers in the earth can tell the archaeologist much about how their contents relate to each other through time. (Courtesy of Brian Schaeffer and the author)

Who's in My Bed?

A layer can also be roughly dated by its content. This was important in the early days of paleontology, when scientists would develop chronologies by matching layers in various places based on their fossil contents. So too in archaeology, where such things as artifact content or plant and animal remains can sometimes be matched between sites.

Layers of volcanic ash can provide another useful date marker. Each eruption tends to produce a specific chemical "signature" in its far-flung debris, so it's possible—in the American Northwest, for example—to distinguish between ash produced by a specific eruption of Mt. Rainier, Mt. Mazama, or the infamous Mt. St. Helens. If we know the date of the eruption, then the layer of ash tells us that the stuff deposited above is younger and the stuff deposited below is older, and anything found within probably dates to the time of the eruption.

Pitfalls and Pointers

If a layer contains a coin from 1890, this doesn't mean that the layer dates to 1890. It does mean that if the layer is undisturbed, then it can't be any older than that date.

Stylin'

Another useful form of relative dating is by artifact style. Most people can probably tell the difference between a Model T, a convertible with fins, and a modern sport utility vehicle, and they could probably tell you not only which is older, but in what order they appeared. That's because styles change through time.

Few items of human manufacture are immune to such change. Some things, in fact, tend to change almost regularly. Pottery, for example, an extremely common component of many ancient cultures, is capable of being shaped and decorated in any number of different ways. Not only that, but it tends to break, and the pieces, known in the trade as *potsherds,* or simply *sherds,* often are tough enough to survive.

Jargon Unearthed

Style refers to the shape and decoration of an object. *Typologies* are ways of organizing artifacts based on details of their style. *Seriation* is the dating of associated groups of objects based on changing styles.

So here's a good situation. You're digging through an ancient mound. There's pottery in the successive layers, and the shapes and decorations change gradually as you go deeper. You can then develop an inventory of pottery styles for your site, and maybe even use it to date other sites, since a layer of the same style of pottery in a neighboring site can be assumed to be of similar age.

If other dating techniques are used to define an exact date for the layer which holds the pottery, then the pottery style becomes an even more useful time marker. And it gets really exciting when we find that same pottery long distances away, thus indicating that people are engaging in trade or some other long distance transport mechanism.

You're My Type

Real experts in pottery styles can sometimes pick up a sherd and, with just a quick glance, determine when it was made and by which group of people. (Kind of like antiques appraisers.) They look at all of the features of a given kind of artifact and develop *typologies,* which are groupings of artifacts based on their common characteristics or style. The typologies can be used to identify and compare similar objects, whether prehistoric stone tools or Roman cloak pins.

Flinders Petrie is credited with contriving one of the more clever ways of using style to arrange objects in time. Confronted with a series of prehistoric graves in Egypt, each containing a collection of pots of different sorts, he noticed that the styles changed among the various graves. By creating a sort of graph in which the graves were ordered to reflect changes in style, he was able to determine the relative dates of each.

This sort of relative dating, which makes use of style changes in groups of objects, is known as *seriation.* It can be a simple procedure, such as listing and arranging each group of objects on sheets of paper, or a complicated statistical analysis involving your computer. It's a useful technique, but by itself it doesn't tell you which end of the ordered series is the youngest or oldest. You usually have to use some sort of additional information, such as stratigraphy, to do that.

Style and Substance

In some ancient cultures, especially where there is an abundance of painting, sculpture, or other detailed crafts, art historians can attempt to date objects based on their style alone. In some cases they can even identify the work of a particular artist or give a name to the subject of a piece known to be living at a particular time. Individual painters of Greek vases have been identified two thousand years later, and unnamed statues of Egyptian pharaohs have been recognized by subtle facial features.

But just when you're comfortable, there are occasionally periods of anachronistic longing for the "good old days." During the Twenty-sixth Egyptian Dynasty, for example, the style of the Old Kingdom, almost 2,000 years previous, was often imitated. But fortunately, not usually with sufficient accuracy to fool the experts.

Dating written documents, too, is often a matter of style. The use of words, the spelling, content, and even the shape of the characters can give valuable and often specific clues to the date and origin. If the text on your ancient Mesopotamian clay tablet mentions a photocopy machine or a hot-rod, it's probably neither ancient nor Mesopotamian.

Pitfalls and Pointers

In Egypt, dating is often a matter of simply reading the walls. The names of a pharaoh are often boastfully noted on temple walls and in their own tombs and those of their functionaries. But watch out! A later pharaoh may have saved a lot of time and money by simply recarving his own name over that of a builder.

Bones and Black Stones

Bones within a given site can be relatively dated by measuring their nitrogen level—which decreases over time—and fluorine and uranium level, which accumulates via ground water. The levels should be about the same in bones of similar age and different in those that are dissimilar. Since this method relies on the specific environmental conditions within a particular site, it is best used within, but not between, sites.

This technique was used to expose the famous Piltdown Man hoax. Early this century, someone artificially "aged" a human cranium and the jawbone of an orangutan, planting them in an English gravel pit. The bones were uncovered between 1912 and 1915. For years the two together were considered to be fossil evidence for the evolutionary "missing link" between ape and man. By measuring the elements mentioned above, however, it was determined that the jawbone and the cranium were of unrelated age. (Although there are suspects, the identity of the hoaxster has never been absolutely determined.)

Water absorption in fragments of volcanic glass can be measured using a technique known as obsidian hydration dating. Freshly flaked obsidian can absorb water at its surfaces from its surrounding environment. The thickness of this "hydration layer" can be measured. If the environmental conditions are similar in a given area within or between sites, then the relative amounts of hydration can be compared. The thicker the hydration layer, the older the date. And, if other more specific dating techniques can be used, then actual dates can be used to date other specimens with similar hydration rates.

Diggers

The possible suspects behind the Piltdown Man hoax are a distinguished lot. Among them are lawyer Charles Dawson, Arthur Smith Woodward of the British Museum, a Jesuit priest and scientist named Pierre Teilhard de Chardin, the anatomist Arthur Keith, and even Sir Arthur Conan Doyle, the writer who invented Sherlock Holmes!

Absolute Dating: That's Commitment

Knowing that one thing is older than another is a good place to start. But the more specific we can get in terms of an actual calendar year, the better we can develop a chronology which can be used to study, describe, and explain the long history of the Earth and its life-forms. Absolute dating is achieved by methods that can produce a specific (or approximately specific) date. Most are very clever and have been improved over the years. Here are some of the best-known ones:

➤ dendrochronology

➤ radiocarbon dating

➤ potassium-argon dating

➤ fission-track dating

➤ archaeomagnetic dating

➤ thermoluminescence

Let's take a look at how they work.

Dendrochronology: Tree Ring Dating

Certain annual cycles in nature are useful to the archaeologist looking for a date. Perhaps the most famous technique is tree-ring dating, or dendrochronology. If you've ever been to a national park, you may have seen the popular exhibit that features a cross-section of a giant log in which hundreds of concentric rings are visible. Popular dates like 1776, 1492, and 1066 are marked by labels moving toward the center, ending in some surprisingly early date for the tree's first year.

Well, that's basically how it works. Many trees accumulate a new ring each year until they are cut down or otherwise die, so one can count the age of the tree by the number of rings.

But, you might ask, don't you need to know what year the tree was cut down in order to start counting in calendar years? Here's where the interesting part comes in. The tree's rings will appear thick or thin depending upon climatic conditions. So, in cases where we know what year the tree was cut down, we have an added bonus to help us with reconstructing the ancient environment. And because these patterns of thick and thin rings occur across many trees, the patterns can be cataloged from trees of various overlapping ages so that a ring chronology can be established, going way back through time. As a result, you can look at an old log and match the pattern of ring sizes in its cross-section to the chronology and come up with the year the tree began and ended its growth.

Jargon Unearthed

Relative dating methods are those which can indicate that an artifact is younger or older than another, but not by how much. *Absolute dating* methods provide dates that can be related to calendar years.

Dendrochronology

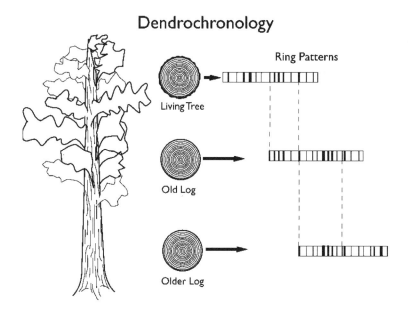

Living Tree

Old Log

Older Log

Ring Patterns

Dendrochronology compares widths of annual tree rings. (Courtesy of Brian Schaeffer and the author)

This works great and gives nice exact dates, but as with most things, there can be some problems:

➤ It only works with trees that produce annual rings. It doesn't work with palm trees, for example.

➤ To develop a good chronology, it helps to have tree species that live a very long time and thus contain many rings, such as the American bristlecone pine or oaks, which are used in Europe.

➤ You need specimens that show a good cross-section of rings, such as old logs.

➤ Like everything else in archaeology, context is important. If you are dating a beam from an old Anasazi cliff dwelling, you are dating the log and not necessarily the building. The log could have been reused from another structure centuries older.

Dendrochronology was originally developed in the American Southwest, and tree chronologies have since been developed in Europe and the Mediterranean area. The American chronologies have been pushed back over 5,000 years, and those in Europe go back even further, to almost 12,000 years.

Radiocarbon Dating

In 1949, Dr. Willard Libby changed the face of archaeology forever when he introduced the revolutionary technique known as radiocarbon dating, often referred to as carbon-14 dating. In simple terms, this is how it works: The earth is continually bombarded with cosmic rays that that produce neutrons which interact with nitrogen in the upper atmosphere to produce carbon-14 (C^{14}). C^{14} joins together with oxygen to produce a form of carbon dioxide which enters plants (along with ordinary carbon dioxide) by way of photosynthesis. Plants absorb C^{14}, and so do the animals that eat the plants and the creatures that eat the plant eaters. This process of C^{14} absorption continues until the living organism dies, and then it stops.

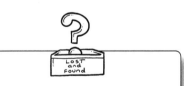

Lost and Found

The bristlecone pine (*Pinus aristata*) is one of the longest-living trees on earth. With some trees living close to 5,000 years, this species, which grows in the western United States, is useful in tree-ring dating.

But that's not the end of the story. C^{14} is an unstable radioactive material, and it decays back into nitrogen. We can measure this transformation and we know how long it takes: 5,730 years for half of the C^{14} to decay. This is called it's "half-life." In 11,460 years, one quarter will be left, in 17,190 years, only one eighth, and so on. So, if we can measure the amount of carbon-14 remaining in a sample, we can determine its age. As you can imagine, this procedure involves a sophisticated laboratory set-up, and it's not inexpensive. But it does produce dates.

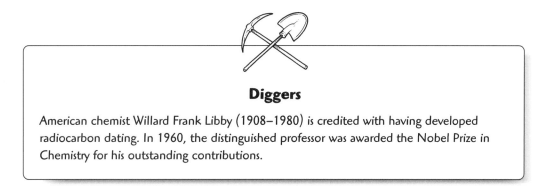

Diggers

American chemist Willard Frank Libby (1908–1980) is credited with having developed radiocarbon dating. In 1960, the distinguished professor was awarded the Nobel Prize in Chemistry for his outstanding contributions.

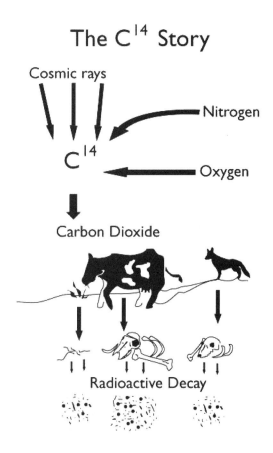

Radiocarbon dating: how it works. (Courtesy of Brian Schaeffer and the author)

Although radiocarbon dating is indeed a wondrous and magnificent thing, there are a number of important considerations to keep in mind:

➤ This dating method can only be used to date material that was once living. Charcoal and wood are real favorites.

45

➤ Given the relatively short half-life of carbon-14, it's difficult to date things more than 50,000 years old, because by that time, there's very little left to count. Things 400 years old or less are also difficult to date, for the opposite reason.

➤ Although techniques have improved, you need a certain minimum amount of material in order to date an object, and that material will typically be destroyed in the process.

➤ The sample must be uncontaminated by other materials that might mess up the date: modern plant roots growing into an old piece of wood, for example.

➤ And, very important in terms of interpretation: The sample must be relevant to whatever it is you hope to date. If, for example, you wish to date a layer in your excavation and you choose a piece of wood, it's possible that the wood itself is from a tree that stopped living hundreds of years before it was incorporated into the site, thus giving you a date too old.

So, let's assume you have submitted your uncontaminated, relevant organic sample of sufficient size to the lab. Eventually a date will be returned. The date might look something like this: 1200 B.P. +/– 100. First, notice the B.P., "Before Present," date. Since the amount of radiocarbon left in your sample will be different if measured 50 years from now, the Before Present date makes sense here.

Unfortunately, since radiocarbon dates have been, are, and will be measured in different years, "B.P." is always changing. So scientists have established the year 1950 as the standard time from which the dates are calculated. To work with it, the best thing to do is simply convert your B.P. date to a calendar date.

The plus-or-minus attached to the dates relates to a statistical probability of error. Without delving into statistical theory, I can tell you that the error range means that there is a 68 percent chance that the date actually falls between the given date and the plus or minus range. So, if we have a converted calendar date of A.D. 1000 plus or minus 100, there is a 68 percent chance the date falls between A.D. 900 and 1100. If we double the possible error, we have a greater statistical

Pitfalls and Pointers

Atomic bomb testing didn't help archaeologists. In some places, the testing produced extreme amounts of radiocarbon in the atmosphere, so much in fact, that some contaminated samples have produced dates in the future! Upon receiving such a date from a lab, one archaeologist commented that he should go out to the archaeological site and wait for the ancient people to show up.

Pitfalls and Pointers

Discrepancies have been found in radiocarbon dates that seem to reflect variations in the amount of cosmic radiation entering the atmosphere through time. Fortunately, correction formulas are available. Dendrochronology has been especially helpful, allowing us to check the accuracy of radiocarbon dates on wood of known age.

confidence rate of 95 percent, but the date will fall between A.D. 800 and 1200. The older the sample, and the less radioactive decay there is to measure, the higher the statistical range of error, so for instance one might find a date of 45,000 B.P. +/– 1,500.

More Radiation, Please!

There are other techniques that make use of the decay of unstable radioactive isotopes. Potassium-argon dating measures radioactive potassium-40 as it decays into argon-40 gas. The technique is used for dating volcanic rock, and with a half-life of approximately 1.3 billion years, it can date some very old rocks indeed. In fact, a rock needs to be at least 100,000 years old before the technique can be applied. It's useful mostly in dating the remains of the early human ancestors in places such as East Africa. There, early stone tools and fossils sandwiched between layers of volcanic material can be given approximate dates based on potassium-argon results.

A method measuring the decay of uranium has proved useful in dating calcium carbonate deposits, especially in limestone caves between about 50,000 and 500,000 years old. Another method, fission-track dating, can be used to determine the age of certain types of minerals, volcanic glass such as obsidian, and human-manufactured glass.

As the uranium decays, it divides in half (fission), creating a sort of small explosion which leaves a mark or track in the glass. Since we know the rate of decay of the uranium isotope, the date can be calculated by counting the tracks. The method is most frequently used on materials several thousand to over a billion years old, but has also been applied to more recent materials.

As is the case with radiocarbon dating, these techniques have a range in error which tends to increase with the age of the sample. But when you're dealing with millions of years, what's a few thousand years here or there? For the moment we can live with it, and in the future, who knows what sort of amazingly precise dating techniques might be developed?

Light and Magnetism

Archaeomagnetic dating is an interesting technique that involves a remarkable physical phenomenon. Did you know that the position of the magnetic pole, at present located in the north, has shifted from time to time in the past? That's right—north, one of the fixed poles of our compass, wanders all over the place, and sometimes even becomes south.

This is important for our purposes because when clays containing iron particles are heated, the particles align themselves to the magnetic pole. So, if we know where the pole has been through the years, and if we can measure the direction of alignment in a clay artifact, then we can date that artifact.

Obviously, the artifact needs to be an immovable structure, typically a kiln. A pot being baked in the kiln will behave similarly, but once you take it out and spin it around, the pot will no longer be aligned and will therefore not be useful for this sort of dating. A lot of information has had to be accumulated for this method to work, and radiocarbon dating of organic materials associated with the kilns has assisted in discovering the patterns.

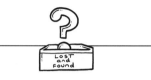

Lost and Found

At some sites, archaeologists find literally millions of broken sherds, making it sometimes nearly impossible to locate and reconstruct the pieces of individual pots. In such cases, pottery experts rely on "diagnostic sherds" for their information. These are the bits of pots such as handles or decorated pieces that will give the expert an idea of what kind of pot is was based on its style, size, and so forth.

Thermoluminescence dating is often used to date pottery. Unlike radiocarbon dating, which measures the amount of radioactive decay, thermoluminescence measures the amount of natural radioactive absorption in substances such as burnt or fired clay and flint. The clock is set, so to speak, when the material is fired, after which the radioactive absorption resumes. When reheated in a laboratory, accumulated trapped electrons can be measured by the intensity of the light they emit. You need to know the radioactive content of the surrounding soil for comparative purposes, but the technique can often be effective, although with a wide range of error.

As you can see, we use a variety of techniques to date a variety of materials. And why not? Determining age is essential for our study of the past. Let's hope even more clever and precise techniques will be developed in the future.

The Least You Need to Know

➤ Relative dating gives you an idea that something is older or younger than something else.

➤ Absolute dating methods are those which try to provide a more or less exact date.

➤ Different dating techniques are used for different kinds of materials.

➤ Most dating techniques have their limitations and consequently must be used with care.

Part 2
Sifting Through the Evidence

In Part One, we laid some groundwork, so to speak, for viewing the past. We also discussed ways of finding the leftovers from ancient times and determining their age. So what else can we do with this stuff so that it makes sense? In this section, we're going to address some specific kinds of evidence. Every piece of data has at least a little story to tell, and different approaches and techniques are required if we're going to find out what it is.

What can human or animal bones tell us? What sort of things can give us clues about the environments in which ancient humans lived? How does the evidence survive? And what about artifacts and other examples of human technology? In the next few chapters, we're going to take a look at some of the ways in which these questions can be addressed, if not answered. And before we're done, we're also going to get our feet a little wet when we try to do the same thing underwater!

Chapter 5

Tales from the Earth

In This Chapter

➤ Geologists share their knowledge of dirt

➤ How plants help us reconstruct the environment

➤ Working with animal remains

➤ Ancient art and dung, too!

➤ Human impact on ancient environments

When we study the human past, we want to know as much of the story as possible. Apart from the people themselves and the things they made, we want to know about how they lived. What was the environment like? What kind of plants and animals lived in the vicinity? How did people interact with their surroundings? What was their relationship with the local plants and animals? Did they eat them, ignore them, or have them as pets? What was the weather like? It takes the skills of a number of specialists to extract this sort of information from the surviving bits of the past, and it's both surprising and exciting how much can be learned.

Let's Talk Dirt

Geoarchaeologists concern themselves with dirt: *soils* and *sediments* found in the archaeological record and what they can tell us. Soils, for example, are good for figuring out previous environments. Some soils can indicate whether there were such things as forests or grasslands in a given area in earlier days.

Geoarchaeologists apply geological principles to archaeological sites and come up with all kinds of information. But they're not just interested in individual sites. They also seek to explain the Earth on global, regional, and local scales.

Jargon Unearthed

Sediments are the materials deposited on the surface of the earth, and *soils* are the uppermost life-supporting layers of sediments.

During the Ice Age, for example, sea levels dropped during the periods of glaciation, exposing land that might have been key in the spread of humans and animals between continents. Subsequently, sea levels have risen as the glaciers melted, thus perhaps stranding some of the evidence underwater. Earthquakes, droughts, floods, fires, and volcanoes also shape the planet, and these, too, are of interest.

Geoarchaeologists are especially useful for reconstructing what are called *site formation processes*. These are the things that make the archaeological record look like it does, and they can help sort out what was the result of human activity and what was caused by nature. For example, an area might have been initially glaciated, and then as the climate changed, people moved into the area at the edge of a stream. Later the stream turned into a river and inundated the site. But when the river changed course, people moved back in and built a village, which was eventually overwhelmed by a sand dune, which gradually was blown away and replaced by a thin layer of fertile soil, and so forth. You get the picture. The geoarchaeologist can help us reconstruct most of this.

Jargon Unearthed

Site-formation processes are those processes that create the physical nature of the archaeological site. These can be of both natural and human origin.

How Does Your Garden Grow?

Nature provides annual environmental information in such places as glacial ice and some lake beds. Glaciers are composed of accumulated layers of snow compressed into ice, and the annual accumulation provides a layer-by-layer record that is often loaded with climatic data. Some lakes that are fed by glacial melting also tend to form annual layers of sediment in their beds. Pollen and other material included in the layers can tell us a lot about the environment.

Cores drilled from lake beds can provide a stratigraphic record of pollen that can show the coming and going of various plant species, including those which might have been introduced by humans. Cores have also been taken from the sea floor, where climatic information can be retrieved from within slowly accumulating layers of muck.

And let's not forget about the trees. As you may recall from the section on dendrochronology in Chapter 4, some trees produce annual rings that give us clues about things like temperature and rainfall based on their thickness.

Sticks, Leaves, and Seeds

If bits and pieces of plants survive, they can provide a lot of information. Paleo-botanists look at such things as wood, leaves, and seeds. And if they can identify them, these things can be good indicators of the ancient environment. Many plants and animals today live in a particular environment, with a certain range of temperature, elevation, or moisture requirements. If, for example, we find evidence of coconuts and papayas in our archaeological site, we can speculate, based on the fact that these plants now grow only in tropical environments, that a tropical environment once existed there. Heather and alpine flowers might suggest a completely different environment.

Retrieving plant remains from an archaeological site requires special attention. Sometimes they can be picked right out of sifting screens (tools for sifting dirt, like big sieves), especially if they're big and visible to the naked eye. Another technique is called flotation. Dirt from the dig is placed in a special bucket containing screens of varying size. As the dirt is screened, the botanical material tends to float and can be caught in the screens.

Most identification is done by comparing the seeds and other materials to known modern species. Woods and plant parts can be examined by slicing off a very thin piece, called a section. When viewed under a microscope, many specimens can then be identified by their specific anatomy.

Some animals, such as pack rats, gather sticks and little plant pieces and drag them to their nests. Finding an ancient midden of this sort can be a real bonanza for the paleobotanist. The rats collect from the local environment, so the material they collect should give a good indication of what it was like nearby. And as a big bonus, this organic material can be radiocarbon dated, that is, after you dissolve the dried rat urine that glues the nest together!

Plant remains are often counted by archaeologists. Their abundance or lack thereof in a given part of a site might suggest what activities went on there, such as finding a lot of chaff in an area where threshing took place. A change in the quantities or types of species through time might indicate a change in how they were used, or perhaps a change in the environment.

Lost and Found

A number of natural processes can move things in a site, and geo-archaeologists, like other specialists, have their own special terms for them. "Cryoturbation" involves frost-heave, and "argilliturbation" describes swelling clays. "Graviturbation" is the effect of dirt creeping down a slope, and "bioturbation" describes the site-disturbing activities of living things, including burrowing animals, earthworms, and plant roots.

Pitfalls and Pointers

Although paleobotanists try to reconstruct the environment based on the known distribution of modern plants, we must also consider the possibility of different kinds of environments, examples of which are not found on earth today.

Pollen Is My Pal

Many plants produce pollen, and it's a great way to look at the ancient environment. Pollen is often produced in great quantities, and it's tough and therefore tends to survive quite well. Most importantly, pollens produced by different kinds of plants tend to look different, thus making it possible to identify what was growing in the vicinity.

Pitfalls and Pointers

Finding a bunch of pollen in a site can be deceptive. Some plants produce more pollen than others, and one or two such plants in the vicinity might produce the majority of the pollen in a sample. Furthermore, just to keep you on your toes, the wind can blow pollen around from another environment where it eventually ends up in your sample.

People who study pollen are called *palynologists.* These folks need to have good eyes and a lot of patience, because they spend loads of time with their eyes parked over a microscope looking at thousands of little pollen grains. They count and identify them, draw huge diagrams, and come to their conclusions.

Other parts of plants can be useful, as well. Little silica structures called phytoliths are produced by some leafy plants and grasses and grow inside the plant. Because they are hard, they often survive long after the plant has rotted away. Like pollen, there are differences between the phytoliths of different kinds of plants which allow them to be identified. Some have even been found adhering to stone tools and teeth!

Bug Story

Insects have a story to tell, too. Some tend to be very sensitive to environmental conditions. Some sensitive bugs such as beetles can often be identified by examining their tough shell-like exoskeletons. The shells of land snails are also helpful. Since they don't move very fast, it might be assumed that they represent the environment in the local area.

Pitfalls and Pointers

Some animals have a high temperature or environmental tolerance range and seem to be able to survive almost anywhere, and therefore aren't particularly good environmental indicators for archaeologists. And then there is the perennial problem of flying bugs, who might have entered the site from afar.

Bone Jour!

It is not unusual to find many animal bones in archaeological sites. Their study is known as *zooarchaeology,* and it is the duty of the *faunal analyst* or *zooarchaeologist* to deal with this sort of material. The remains of animals not only have the potential to tell you about the environment, but also how the animals lived (or died) with humans. Given the right conditions, bones can survive in profusion, and if certain animals were used for food, we can often find their remains in garbage dumps, sometimes with evidence of butchering and cooking or other methods of food preparation.

A good faunal analyst can extract a tremendous amount of information from a collection of bones. It's usually not too difficult to sort out the mammals from the birds from the fish and so forth. And, being familiar with the usual animals in an area, most can readily identify the various bones or teeth and can figure out anything unfamiliar by consulting reference materials. It is often possible to determine the age of a given animal, and sometimes it is even possible to tell if a bone belongs to a male or female of a given species.

The types of animals found in an archaeological site can give you an idea of cultural practices and perhaps even help identify some of the early occupants. In Israel, for example, you can't expect to find the bones of taboo pigs in places occupied by Jews or Muslims. If you've got pigs in a layer of your site, you're probably dealing with some other group.

The existence of a particular animal can be telling in other respects. At the ancient site of Ashkelon on Israel's Mediterranean coast, over 800 dogs were buried in what is the ancient world's largest known dog cemetery. Each animal was carefully placed, suggesting that they were highly respected or sacred. The cemetery dates to the fifth century B.C. and might be related to Persian religious practices.

One of the most amazing collections of Ice Age creatures was found superbly preserved in natural asphalt seeps known as the La Brea Tar Pits, located today in the middle of downtown Los Angeles. Researchers have recovered millions of bones of now-extinct mammoths, saber-toothed cats, lions, and giant ground sloths, along with birds, insects, and numerous other creatures of all kinds and sizes, trapped in the tar thousands of years ago.

When scientists examined the collection, they unexpectedly found a strange overabundance of carnivores when compared to herbivores, which suggested that when the plant eaters got stuck, carnivores individually or in packs attacked the trapped beasts, only to become trapped themselves. Only one human has thus far been recovered from the tar pits: a 9,000-year-old female known as "La Brea Woman."

Jargon Unearthed

A *zooarchaeologist*, *archaeo-zoologist*, or *faunal analyst* is a specialist who studies the remains of animals, typically bones, found in archaeological sites: a study known as *zooarchaeology*. *Palynology* is the study of pollen, and a *palynologist* is one who studies palynology.

Lost and Found

Taphonomy is the study of what happens to living things after death. It can give us great insights into what might survive in the archaeological record and what might not. For instance, certain parts of bones, such as the dense ends of the long bones, tend to last longer.

A dead dog of Ashkelon.

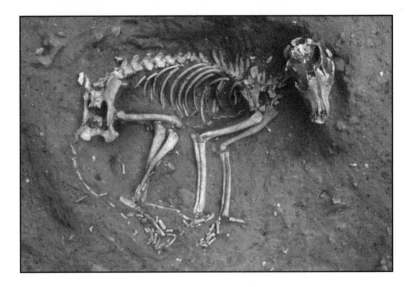

Harvesting Information

One of the great questions of archaeology is how, when, and why plants and animals were domesticated. After long millennia of hunting animals and gathering other natural resources, plants and animals were finally modified to suit human convenience, and human societies would be radically transformed, for better or for worse. But is it possible to detect such a thing in the archaeological record? Some faunal analysts believe that evidence of domestication can be detected in some animals' bones.

Domesticated animals tend to be smaller in size than their wild counterparts, and if they've got horns, they tend to be shaped differently. Doing a "mortality profile" for a site, that is, noting the age of death for animals you think might be domesticated, might provide a clue. Since only a few adult males are needed for reproduction purposes, an abundance of slaughtered young males might suggest that animals were being kept in the vicinity.

As with animals, it can sometimes be hard to tell if a given plant is domesticated. Some forms of domesticated plants, such as maize and wheat, have developed tougher parts than their wild counterparts which serve to retain the bits of use to humans: the kernels, seeds and grains. The nature of the ancient site and telltale artifacts such as grinding stones and storage containers might also help to build a case.

Pitfalls and Pointers

Although you and I can probably recognize the difference between a sheep and a goat from a long distance, it's very hard to tell the difference between the two from their bones. Yes, without their woolly coats or wiry hair, they look pretty much the same; thus many faunal analysts note their remains as Ovis/Capra: sheep/goat.

Fish That Talk

Fish have a lot to say. I was certainly surprised to find fish bones in the remains of an ancient campfire in the Egyptian desert, many miles from any water. The campers of old had once lived on the edge of a huge lake, which has diminished considerably over the last several thousand years. Like mammals and birds, fish can often be identified by their bones, and their presence can be suggestive of past environments and possible cultural uses.

But fish also have some especially neat features. Otoliths are little stone-like objects that form in the ears of fish and are distinct enough to assist in identification. And fish produce annual rings in their vertebrae which can be counted to age the individual. The scales, too, can provide information about the type of fish, including whether it's a saltwater or freshwater species and its size and age.

Artistic Clues

Sometimes, in addition to the remains of plants and animals, we find a different kind of evidence. In some places, ancient art can give us wonderful depictions of the ancient environment. Cave dwellers in Europe painted on the walls and often depicted types of animals that are now extinct or no longer found in that area. Some rock art in North Africa shows an abundance of wild animals in areas which are now mostly covered by desert. Four-thousand-year-old Egyptian tomb scenes illustrate a world where hippos and crocodiles roamed in papyrus swamps, an environment which has now vanished in modern Egypt, but which survives thousands of miles southward in central Africa.

This ancient Egyptian tomb scene shows an environment that no longer survives in modern Egypt. It's a papyrus swamp. Note the hippo under water in the corner. (From Adolf Erman, Life in Ancient Egypt *[1894], p. 210)*

Clues from Dung

Once in a while, animal or human dung survives, and it can be quite instructive. These remains are known as *coprolites,* and their contents can tell us lots about food choices, the environment, and even the health of the dung provider. Parasites, seeds, hair,

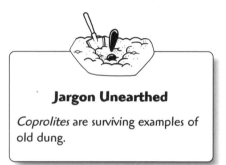

insect parts, fish scales, and indigestible plant bits often pass through in an identifiable state, to the delight of the brave researchers who pursue this line of work. It's also a great source of pollen.

Jargon Unearthed

Coprolites are surviving examples of old dung.

Laboratory techniques are used first to determine if the dung belongs to a herbivore, a carnivore, or a human, and then the fun begins. It takes a special archaeologist with a devotion to dung to deal with this stuff. It's one of those things that you're grateful someone else is doing, so long as they're willing to share the results.

A World of Change

Among the things archaeologists are interested in is the impact of humans upon the environment. While the surroundings have a big influence on the human activities that go on in an area, sometimes those activities can in turn reshape the surroundings, as when overgrazing turns fertile grasslands into barren deserts. On lonely Easter Island in the Pacific, it has been suggested that the cutting down of most of the trees (for use in statue moving) or the coming of rats in colonist's canoes may have played important roles in an ecological transformation of the island. (For more on this fascinating place, see Chapter 19.)

Where'd They Go?

Another way humans have shaped their environment is by causing the extinction of animal species, including the over-hunted ostrich-like giant moas of New Zealand and certain birds whose beautiful colored feathers were highly prized by the early Hawaiians. And let's not forget the dodo and passenger pigeon. Archaeology provides evidence of such human activities even in ancient times. Animals such as lions were hunted to extinction in Mesopotamia, where they are depicted in art from 2,700-year-old royal Assyrian palaces. They certainly don't live there anymore, although a changing climate might have also played a role. The later Romans also helped to bring about the extinction of several species in certain regions by their capturing of them for use in brutal coliseum shows.

Adios to the Mammoth

During the latter part of the Ice Age (ca. 2.4 million to 10,000 years ago) humans coexisted with a wide variety of creatures that no longer exist today. In Europe, woolly mammoths wandered about along with giant cave bears and other great creatures. In the Americas, there were several elephant species, lions, camels, horses, and lots of other big animals that have since disappeared.

What happened? There are several theories. One suggests that changing climates during the Ice Age led to extinctions. Others propose that diseases or humans hunters killed certain animals off and disrupted the food chain. Perhaps the truth lies in a combination of several such factors. Fortunately, archaeologists have a wide variety of tools and techniques that are helping us find the answers.

Lost and Found

Mammoths died off at the end of the Ice Age 10,000 years ago, or so we once thought. Archaeologists have found that a species of pygmy mammoth survived on Wrangell Island, north of Siberia, until about 2,000 B.C.

The Least You Need to Know

➤ In studying the past, we are interested in learning about the big picture, including what the environment was like.

➤ Many different fields of study contribute to our search for ancient environmental knowledge.

➤ Geoarchaeologists can help us understand the changing face of the planet and the nature of the archaeological record.

➤ The remains of plants and animals can give us many clues about the way things were and how humans interacted with the natural environment.

Voices from the Grave

Since we're interested in studying the human past, what better way to scrutinize our ancestors than by looking at what's left of them personally? Everybody who ever lived up to about 120 years ago is dead, after all. That's a whole bunch of dead bodies, many hundreds of millions, and counting.

The study of human remains is most often the domain of the physical anthropologist or forensic anthropologist. The latter term is usually associated with crime scene investigations or the coroner's department, but both do much of the same thing. A lot of work is with bones, a study known as *osteology*. Human osteology, of course, deals with the human skeleton, or whatever's left of it.

In this chapter we'll take a look at what those skeletons can tell us. How old were people when they died? Were they male or female? Did they have any health problems when they were alive and how did they die? To whom are they related?

That Which Remains

Obviously, if the remains of everything that ever died survived, we'd be walking on a very thick layer of bones. As it works, we're all part of a natural cycle that reduces us to dust. Sooner if not later, the remains of dead things are going to disintegrate, unless

Lost and Found

In the Biblical book of Genesis (3:19), God gives disobedient Adam a little taste of the future: "In the sweat of your face you shall eat bread till you return to the ground, for out of it you were taken; you are dust and to dust you shall return."

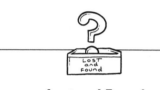

Lost and Found

Some boney facts:

➤ At birth, a human baby's skeleton has 460 growth centers, which will eventually fuse into the 206 bones of an adult.

➤ Your skull is composed of 22 single and paired bones.

➤ The "hyoid" bone is perhaps the least known bone in the body. It connects with no other bone, but serves to anchor your tongue and other muscles involved with speech.

unusual processes intervene. Dinosaur skeletons and other fossils are the exception rather than the rule, and they owe their survival to rare fortuitous conditions that saved them from total decay.

The same thing applies to dead people. Unless the conditions, or *environment of deposition*, are just right, human bodies will dissolve, including, eventually, the bones. A body left in the woods, for example, will be subject to the effects of bugs, bacteria, and various scavengers, and can completely vanish in a matter of months.

Ancient people were buried or otherwise disposed of in all sorts of interesting ways—everything from a simple hole in the ground to amazing artifact-rich burials in large tombs. Bodies can be cremated, left in trees for vultures, or buried in jars or coffins, sometimes with favorite toys or tools. Other times the dead are allowed to rot, and their bones are later collected and bundled together. Occasionally, a whole bunch of people are buried at the same time after some sort of natural or man-made catastrophe.

Given the right artificial or natural conditions, whole humans can be preserved. Bodies buried in desert sand, in cold dry conditions, or even directly in ice can survive for thousands of years. In several instances, relatively intact bodies have been preserved in peat bogs. In some well-preserved bodies, even the soft internal bits survive. And then there are the human attempts to artificially preserve the body, such as mummification, which sometimes, amazingly, succeed. In most cases, though, we are left only with bones. Fortunately, bones can tell us a lot.

Young or Old?

Let's assume we've uncovered a human skeleton in the course of our excavations. One of the basic questions we'll want to ask is how old this individual was at death. To answer that, we need to know something about how the human skeleton develops.

The fully developed human skeleton is composed of 206 bones, many of which are composed of fused sections. The rate at which the various bones develop and fuse, from the fetus through adulthood, can give us a good idea about age. The ends and shafts of the long bones in the arms and legs fuse together at known rates. For instance, the humerus, or upper arm bone, tends to be completely fused by age 25, and the upper leg bone, or femur, by about age 22.

Bone Fusion!

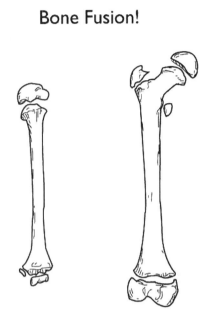

The ends of long bones fuse at known rates and help to determine the age of an individual.

10 year old Humerus   15 year old Femur

You may have noticed the "soft spot" on a baby's head. This is an area where the bones of the skull have yet to fuse together. This happens at a fairly predictable rate and can be measured by the degree of fusion of the *sutures*, the wavy cracks noticeable on the top of skulls where the bones are joining. In the skulls of older individuals, the top of the head can be completely smooth, with no indications of the plates.

In children, whose bones are generally unfused, the cycle of tooth eruption is telling. The baby teeth come and go at a typical rate, to be replaced in stages by the permanent teeth. The baby teeth tend to be completely gone by age twelve and the permanent teeth, including the infamous "wisdom teeth," by age 21. After that, we can measure relative wear on the adult teeth.

Most bones tend to get thinner as they get older, and others, such as the end of the ribs, become somewhat eroded where they join with the breastbone. The place where the two pubic bones meet on the pelvis has also been used for dating skeletons, because its rough surface becomes smoother through time at a predictable rate.

Jargon Unearthed

Osteology is the study of bones.

Boy or Girl?

In spite of what your politically correct social engineering professor in college may have told you, boys and girls are very different. If you don't believe me, stand in front of a mirror naked with one of your opposites. Some scientists are even suggesting that the male and female brains are "wired" differently. The differences between the two are certainly reflected in the bones. Females, for example, are physiologically designed for giving birth; consequently, their pelves (plural of "pelvis") are a bit different than males. The pelvis, in fact, is the best indicator of the sex of a skeleton.

Female pelves are usually broader than males, and certain notched or curved areas have wider angles to accommodate the requirements for bearing children. Since the ligaments at the joining of the two pubic bones are often strained during childbirth, scarring is occasionally visible there, indicating that the woman has given birth at least once in the course of her life. Some investigators even claim that they can determine how many children a woman bore, but not all agree that this is possible.

Women's bones are usually less robust than males, and women typically have smaller teeth. Their foreheads are apt to be more vertical than the typically sloped male. There are a few other things on the skull that are indicative of males, including square jaws, larger and more pronounced brow ridges, and other features. In determining the sex of a skeleton, as many variables as possible should be considered together.

Of course, there are females with narrow hips and sloped foreheads and males with wide hips, so sometimes determining the sex can be tricky. Real bone experts, though, can in many cases tell nearly at a glance—as long as they're dealing with an adult skeleton, that is. The bones of prepubescent children pose a real problem, because their secondary sexual characteristics haven't yet manifested themselves in their skeletons.

Pitfalls and Pointers

One of the most controversial discoveries in Egypt is "Tomb 55," which was discovered in the Valley of the Kings in 1907. Much of the grave furniture found within belonged to Queen Tiye (ca. 1350 B.C.) and a damaged coffin was found containing a mummy. The bones of this poorly preserved mummy were originally identified as that of a woman. Subsequent studies seem to indicate that the body is that of a young man in his twenties, but his identity is still wildly debated.

Male and female pelves: There is a difference.

Male Pelvis   Female Pelvis

Tall or Small?

There tends to be a relationship between the length of certain bones and the size of an individual. Charts have been developed that can generally predict what the height of someone was based on, say, the length of a femur. There are differences in average proportion between various populations, though, and it helps to know if the bones belonged to a certain group—for example, Caucasian, African, Asian, and so on—so that the appropriate formula can be applied.

The height of mummies and other preserved dead folk isn't too hard to estimate, but you do need to account for shrinkage. Once in a while, rare "trace fossils," such as footprints, are found which can allow us to make a size estimate. The prints of ancient feet have been found in caves and also, tragically, in lava.

The Race Is On

Although we are all part of the same human family, there are some physical differences between population groups that can be seen in the bones. Some African populations tend to have wider nasal apertures and longer leg bones than Caucasian peoples, and many Asians have incisor teeth that are shovel-shaped in the back. A distinguishing characteristic of Polynesian skeletons is a "rocker jaw." Unlike most Caucasian jaws, which will sit flat on a table, the rocker jaw is curved along its base.

It Was a Tough Life

Human remains can tell us not only about the basic characteristics of an individual, such as age, sex, and race, but also sometimes about lifestyle, health, and cause of death. If we have a whole group of remains from a specific area, an ancient cemetery, for instance, we might be able to determine the average life span. Compared to today, life spans in the past could be relatively short, and survival through childhood was by no means guaranteed.

When we find whole bodies frozen, dried, mummified, or whatever, all kinds of interesting information can be obtained. Parasites, worms, and diseases can often be detected within soft tissues or in human coprolites. Bones, though, can tell a surprisingly

Lost and Found

Footprints 3.6 million years old belonging to pre-human creatures were discovered preserved in solidified ash at Laetoli, Tanzania. These rare "trace fossils" demonstrated that these creatures were walking on two feet quite similar to our own. An estimation of height based on the size of the footprints suggests that their makers were about 4 to 4¹/₂ feet tall.

Pitfalls and Pointers

Scientists were in for a big surprise when they examined a small Egyptian mummy labeled with the name Moutemhet. The mummy was thought to be the infant daughter of a woman named Makare, with whom she was buried. X-rays revealed that the little mummy bundle contained the remains of a female baboon.

large chunk of the story. Fractures, healed or otherwise, can be seen, as well as other traumatic injuries. Degenerative diseases, such as arthritis and leprosy, can be detected. Syphilis can leave its mark on bones, as can abscesses. Episodes of malnutrition are sometimes visible in tiny microscopic lines, known as Harris lines, which appear when growth is halted.

Teeth can provide a lot of information as well, in addition to evidence of age. For example, they can suggest the nature of the diet. If the teeth are worn down at an early age, it might indicate that the person ate a lot of coarse or gritty food. Cavities and other forms of decay might indicate a poor diet, or one with a lot of sugar or other notorious sources of dental problems.

Untimely Ends

Cause of death is always of interest. Arrowheads found imbedded in bones, sword slashes, and bashed heads all suggest an unpleasant end. Mass graves of dead Egyptian warriors have been found, and one royal mummy bears the gash of a battle axe across his skull. It's even been suggested that the famous King Tut was conked on the head, as evidenced by a bone fragment detected in X-rays.

Fortunately, not everyone meets their doom in a violent way, and we also study bones carefully to look for injuries, disease, and just plain old age.

Diggers

In 1845, the Arctic explorer Captain Sir John Franklin set out from England in two ships with 134 men to search for the Northwest Passage. They never returned. Several expeditions went in search of them and eventually found a few clues indicating that all involved had gradually died off. The graves of three expedition members were found on Beechey Island, and in 1984 and 1986 the well-preserved, frozen bodies were exhumed and examined. All three apparently died of tuberculosis. The bodies also contained a very high measure of lead, which might have been absorbed through food stored in tin cans sealed with lead. The resulting poisoning may have contributed to the men's death. The remains of still more of Franklin's men, found at Erebus Bay on King William Island in 1993, attest a more gruesome fate. Of the more than 400 bones and bone fragments recovered there, 25% had cut marks, suggesting that the bodies had been intentionally dismembered and defleshed—cannibalized.

Radical Surgery

Evidence of ancient surgery is occasionally found. *Trepanation* was practiced here and there—a procedure in which a chunk of skull was removed to relieve headaches, release evil spirits, or for whatever reason. I can't imagine that the procedure was particularly pleasant, but there are many skulls that show healed holes in the head, so people did survive it. Some skulls even provide graphic evidence that an individual underwent and survived multiple trepanations.

> **Jargon Unearthed**
>
> *Trepanation* is the surgical removal of a piece of bone from the cranium.

Beautiful Bones

Some ancient people engaged in cultural practices that left dramatic marks on their bones. Skull deformation was performed in a number of places in the world. In some cases, a baby's skull would be bound while the plates in its skull were still growing, and the end result was a flat or oblong head that someone must have thought looked pretty good. Feet could likewise be bound to keep them small, as was done in China. Teeth were sometimes knocked out or decorated by cutting and shaping to achieve a desired effect. Elite Maya of Mexico and Central America often had their teeth inlaid with turquoise or other semi-precious materials.

DNA: Unzipping Your Genes

Who you are and how you are related to everyone else is one of the more interesting subjects that archaeology can address. If we believe in an ultimate common ancestor for all of us, than we are ultimately all related. But through time, what with genetic mutation and the mixing and matching of genetic material among and between groups, we have developed a tremendous wealth of human variety.

Comparing skull shapes and bone measurements was for decades a common way of identifying and relating groups of people. Noting differences in blood types was and is especially useful. But today, with advances that allow us to look at the very genetic code in each and every one of us, we can attempt to unlock all sorts of secrets about our past.

> **Jargon Unearthed**
>
> *DNA*, or deoxyribonucleic acid, is the chemical genetic code housed in our chromosomes.

Who Are You?

Half of our individual genetic code is passed on to us by each of our parents, which they, in turn, inherited from their parents. This information, which determines our physical makeup, is housed in the center of each of our cells in the form of *DNA*.

DNA (a.k.a. deoxyribonucleic acid) is composed of various combinations of proteins within our chromosomes that determine everything from facial structure and height to inherited diseases.

If we can sample DNA from ancient people, we might be able to tell who is related to whom. It's not always easy to extract DNA from human remains, but it has been successfully performed many times with samples from mummies and other bodies retaining soft tissues. And now there are techniques that can even extract DNA from old bones.

Pitfalls and Pointers

When tombs in Egypt's Valley of the Kings were robbed in ancient times, the priests would gather up the ransacked mummies, rewrap them, and store groups of them together. When the mummies were x-rayed, scientists discovered that the ancient priests might have mislabeled the pharaohs. The expected ages and facial structures of the mummies did not always fit. This is something that we hope DNA will sort out.

Jargon Unearthed

A type of DNA that is inherited unmixed from one's maternal line is *mtDNA*. It can provide evidence of long-term inheritance.

The comparison and matching of DNA has been used to solve some interesting historical problems. DNA was used recently to identify the bodies of the murdered family of the last Russian czar by comparing their DNA with known living relatives. In another example, DNA was recently extracted from a 9,000-year-old skeleton found in a cave in Cheddar, England, and a modern relative was identified living nearby.

The problem of figuring out who was related to whom among ancient Egyptian royalty might ultimately be solved when DNA samples taken from the mummies are analyzed. Information from DNA has also allowed us to determine how genetically different or similar we are to Neanderthals and other primates such as chimpanzees.

On Your Mom's Side

There is another type of DNA which is producing a lot of interesting results. "Mitochondrial DNA," or *mtDNA*, is found outside the nucleus of a cell and contains genetic material inherited only from the mother. This is useful for identifying relatedness of people over the long term, because the material isn't constantly being recombined with the genetic code of a father.

Information from mtDNA can be used to trace migrations of ancient people all over the world, even back to the proposed homeland for humans on the African continent. A genetic mutation originating in Asia, for example, might be found in subsequent generations who had established themselves in such places as the Americas or Polynesia. With evidence from deceased individuals and their living descendants, an interesting story of personal or group heritage, and perhaps even ancient migrations, might be told.

Mummies and Grand-mummies

When it comes to dead people, mummies are by far the most popular. Although natural mummies can be produced by dry, cold, and other special conditions, intentional mummification was practiced in such places as Egypt, the Canary Islands, and Chile. In Egypt, untold thousands, if not millions, of mummies were prepared over approximately 3,000 years. The internal organs were removed and the bodies dried out with chemicals and then wrapped up, placed in a coffin, and sealed in a tomb. Many of the royal mummies of Egypt were given the "deluxe" mummification treatment, and their bodies are usually superbly preserved.

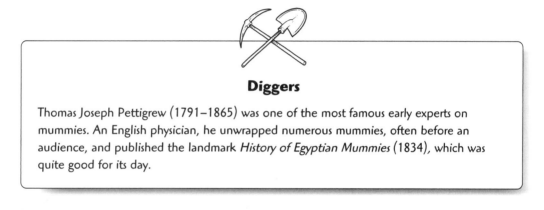

Diggers

Thomas Joseph Pettigrew (1791–1865) was one of the most famous early experts on mummies. An English physician, he unwrapped numerous mummies, often before an audience, and published the landmark *History of Egyptian Mummies* (1834), which was quite good for its day.

The author uncovered this well-preserved mummy in Egypt.

Although we're usually glad to have some flesh survive once in a while, it makes it harder to look at the bones, which give us a lot of the age and sex information that I mentioned above. The use of X-rays and CAT-scans can assist tremendously in this regard. Even wrapped mummies can be studied quite well without having to take them apart. These techniques, which allow us to see right through the mummies, often reveal artifacts or other surprises in the wrappings or in the mummies themselves.

Lost and Found

Mummies from ancient Egypt were once plentiful, and many were exported to Western countries as curiosities. Ground up mummies were popular in Europe for medicinal purposes, thus sparking an interesting export business in Egypt. Mummy wrappings were once recycled in an attempt to make paper, and Mark Twain commented (jokingly?) that the numerous mummies themselves were being used to stoke the engines of steam locomotives.

Faces of the Past

The incredible variations possible within the basic human face allow you to tell the difference between your brother, the guy next door, and the foreign exchange student down the street. With a relatively intact skull, it is sometimes possible for skilled artists to reconstruct the face of an individual with some degree of accuracy.

Known soft tissue thickness and facial muscles can be plotted on the actual skull or a cast. Eye and hair color can be guessed if a given racial or ethnic group is suspected, and a model head can be produced. These reconstructions have been occasionally effective in identifying murder victims, and have been used to give us a glimpse of the very faces of our ancestors.

Taken as a whole, though, we are not merely interested in individuals, but in groups of people as well. Are there patterns in how long they lived or how they died? Did they tend to suffer from one affliction or another? How did they differ physically from other groups of people in time and space? These are all good questions, and they can all be addressed by the fascinating remains of our own species.

The Least You Need to Know

➤ Dead bodies provide useful insights into how people looked, lived, and died.

➤ Except under special circumstances, most human bodies survive as bone at best, and most often not even that.

➤ Examination of human bones can often reveal the age, sex, race, diet and lifeways, and cause of death of an individual, along with other specific information.

➤ Studies of DNA provide the chance to determine who is related to whom and to trace ancient migration patterns.

Artifacts with Tales to Tell

Everybody knows that archaeologists study artifacts, among other things. But what exactly is an artifact? In this chapter, we'll explore that issue and discuss what different kinds of artifacts can tell us. We'll also take a brief look at the experimental side of archaeology, a subject that is often fun and provocative.

What's an Artifact?

We've talked about artifacts and such in the previous chapters, but what are they exactly? One definition holds that an artifact is anything used, manufactured, or modified by human beings. Sounds simple, eh? Not necessarily. There are a lot of things out there that look just like humans made them, but are actually natural objects.

Ask any archaeologist or paleontologist working as a museum curator and they can tell you stories about people bringing in rocks, pieces of wood, and other objects shaped like animals, ancient weapons, tools, or pieces of art. Some curators even keep a shelf of these sorts of things, some of which in fact are nearly convincing.

Separating what occurs in nature and what is truly an artifact is obviously an important question. There are several sites in the Americas that contain what appear to be ancient stone tools. And if they could be positively determined to be of human manufacture, they would dramatically push back the age of humans in the New World and radically alter our ideas.

The Calico site in California's Mojave desert is one such site. There, chipped stones resembling tools were found in the gravel dating to perhaps 70,000 years ago. Critics dismissed the dubious context of the find, but more importantly, they argued that the so-called "tools" were natural.

There is also some ambiguity about how much a natural object must be modified by humans before it becomes an artifact. Think about this one: If someone picks up a stone and skips it across a pond, where it sinks and lands on the mucky bottom, is it an artifact? Its location was modified by a human, after all, and it served as a toy, a tool of amusement.

I've had students argue both sides, including those who insist that since we probably won't be able to determine that the skipped stone is an artifact, then it isn't. I disagree. Our ineptitude doesn't change the fact that the stone was used by a human. I would define an artifact as anything used, manufactured, or modified by humans.

In practice, the term casually refers to objects that are fairly small and portable. Archaeologists use a couple of other terms when discussing other kinds of artifacts. A *feature* is a non-portable artifact. Fire-pits and kilns, for example, would fit this definition. A *structure* is some sort of building.

In discussing artifacts, we often divide them up by the materials they are made of. The major groups include:

➤ stone

➤ pottery

➤ metal

➤ fibers

➤ bone and ivory

➤ wood

Let's take a look at what we can learn from some of these groups.

Pitfalls and Pointers

At the site of Old Crow in the Yukon, the big debate is whether broken bones resembling tools were produced by the action of animals or other natural forces, or by human effort. The alleged tools were created with a spiral fracture, a kind of break seemingly rarely produced in nature. Experiments conducted by throwing bones to zoo animals, however, demonstrated, that bears can create similar "tools" with their bite.

Jargon Unearthed

An *artifact* is anything used, manufactured, or modified by human beings; a *feature* is a non-portable artifact; and a *structure* is some sort of building.

Stone Faces: Lithics

Among the oldest and most commonly found and preserved kinds of artifacts are stone tools. Archaeologists refer to them as *lithics,* and their manufacture as "lithic technology." A variety of stone has been used for tool manufacture, including flint, basalt, and obsidian. Crude stone tools apparently made by pre-humans in East Africa date back to around 2 to 2.5 million years ago.

Most tools begin when a chunk of stone is modified by chipping and shaping. The chips themselves can often serve as tools, or material for the finished tool. The end result can be a big clunky hand axe or a delicate little cutting blade, and everything in between. A great deal of variation is possible, and the styles of different people at different times and places can often be discerned.

The simple Olduwan pebble tools of ancient East Africa can be easily distinguished from the masterfully chipped Clovis spear points of early American hunters or the complex ceremonial obsidian knives of the Maya. Archaeologists have developed typologies of stone tools, with descriptive categories based on shape, number of edges, and so forth, that can be used for stylistic dating and comparison between sites.

Knapping the Flint

Lithics experts often engage in a lot of experimentation by manufacturing their own tools. This process of manufacture is called *flintknapping,* and trying it will quickly instill an appreciation for the skill of our ancestors. In replicating stone tools, experimental flintknappers gain insights not only into how a tool is shaped and finished, but also about what kind of marks are left on a stone as a result of human activity (as opposed to nature at work) and what sort of debris is left over. The latter is especially important, because when the tool is made and its maker walks away, a mess of little flakes, called "debitage," often remains, and this debris can sometimes tell us about what was being made and how.

What Was It Good For?

So we've found some stone tools. What do they mean? What was their function? Suppose someone

Pitfalls and Pointers

Flintknapping is an art, and sometimes a dangerous one. Cuts are common, especially when working with obsidian (volcanic glass). If you want to try it, it's good to learn from someone, or at least consult a good book. And when you're done knapping your flint, clean up the mess, or you might seriously confuse an archaeologist of the future.

Jargon Unearthed

Lithics are stone tools. *Flintknapping* is the art of creating them.

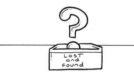

Lost and Found

Humans were using stone tools tens of thousands of years before pottery or metal was in use. But Stone Age people probably also used other materials, some of which simply did not survive the ages. Wood and bone, for example, can disintegrate quickly. Perhaps the "Stone Age" is the Stone Age because that's what has survived best.

manufactures an arrowhead to wear around their neck as a pendant. Is it still an arrowhead if it's never been used as such? Can we just look at a tool and determine its function based on common sense? Is that hand-sized thing used to scrape hides or was it a cute paperweight?

Determining the function of stone tools is very important, and it isn't just a matter of guessing or making up a likely story that seems to make sense to you. Archaeologists typically address this crisis by exploring the physical parameters of the material (is it strong? brittle? flexible?, etc.) as appropriate for a given function, and also by looking for actual traces of use.

The edges of a stone tool can be examined to look for evidence of wear. Markings parallel to an edge, for instance, might indicate that it was used with a cutting motion, while edge breakage patterns might suggest a different kind of motion. Ancient residues adhering to stone artifacts can sometimes be detected, including plant parts and even blood.

Some archaeologists have made replicas of ancient tools and then experimented to see what sorts of marks different kinds of materials leave on them. Bone and wood might leave distinct patterns wholly different from those left by animal hide or grass. This is also a good way to see how different tools work for different jobs.

Pitfalls and Pointers

The term "arrowhead" is rarely used by archaeologists. Instead, the preferred word is "projectile point." The latter term can encompass not only the pointed stone tools that were fitted on the ends of arrows, but also the tips of spears and other weapons.

A prehistoric projectile point from Egypt.

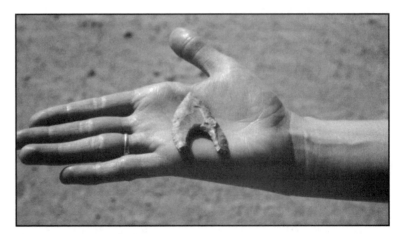

Pots: Making 'Em and Breaking 'Em

Humans started making pots about 12,000 years ago, and pottery became increasingly important and abundant as people began to establish themselves in permanent settlements. The possible functions of pots are endless. They can be used to hold water or food, or simply for decoration. Residue traces can sometimes be detected, which can give us an indication of the artifact's function or contents.

Sorting It Out

Pottery and archaeologists are good friends. Ceramic vessels and other objects manufactured from baked clay are durable and survive very well. Clay can be molded in an infinite variety of shapes, and it can be decorated as desired. It also tends to break eventually, so there's a whole lot of it and people have to keep making more! You may recall from our discussion of dating (Chapter 4) that noting changing styles is an important tool in archaeology, and the pottery of a specific people at a specific time is often very distinctive.

I have met experts who can pick up a single distinctive shard of pottery and tell who made it, and when, to within a decade or so. One famous old archaeologist even conducted surveys in the desert by identifying surface scatters of pottery from horseback. I once participated in a big dig which employed three full-time pottery "readers," whose job was to sort out what was what. As with stone tools, pottery can be classified in detail for descriptive and comparative purposes based on materials, shapes, color, glazes, type of decoration, and so forth.

Lost and Found

One of the most recognizable pots of antiquity is the Mediterranean amphora. These elegant tapering jars came in many styles and typically had two handles and a pointed base. Amphorae can be found just about anywhere Mediterranean seafarers (such as the Greeks, Carthaginians, and Romans) went, and were often filled with wine, olive oil, or exotic products.

A remote site in Egypt where the ground is thoroughly covered in broken Roman potsherds.

Tracing the Source

As with lithics, experiments with ceramic technology have provided great insights into its ancient manufacture. Several important techniques have been developed which can analyze ancient pots and determine whether the clay was from a local source or from elsewhere.

This kind of information has important implications for tracking ancient trade. In some cases, specific sources of clay can be identified. Since pots are portable, are often distinctly shaped and decorated, and sometimes have an identifiable clay source, they are wonderful for tracking interactions within and between peoples.

Metallica

Many ancient people eventually made use of some sort of metal, if it was available. Copper was commonly used, as was silver, gold, iron, lead, and tin. Evidence for the use of metal is first found about 9,000 years ago in the Near East. Copper seems to have been the first and most easily used metal. Eventually it would be combined with tin to produce bronze and with zinc to produce brass.

The use of metals would revolutionize human relations, with the spread of metal tools changing the scope of activities such as agriculture. And weapons with strong sharp edges assisted in threatening and conquering the neighbors, particularly if the new technology hadn't reached them yet.

As techniques got more advanced, molds were made in which molten metals could be formed and tools mass-manufactured. Techniques for casting would be developed that would produce splendid artistic pieces, and the variations in those techniques can also help us determine an object's source.

Analyzing an object made of metal can be complicated, and we are especially interested in what sort of materials or combinations thereof were being used. The microscopic study of thin-sections taken from metal artifacts can be useful, but sophisticated laboratory procedures are also often employed. Here are a couple of examples:

Pitfalls and Pointers

Gold has long been considered a precious material with its beautiful shiny properties and its ability to be hammered thin and shaped to perfection.

➤ Neutron activation analysis is quite effective and doesn't damage the artifact. Unfortunately, it requires a nuclear reactor, and some kinds of artifacts can be made temporarily radioactive.

➤ X-ray fluorescence spectrometry irradiates the artifact or sample with X-rays. Afterwards, the sample glows, or fluoresces, with wavelengths that indicate specific elements within the sample. It is relatively cheap and non-destructive.

As you can see, the analysis of metal is often one of the more difficult tasks an archaeologist might face in the laboratory. The effort, though, often proves worthwhile.

Rope Story

Apart from lithics, pots, and metals, other materials can be subject to similar analyses of their materials, manufacture, and function. Wood, baskets, cordage, and textiles are commonly studied, and there are experts who specialize in dealing with each.

Sit back and let me tell you a little story about an archaeological analysis of technology and materials. As a mountain climber, I've always been interested in ropes. As an archaeologist, I recognize that "cordage" of all sizes has been an incredibly useful technology through the ages that can be used to tie shoes or haul huge blocks of stone. I've had several opportunities to study surviving examples of rope from ancient Egypt, and this is how we did it.

The useful characteristics of rope are its strength and flexibility. To study these things, we needed to examine the size, material, and construction of each specimen. The size was simply a matter of measuring the diameter. Determining the construction method required examining how the materials were twisted and combined to form the finished rope.

The most difficult part was determining the material. Thin sections of fibers taken from each artifact were examined under a microscope and compared with thin sections of modern plants collected in Egypt. The comparisons allowed us to match the old materials to the very plant species from which they came.

So what, you say? Apart from giving us the basic information about how and from what materials the ancient Egyptians made rope, individual specimens have interesting stories to tell. One massive rope found in a limestone quarry not far from the Giza pyramids was made of papyrus. Its date was a couple of thousand years too late for it to have been used in building the pyramids, but it told us something about the quarry and its use through time.

Another rope specimen was found hanging into a shaft in a royal tomb in Egypt. When that specimen was dated, it proved to be from the period when the tombs were being robbed in ancient times, and could have been used by the robbers or by the priests who came later to clean up the mess.

Lost and Found

The wealth of inscriptions in Egypt often makes it easy to date monuments and gain insights into the past. Consequently, archaeology developed much differently there than in places like Israel, where written material is rare. There, the study of pottery is exceedingly important and well-refined. In Egypt, on the other hand, pottery experts are scarce, and the study of "mundane" technologies like cordage is rare.

Trade: Swapping Goods from Near and Far

It's often possible to trace the material of an artifact to its original source. This is called *characterization,* and the procedures for this differ for different materials. A thin-section of pottery might be taken and its mineral content examined under the microscope. This technique helps trace the artifact's origin because the composition of various clay beds can differ markedly.

Jargon Unearthed

Characterization is the science of identifying unique characteristics in the fabric of artifacts which allow them to be traced to their original source material.

Pitfalls and Pointers

The fact that you find an Egyptian pot in some unlikely spot in the middle of Europe doesn't mean that the Egyptians were trading with Celts and Goths. A portable artifact can change hands any number of times from source to endpoint.

The same can be the case with such materials as obsidian, with each bed containing slightly different trace elements. Even metal ores can sometimes be tracked to the site they came from. Most of these studies involve lots of sophisticated laboratory techniques, but this information is incredibly valuable for tracing interactions between different areas.

Actually determining whether an item has been traded is not always as easy as it might seem. Artifacts from one area might change hands many times before reaching their destination. Goods might be captured and taken home as booty or souvenirs, or they might be sent off as tribute or tax payments. Designs might be admired and copied. Ideas of all sorts can be exchanged and leave very little trace of the process. Given such possibilities, we need to closely evaluate all of the evidence at hand before forming conclusions about what kinds of exchange we are seeing.

Experimental Archaeology

As we've seen, experimentation is a big part of understanding artifacts. Experiments help us explore what was and wasn't possible and assist us in understanding and explaining what we find in the archaeological record. There is a kind of archaeological research that is called "experimental archaeology" that typically replicates and tests artifacts or ancient lifeways, and a lot of it is very interesting, and sometimes highly exciting! Here are a few examples.

Moving the Big Stones

One of the most popular mysteries of the past is figuring out how ancient people managed to carve and move huge and heavy stones. The Great Pyramid in Egypt was constructed of perhaps 2 million blocks of stone weighing tons each. We're still not exactly sure how they did it. On isolated Easter Island in the Pacific, hundreds of giant statues were carved from a quarry and transported for miles, then set up on impressive stone platforms. England's Stonehenge is another fascinating example, as are the incredible stone structures of the Inca.

Experiments have yet to be absolutely conclusive in each of these cases. Although it's possible for a strong gang using brute force to drag a pyramid block to a building site, the sheer organization required to build such a thing is staggering. On Easter Island, experiments in moving stone statues have included pulling them on sleds, swinging them from tripods, and wobbling them forward in a standing position. (More on this in Chapter 22.)

Seeing If It Will Float

Perhaps the most famous practitioner of experimental archaeology is the Norwegian explorer and scholar Thor Heyerdahl. Based on a variety of evidence, and contrary to most scholarly opinion, Heyerdahl proposed that there was important contact between the Americas and the Pacific islands. In 1947, he successfully sailed a replica of a South American raft from Peru to Polynesia. The voyage of the *Kon-Tiki* demonstrated that it was possible for a seacraft of this sort to survive such a journey.

In 1969 and 1970, Heyerdahl built boats of papyrus and followed the natural currents across the Atlantic from Africa to the New World. His second attempt, in the boat *Ra II*, demonstrated the seaworthiness of this sort of craft, which was used in various parts of the world in ancient times. Heyerdahl's last experimental reed boat, the *Tigris*, was easily navigated from the Persian Gulf into the Indian Ocean to Pakistan, and then to the Red Sea.

Pitfalls and Pointers

Many people tend to think of ancient people as ignorant and technologically inferior, if not stupid. This is certainly not the case. Modern people would have a hard time organizing and building something like the Great Pyramid even with our more "sophisticated" tools. The secret of the pyramids probably lies in the realm of the clever and efficient use of simple technologies.

Diggers

The much-celebrated and often controversial Thor Heyerdahl was born in Larvik, Norway, in 1914. Apart from his famous experiments on the *Kon-Tiki*, the *Ra* expeditions, and the *Tigris*, Heyerdahl is also noted for his important archaeological work on Easter Island and elsewhere in the Pacific, the Maldive Islands, Peru, and most recently on Tenerife in the Canary Islands. His wonderfully compelling and inspiring tales of his adventures have sold many millions of copies, and the man is still very active today.

None of these voyages in and of themselves actually proved that contact took place, but they have opened our minds to practical possibilities. The voyage of the *Kon-Tiki* has been repeated many times, and others have carried out experimental projects with different kinds of ships. Oar-propelled Greek "trireme" warships have been reconstructed and tested for speed and mobility. Replicas of Chinese junks have been sailed to the New World, as have Viking ships and Irish skin-boats. Each of these efforts has provided us with not only useful insights, but darn good adventure stories as well.

Back on the Farm

Another kind of experimental archaeology is taking place on dry land. In Hampshire, England, a whole Iron Age farm, the "Butser Farm," has been replicated to the conditions of about 300 B.C., including a thatched roof farmhouse and other structures. This farm has provided many insights into such matters as ancient crop yields and the effectiveness of various old farming implements and techniques. The replica buildings have provided information about their strength and the application and reliability of materials.

Not for the Queasy

One of the most singular and intriguing recent examples of experimental archaeology was conducted in 1994 by a team led by American Egyptologist Bob Brier and anatomist Ronald Wade. Using ancient tools and procedures, they conducted experiments in ancient Egyptian mummification on the cadaver of a 76-year-old human male.

Most of the entrails were taken out through a small incision in the abdomen, and the brain was removed through the nose. The body was then covered with a natural dehydrating agent known as natron, which was imported from Egypt. The experiments were a great learning exercise and were successful in producing a modern-day Egyptian-like mummy.

Diggers

Dr. Bob Brier is a professor at Long Island University and an expert on Egyptian mummies. Having studied numerous mummies, Brier decided to try to re-create ancient methods by mummifying a modern body. One of his recent books chronicles the forensic analysis of the remains of King Tut, and Brier suggests that the boy king was murdered, possibly by the official who would replace him as pharaoh.

Most experiments aren't that radical, but they, along with the information we get from artifacts, all contribute to the big picture. And there is as much room for new approaches as there are creative people!

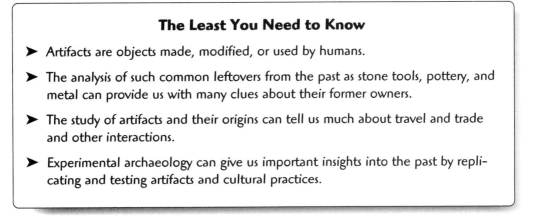

The Least You Need to Know

➤ Artifacts are objects made, modified, or used by humans.

➤ The analysis of such common leftovers from the past as stone tools, pottery, and metal can provide us with many clues about their former owners.

➤ The study of artifacts and their origins can tell us much about travel and trade and other interactions.

➤ Experimental archaeology can give us important insights into the past by replicating and testing artifacts and cultural practices.

Chapter 8

Some Like It Wet

In This Chapter

➤ The joys and hazards of underwater archaeology

➤ Finding and excavating underwater sites

➤ The difference between treasure hunting and underwater archaeology

➤ Some famous shipwrecks and sunken cities

The majority of the earth is covered with water, and humans have been traversing it for thousands of years, so it's not surprising that a bit of the human past can also be found underwater. In this chapter, we're going get a glimpse of some of the exciting things that have been found beneath the waves, and how archaeologists have had to adapt their tools and techniques to this special environment.

Archaeology Underwater

It's not known exactly how long human have been going about in boats, but we're probably looking at hundreds of thousands of years. Just recently new evidence has been uncovered that suggests that seafaring may have played a very important role in the spread of humans across the globe in prehistoric times. Here are a few provocative examples:

➤ Archaeologists once assumed that humans entered the American continents around 12,000 years ago by way of an exposed land bridge from Asia during the lower sea-levels of the Ice Age. However, the recent discovery of South American sites that predate those in North America suggests that this scenario is far too simplistic. Rather than travelling overland as previously thought, some scholars believe that America's earliest inhabitants may have voyaged by sea, travelling southward along the coast and exploiting the rich marine resources along the way.

➤ Evidence in Australia suggests that humans were there perhaps as long as 60,000 years ago. And they didn't walk there!

➤ Even more startling, a site linked to early humans (*Homo erectus*) has been found in Eastern Indonesia at a site on the island of Flores dating between 800,000 and 900,000 years ago, in an area that would have required transport across water.

Pitfalls and Pointers

Humans have been traveling on water for hundreds of thousands of years. The earliest kinds of watercraft, though, were constructed from perishable materials such as wood, reeds or animal skins so it is very unlikely that any of their actual remains will be found except under the most extraordinary of circumstances.

So, humans have been building boats of some sort for eons. What sorts of watercraft were they using? Log rafts? Inflated animal skins? Boats made from bundles of buoyant reeds? Canoes or kayaks? Probably all of the above. Later on, ancient people built huge ships and engaged in long-distance trading, exploration, and warfare. Unfortunately, most of the earliest stuff has disappeared, and when you think about, it's surprising that so much has survived even from the last several thousand years.

The study of all aspects of ancient seafaring is called *maritime* or *nautical archaeology*. Not all of maritime archaeology takes place underwater. Big ships have been excavated on land. Some very famous examples include the 1,300-year-old ship buried at *Sutton Hoo* in Britain and the 1,200-year-old Viking burial boats in Norway, described in Chapter 14.

Jargon Unearthed

Maritime or *nautical archaeology* is the study of all aspects of ancient seafaring. *Underwater archaeology* is any archaeology that takes place underwater.

But not all underwater archaeology deals with boats. Sunken cities like Port Royal in Jamaica are not shipwrecks, nor are the artifacts recovered from the freshwater springs of Florida or the natural limestone sinks in Central America, called "cenotes." *Underwater archaeology*, then, is any archaeology that takes place underwater.

Searching the Depths

The approach to archaeology underwater is much the same as that on land, except that it's much more difficult and hazardous. The rewards, however, can be great. Since many shipwrecks are the result of some sort of catastrophe, they sink to the bottom with their contents intact, and if they are preserved, they can serve as a sort of time capsule. Archaeologists call such remains "closed deposits," since human activity associated with these sites ceased at the time of disaster.

Humans, of course, are not by nature suited for living underwater, but fortunately, inventions of the twentieth century have changed things. The invention of scuba gear, in particular, has revolutionized our ability to explore the shallower depths of watery environments. As with most things, there are hazards and limitations with working under water, and I'll mention a few of them before turning to the happier topics of advantages and big discoveries.

Hazards and Limitations: The Bad News

First of all, there is a limit to the depth to which a free-swimming diver can go. Due to the limitations of the typical scuba apparatus, the maximum time one can spend underwater is a few hours. The deeper one goes, the less time one can stay at that depth. And even with a short stay, a slow ascent with stops for decompression might be necessary. Scuba diving at great depth can affect one's thinking ability and cause bubbles in the bloodstream that can be fatal.

Diving in cold water can be dangerous and exhausting, and the time a diver can spend in cold water is limited. Even in warm water, of course, divers have to come up for air periodically. And then there is the matter of visibility, which can range from crystal clear to so murky you can't see your own hand in front of your face. And did I mention the weather and rough water? Both can put a serious damper on your activities. If you're really unfortunate, maybe you'll add your own modern shipwreck to the one you're exploring.

There are lots of problems, too, with excavating. Digging a trench on land to look at strata is one thing, but digging a hole underwater can be quite tricky, given the instability of seafloor sand, mud, or other sediments. Obviously, the underwater archaeologist needs lots of skills not only in excavation, but in all aspects of working underwater. This kind of archaeologist must be calm and alert and make serious and wise decisions involving the well-being of other people.

Speaking of other people, underwater archaeology often requires a number of individuals in order to be efficient. Apart from the divers below, there's a need for people above to mind the boat, assist the divers, and retrieve artifacts coming to the surface. And given the limited amount of time one can spend underwater, you probably need several divers on your expedition to replace the ones

Jargon Unearthed

Scuba stands for Self-Contained Underwater Breathing Apparatus and consists primarily of a tank with compressed air connected to a mouthpiece which regulates airflow in conjunction with breathing.

Lost and Found

Strange, unexpected things are occasionally found underwater. A number of superb Greek sculptures have been discovered in the Mediterranean by sponge divers, fishermen, and archaeologists. The statues were once part of the cargo of ancient ships that had suffered mishaps.

coming up. What does all this mean? It's expensive. Boats, underwater gear, slow and tedious work, and a schedule that might be a slave to the weather all mean costs that can add up quickly.

The Good News

So what's the upside to all of this? In the right conditions, many things that might not last in a terrestrial environment survive splendidly underwater—the water acts, in effect, as a time capsule. Ceramic vessels several thousands of years old have been recovered with their contents intact, and from a mineral spring in Florida, researchers have recovered a 9,000-year-old human skull with the brain intact inside!

Certain aspects of excavation underwater can even be easier than land excavation. Given the situation of virtual weightlessness, one can hover above or maneuver about the site easily. Buckets of sediment and large objects can usually be moved fairly easily by just one or a few divers.

Your Technique Is All Wet

Despite all of the constraints of working in such an environment, underwater archaeology has the same goals as that performed on dry land: to document, recover, and explain the past. In addition, many of the procedures for excavation are the same. A grid can still be placed over the site, for example, for recording the location of artifacts using drawings or photography.

There are also sophisticated mapping systems that allow a diver to map a site while sending signals to a computer on a vessel above, which collects the data and produces the map. Using gentle techniques to remove sediments, a site can be excavated in layers. From a practical standpoint, this usually means that a grid-frame is suspended over the site, with suction hoses used for removing muck. Air-filled balloons are often used for transporting material to the surface, especially the heavier items.

Conservation of objects recovered from water can be quite different from conservation of objects unearthed on land. Special techniques might be needed to deal with woods, metals, and other materials. Sometimes, the decision might be made to leave all or most of the material where it was found. With shipwrecks, for example, such a decision might be based on how common the remains are, the extent of preservation, the physical size of the remains, the difficulty and danger of retrieval, and, of course, the expense required.

Dating a shipwreck can be done in a number of different ways. If it is a known vessel, then it's not much of a problem. Even if not, the nature of the cargo and style

Pitfalls and Pointers

Objects brought up from the sea floor often require immediate attention. Some materials which were relatively stable underwater will start to decay when exposed to air. Wood in particular is tricky and is often initially kept wet so that it will not quickly dry out and become damaged.

of the boat can be telling. Cannons from European ships are usually quite datable. Dendrochronology has been used occasionally with wooden ships, and radiocarbon dating can sometimes be used if uncontaminated samples can be acquired.

An archaeologist underwater at work on an ancient shipwreck off the coast of Turkey. (Courtesy of the Institute of Nautical Archaeology)

Finding Underwater Sites

So how does one go about locating an underwater site? Some are discovered accidentally by recreational or commercial divers. Other have been found during dredging operations. Many, though, are intentionally sought, either by archaeologists or treasure hunters. Over the 500 years since Columbus first stopped by, many thousands of ships and other vessels have been lost in waters off American coasts or in lakes and rivers. Columbus himself left some of his vessels on the sea floor during his expeditions.

Many Spanish shipwrecks have been located by means of old records. Hundreds of galleons bringing the wealth of the New World back to the Old met their doom in transit. Shipwreck hunters will often look in archives for records related to the various incidents and occasionally find cargo lists and even maps. And, as with archaeology on land, there are special tools that can be used for locating sites beneath the water.

Many of these were originally a product of military research and adapted for civilian use. In clear water, aerial photography can sometimes produce results. Magnetometers can be dragged through the water to look for magnetic anomalies, and metal detectors can be used to find large metal objects such as anchors and cannons. Acoustic sounding and sonar can be quite useful, too. Sound waves are bounced off the bottom in various paths and can map the surface of the sea floor.

Manned underwater submersibles have been effectively used for locating and exploring sites. Submersibles can be equipped with Remotely Operated Vehicles (ROVs), which are unmanned vehicles that can perform underwater tasks and can be rigged with cameras and grabbers. They are especially useful or cost-effective in environments—such as great depths—inhospitable to humans. Submersibles and ROVs got a lot of attention with the exploration of the *Titanic*.

Diggers

The exploration of the *Titanic* required sophisticated equipment that could operate at great depths. A submersible named Alvin was put to use that could carry two or three scientists to the site. Attached to Alvin was Jason, an ROV with cameras that was successful in exploring the *Titanic's* treacherous interior.

Once a site is found, it needs to be marked. In the old days, this could be a tricky thing, and might have involved compass bearings and distances or a buoy marking the site. Neither was foolproof, and lost shipwrecks were sometimes found only to be lost again. Today, though, technology has provided us with such marvels as the Global Positioning System (GPS), which uses satellites to pinpoint with precision the geographical coordinates of anything on the planet; GPS can be used on land or at sea.

Treasure Hunting vs. Archaeology

Archaeologists aren't the only ones interested in underwater debris. Treasure hunters have been active through the years with hopes of finding treasure and making a fortune. Although several have been very well rewarded for their efforts, a great many have spent huge sums of money and years of dangerous effort to find little or nothing of interest.

It's true that some of these people have been successful in finding extraordinary things, but most are not archaeologists, and many treasure hunters have conducted their work as if it were the old days of artifact-collecting in the Middle East, where obtaining the object was more important than the object's context. Valuable information is lost forever when this happens.

Treasure hunting can be quite competitive, with searchers visiting old archives looking for clues alongside other treasure hunters and archaeologists, all searching for the same wrecks. Once found, the locations are kept secret for fear of rivals or looters while the artifacts are collected or legal claims are filed.

Of course, the big differences between treasure hunters and underwater archaeologists lie in their motives and the procedures they use. The archaeologist seeks knowledge of the past, while the treasure hunter hopes to benefit financially from a discovery. Many treasure hunters merely rummage through a site looking for objects of value, while archaeologists record everything *in situ*, carefully conserve those things removed to the surface, and then study their discoveries and publish their findings so that others can study them as well.

Pitfalls and Pointers

Many countries around the world have laws that deal with shipwrecks within their territories. In the United States, the 1987 Abandoned Shipwreck Act gives the government ownership of abandoned wrecks and their cargo within American waters, or any sunken American ship wherever it might be. Laws governing shipwrecks in international waters, however, can be very tricky!

One famous treasure hunter, Mel Fisher, adopted a middle ground. Although financially he benefited tremendously from his discoveries, he made a good effort to share his findings with the public through museums, traveling exhibits, and other educational enterprises. Treasure hunters also occasionally contribute to archaeological efforts. In their zeal to locate things underwater, they have at times developed techniques that can be of use to scientists.

Diggers

Mel Fisher (1922–1998) was one of the world's most successful treasure hunters. Fascinated with diving since his youth, Fisher is credited with opening the first diving shop and training thousands in the developing art of SCUBA diving. In the early 1960s he was successful in locating the treasure of a fleet of Spanish ships lost in a hurricane off the Florida coast in 1715. His biggest discovery was that of the *Atocha*, a 1622 Spanish wreck that has yielded many millions of dollars worth of gold, silver, jewelry, and other objects.

Some Wrecks of Fame

There are literally tens of thousands of shipwrecks around the world. They come in all sizes and degrees of preservation. Some are still full of cargo while others are nothing more than an empty shell. Let's examine a few of the more famous underwater discoveries.

Ulu Burun—Making the Rounds in the Mediterranean

One of the greatest shipwreck discoveries from ancient times was found at Ulu Burun in Turkey. The ship, discovered by a sponge diver in 1982, lay on a slope about 150 feet below the surface. It was excavated between the years 1984 and 1994 by underwater archaeologist George Bass and his team.

Drawing of a portion of the Ulu Burun wreck with artifacts in situ. (Courtesy of the Institute of Nautical Archaeology)

The ship, which sank over three thousand years ago, around 1306 B.C., contained many tons of diverse cargo, including copper ingots (apparently from Cyprus) and ingots of tin and glass. Apart from metals, there were numerous jars containing resins and other products, including what appears to be some very old olive oil.

Hundreds of other items, such as ebony wood, elephant and hippo ivory, plant seeds, and jewelry and other precious objects from Egypt, Palestine, and elsewhere indicate that this was a trading vessel operating around the Mediterranean. The crew might have been from Cyprus or maybe Palestine, with perhaps a couple of Mycenean (early Greek) sailors on board as well.

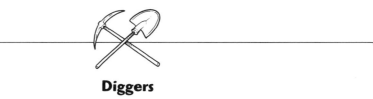

Diggers

When it comes to the relatively new field of scientific underwater archaeology, Dr. George Bass (b. 1932) is a pioneer. For several decades he has excavated at many sites around the world and developed technology and ways of working that have become the modern standard. Bass was one of the founders of the prestigious Institute of Nautical Archaeology at Texas A&M University in College Station.

Lake Nemi—Caligula's Party Barges?

In the late 1920s, two massive Roman galleys emerged from the mud of Italy's scenic Lake Nemi. The ships were long known to exist, and attempts to salvage them began as early as 1446. During the last recovery effort, beginning in 1929, the lake level was lowered using pumps and old Roman conduits, which allowed water to be drained to a nearby valley. The first ship was 230 feet long and about 65 feet wide and very well preserved. The second, not quite as large as the first, was of a different design. Both provided incredible details of Roman shipbuilding, which was technologically very impressive.

How the boats were used is not clear, but they may have dated to the time of that loony Roman emperor, Caligula. It has been suggested that they could have had a religious function, but given their size, and the peculiarities of the emperor, perhaps they were Caligula's party barges (my favorite theory).

Lost and Found

Many small wooden boat models have been found in Egyptian tombs. In the tomb of King Tutankhamun, thirty-five such models were found, some complete with rigging for sails. The ships served to symbolically allow the deceased to sail into the afterlife.

The ships were excavated and removed from the mud, and preserved at the lake shore. Tragically, during World War II both ships caught fire and were destroyed. There are now discussions about building a working reconstruction of the first ship.

The Vasa—Barely Out of the Harbor

In 1628, the mightiest warship of its day was launched in Sweden's Stockholm harbor. This ship, named the *Vasa*, was built to assist in Sweden's war with Poland, and carried 64 heavy bronze cannons. After only a few minutes of sailing, however, the beautifully decorated, top-heavy ship leaned over, and water rushed in through its open gun ports, quickly sending the *Vasa* down 100 feet to the harbor floor. In one of the earlier uses of underwater technology, a diving bell was used between the years 1663 and 1665 to recover many of the ship's cannons.

The *Vasa* was rediscovered by shipwreck diver and amateur archaeologist Anders Franzen in 1956, and a project was organized to raise the entire well-preserved ship in one piece. The raising was accomplished in stages by cables placed beneath the hull, which were then lifted with the help of pontoons.

Once above the surface, the ship was excavated. Thousands of wonderful objects were recovered, and the remains of 25 crew members were found within. The ship and its contents have been carefully preserved, and are available today for all to see at the Vasa Museum in Stockholm.

Titanic—So Famous They Made Movies About It

Perhaps the most famous ship of all time, and the best-known underwater discovery, is not of an ancient vessel at all, but that massive hunk of metal that went down to the bottom of the ocean in April 1912. Who hasn't heard of the *Titanic*? There have been movies about it, the latest setting a box-office record. It has been the subject of numerous books, songs, and even a Broadway musical! The ship, 882.5 feet long, hit an iceberg in the North Atlantic, sending over 1,500 people to their doom, primarily due to the lack of lifeboats in this "unsinkable" monster.

Although the general location of the wreck was known, its specific location was never verified in the deep, cold, rough waters 350 miles off the coast of Newfoundland. In 1985, however, a French and American expedition led by Dr. Robert Ballard managed to locate the *Titanic* at a depth of 12,500 feet below the surface of the ocean.

The ship was broken into two main sections, and debris of all sorts was found scattered on the ocean floor in-between. Mini-submarines and robots have been used to explore the wreck, producing incredible images. Since

Lost and Found

One of the largest collections of sunken ships is in the Truk lagoon in the Central Pacific. The lagoon served as a Japanese naval base during World War II and during 1944/45, allied bombing raids sunk 46 ships. Along with ships were destroyed several hundred airplanes and other military equipment, some of which can be seen by recreational divers in a protected underwater park.

the ship is so well known, individual salons, state rooms, and crew areas could be identified and examined.

While Ballard and his team had hoped the ship would remain a memorial to those who perished on that fateful night in April 1912, the ship has been pillaged. Not only have objects been taken from the wreck, put part of the ship itself, a section known as "the big piece" was raised from the sea floor this past year.

(For additional information, see *The Complete Idiot's Guide to the Titanic*, by Jay Stevenson and Sharon Rutman.)

Diggers

Dr. Robert Ballard (b. 1942) is one of the world's best-known underwater explorers. He has participated in dozens of underwater expeditions, many of which use submersibles that can descend to great depths. His most famous discovery was the wreck of the *Titanic* in 1985. Ballard has also located other important shipwrecks, including the *Bismark* and the Roman *Isis,* the deepest ancient wreck yet known. Ballard is also interested in exploring the sea floor and undersea life and is actively involved in programs to introduce young people to the sea and exploration.

Sunken Cities

Although shipwrecks and their contents are the most common things explored underwater by archaeologists, occasionally there are some dramatic exceptions. Although rare, there are a few cities, or parts thereof, that have actually sunk beneath the waters. This has nothing to do with the many odd theories about lost mythical continents, but with bits of land that have met with natural catastrophes. Here are a couple of the most famous.

Port Royal: Shakin' at the Seashore

In 1692, the town of Port Royal, Jamaica, was perhaps the richest and busiest English town in the New World, serving as a major trade and transit point between the continents. With its pirates, privateers, and slave traders, it also had a reputation as "the wickedest city in Christendom."

Pitfalls and Pointers

When it comes to sunken cities, most people think of the mythological Atlantis, which was more than just a city, it was said to be a whole continent. Contrary to regular reports in the tabloids, Atlantis has not been found. In fact, it probably never existed. You can read more about this in Chapter 24.

On June 7 of that year, a big earthquake shook the area and sent two-thirds of the town, built on a sand spit, into the sea. Thousands of people died in the disaster or its aftermath. Like the volcanic eruptions that bury towns on land, the human tragedy of sunken Port Royal has provided a time capsule for archaeologists to explore.

Beginning in 1956, underwater archaeologists have been able to map the town with its many buildings and streets and excavate complete structures and individual rooms with their contents intact, providing a window on colonial life in the New World. The project has provided a tremendous amount of information about this very important town.

Alexandria: Sphinxes in the Harbor

The metropolis of Alexandria was established on the Mediterranean coast of Egypt in 332 B.C. by Alexander the Great. The city became a cultural center of the ancient world, and was ruled by the descendants of Ptolemy, one of Alexander's generals.

A sizable chunk of Alexandria's ancient harbor sank as a result of numerous earthquakes that struck the North African coast, and is now being explored. Already, the location of Cleopatra's palace has been found on a submerged island and more than two dozen sphinxes, an obelisk, a colossal granite statue of a pharaoh, and other outstanding stone sculptures have been recovered.

It has been suggested that perhaps some of the sunken remains are those of the massive Pharos Lighthouse, one of the Seven Wonders of the Ancient World, which was said to have stood as a beacon on the coast until it was destroyed in an earthquake ca. A.D. 1300. The lighthouse collapsed into the harbor and many of its blocks were reused to construct a fifteenth century Ottoman fort. Although there are skeptics, no one doubts the importance of the wonderful remains which continue to be brought to light from Alexandria's ancient harbor.

The Least You Need to Know

➤ Humans have traveled on water for tens of thousands of years. There are a lot of archaeological sites underwater.

➤ The goals of archaeology underwater are the same as those on land.

➤ Archaeology, whether on land or under water, should not be confused with treasure hunting.

➤ Archaeology conducted underwater can be challenging, productive, and sometimes dangerous.

Part 3
Cradles of Civilization

If you open nearly any textbook on the subject of Western Civilization, and there are many, you might get the impression that ancient Greece and Rome were the be-alls and end-alls of modern society. Typically there are a couple of pages on Mesopotamia, a few about Egypt and the Hebrews, a nod here and there to the Phoenicians, and then hundreds of pages about the toga-clad masses (which we will be discussing in Chapters 15 and 16). But on the big scale of things, the latter are relative late-comers. When the Greeks were building the famous Parthenon in Athens, the Great Pyramid in Egypt was already 2,000 years old! And the Romans were visiting Egypt as tourists to look at the antiquities.

One reason our Greek and Roman friends get so much attention is that a good deal of their writing has survived. But let's not forget where these people got their writing: from the Near East. As for the Christian society that came to dominate Europe, they got their religion and accompanying values from the Near East, as well. Yes, there are many examples to counter the smug fans of ancient Greece and Rome.

In the next few chapters, we're going to take a look at some of the civilizations of the ancient Near East, including Mesopotamia, Egypt, and the lands of the Bible. In doing so, you'll discover many of the roots of our modern world.

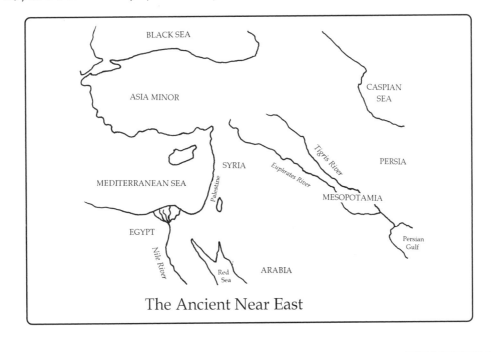

The Ancient Near East

Chapter 9

Big Questions on the Road to Civilization

In This Chapter

➤ Humans colonize the world

➤ Hunters and gatherers do their thing

➤ People settle down to an agricultural revolution

➤ Life gets civilized, and much more complex

We can talk about artifacts, civilizations, and interesting discoveries all we want, but they didn't just magically appear from nowhere. How we got from butchering a mastodon to building the space shuttle is an amazing story, and only the latter part is known in much detail. The facts of our earliest days are most elusive, and offer big questions for archaeologists to tackle. Too big, in fact, for this little chapter, which will only try to give you an overview of some of the most important concepts and terms.

Out of Africa

Most scientists today agree that modern humans evolved from other primates in Africa over the last few million years. Now it's not within the scope of this book to discuss the various "ape-like creature evolves into humans" theories. That's the realm of the physical anthropologist or paleoanthropologist. Besides, those ideas are always changing, it seems, when regular discoveries of new fossils cause the reinterpretation of whatever the current hypothesis might be. So let's stick with humans, or *Homo*, as we are scientifically classified by biologists.

So what makes us *Homos* different from the other primates, both past and present? Well, for starters, we've got bigger brains and we can walk upright. Our opposable thumbs and sense of creativity allow us to make tools and manipulate our environment. And this thing we have called culture has allowed us to adapt to an incredible variety of environments throughout the globe.

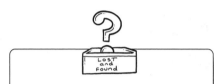

Lost and Found

Biologists have classified humans, along with all other forms of life. This is where you stand: You're an animal as opposed to a plant. You're a vertebrate because you have a backbone and you're a hairy, warm-blooded, milk-drinking mammal. You fit in well with monkeys and apes in the Primate order. Your genus is *Homo* and your species is *sapiens*.

Jargon Unearthed

Our present geologic period is called the *Quaternary* and is divided into two epochs: the *Pleistocene* (or Ice Age), beginning around 2.4 million years ago, and our present time, the *Holocene,* beginning 10,000 years ago.

It's true that other animals can do some of these things: beavers build dams, chimps use simple tools, and so on. It's the combination of talents that produces a qualitative difference in humans. How else are we special? Some will say that we are made in God's image or that only humans have souls. We'll leave that sort of discussion for the theologians.

Wise Guys

The geologic time period during which humans established themselves is known as the *Quaternary Period.* The Quaternary is divided into two epochs, the *Pleistocene* (commonly known as the Ice Age), which begins around 2.4 million years ago, and the *Holocene,* which is our current geological era, beginning about 10,000 years ago at the end of the Ice Age.

Species of *Homo* first appeared around 2 million years ago in East Africa, and within about 200,000 years spread to Europe and all the way to East Asia. This widely traveled variety of early human is called *Homo erectus.* Some scholars believe that *Homo erectus* evolved into our modern human species, *Homo sapiens,* about 400,000 years ago, while others contend that a more clever and resourceful *Homo sapiens* evolved independently and spread out, while *Homo erectus* became extinct.

Whatever happened, anatomically modern humans were living far and wide in the Old World by 100,000 years ago. Along with them lived another variety of *Homo*, the Neanderthals, a stocky, beetle-browed group who died out around 30,000 years ago. Why? It's not known for sure. Perhaps they competed with the *Homo sapiens* and lost. Anyway, humans as we know them today became the sole species of *Homo* after that time.

Meet the Flintstones

In studying the lifestyles of the past and present, anthropologists have been able to classify groups of humans based on the way they organize themselves economically and what kinds of social structures they have. Hunters and gatherers, for example, are groups of humans who get their food primarily from (surprise!) hunting animals and gathering wild produce of various sorts. They are also known as foragers.

One way to examine the social structures of the past is by comparing them to those of similar peoples today. The few surviving hunter-gatherer groups around these days tend to be organized into small groups who more or less live within the natural carrying capacity of the land. They seem to be generally egalitarian, sharing their resources among their group.

Hunter-gatherers tend to move around a lot, probably in search of food during different seasons of the year. As a result, they tend not to have a lot of permanent buildings or large possessions that they would have to cart around with them. But they have left a lot of stone spear points and other stone tools laying around for the archaeologist to find. That's why we call the ancient time period when most of this activity was going on the *Paleolithic*, or Old Stone Age.

A popular image of these times is that of a harsh existence with people on the edge of starvation and a high mortality rate. The social philosopher Thomas Hobbes (1588–1679) described such an existence when he proposed that life in a state of nature consisted of "continual fear and danger of violent death; and the life of man, solitary, poor, nasty, brutish, and short."

Hobbes notwithstanding, studies of modern hunters and gathers have suggested that these people have a relatively content existence, with lots of leisure time. On the other hand, the "short" part might be generally true: Get kicked by an animal you're hunting or catch a bad cold, and it might be all over. Studies of the remains of early people suggest that they didn't live all that long.

Pitfalls and Pointers

Modern human beings are classified *Homo sapiens sapiens*, the last "sapiens" naming our sub-species; it literally means "wise man," although a quick perusal of the daily news might cause one to doubt the accuracy of this name. Neanderthals are classified *Homo sapiens neanderthalensis*.

Jargon Unearthed

The *Paleolithic*, or Old Stone Age, is characterized by the use of stone tools and hunting and gathering. It extends from about 2 million years ago to 10,000 years ago, roughly corresponding to the Pleistocene epoch.

Paleolithic technology.
(From Charles Lyell, The
Geological Evidences of
the Antiquity of Man
*[London: John Murray, 4th
ed., rev. 1873], p. 150, fig.
15)*

Settling Down

As far as we can tell, humans hunted and gathered on this earth from their earliest
days, until something dramatic, and still somewhat mysterious, occurred about 10,000
years ago. At that time, a major shift in lifestyle oc-
curred. In just a few places at first, people started
settling down, raising crops, keeping animals, and
constructing permanent buildings and villages.

One thing led to another. People needed to harvest and
store grain, so they produced a lot of pottery and
different kinds of tools. The food surplus created by
domestication and agriculture meant that more people
could live together in much larger groups. This revolutionary new way of living is often referred to as the
Neolithic, or New Stone Age, and is sometimes called the
Neolithic Revolution.

Lost and Found

The Kalahari Bushmen of southern
Africa are among the few hunter-
gatherer groups around today. The
Australian Aborigines have also been a
focus of attention in the search for
analogies which can illuminate the
past. Unfortunately for anthropologists, it wouldn't be surprising to see
members of either group today living
in towns, drinking soda pop, and
wearing T-shirts, thanks to their
increased exposure to modern society.

Cereal in My Bowl

The earliest known evidence for this Neolithic phenomenon is from the Near East, in the area around modern
day Iraq. From there the notion of agriculture apparently gradually spread to neighboring areas, or was
independently invented. Over the next several thousand
years, it caught on through much of the world. In

Europe and the Near East, wheat was the crop of choice. Rice was popular in Southeast Asia. In the New World, maize (Americans call it "corn") was a real favorite. This change is profound stuff!

Plants are domesticated when their lives are altered in some way that makes them more useful to humans. It can involve something as simple as pulling weeds from a favorite stand of wild wheat, or as complicated as organized agriculture involving the selective breeding of crops.

Many domesticated plants are distinguished from their wild brethren by attributes that, while making them useful to a hungry human, make it difficult for them to survive on their own in the wild. For example, humans want the seeds and kernels of wheat and maize to stay on the plant where they can be removed at will, rather than having them disperse as nature would require in the wild. Some plants became completely dependent upon humans for their existence—and vice-versa!

Taming the Beast

Apart from plants, a number of animals were domesticated as well. You might be surprised to learn that the wild equivalent of that peaceful, slow-moving, domesticated cow in the field can be a ferocious untamed animal. To make cattle more useful to humans, a process took place that probably involved the capture and breeding of the slow, fat ones to the point where a cow gives milk, provides meat, and is well behaved, if not trustworthy. This process took place with goats, sheep, dogs, pigs, chickens, and several other popular beasts.

Pitfalls and Pointers

The *Neolithic* is a period in a given culture when the hunting and gathering lifestyle has given way to permanent settlements and the tending of plants and animals. Stone tools are still widely used, and pottery and other new kinds of tools reflect the new way of life.

Lost and Found

Scholars use the term *Mesolithic* to describe certain cultures, such as those in Europe, where there was an extensive period between the end of the Pleistocene and the adoption of agriculture. During that time, many groups adapted to the new post-Ice Age environment by exploiting the environment in novel and creative ways.

Life in the New Stone Age

Although you might think that the farming life sounds pretty good compared to a hunting and gathering lifestyle, there are some who consider the Neolithic to be the downfall of the human species. Archaeologists have found ample evidence that with growing populations living in permanent settlements and accumulating private possessions and differing levels of wealth, disputes and fighting become commonplace.

The assumed egalitarian existence of hunters and gatherers is transformed as chiefs or leaders with more power than others emerge. And furthermore, we find that humans begin to alter and transform the natural environment in very big ways. Trees are cut down, fields are cleared, and expanding populations heavily exploit natural resources.

Çatal Huyuk: Urban Legend

A classic example of an early Neolithic village is that of Çatal Huyuk in central Turkey. Actually, it's bigger than most such villages (32 acres), but it's been well studied and is mentioned in most every book on this subject, so why not this one too? About 5,000 people lived in this town in around 6500 B.C. Wheat and barley were the agricultural crops of choice, and cows were kept. There was a volcanic source of obsidian nearby, and the town apparently traded in the black volcanic glass.

The houses were made of mud brick and were entered by ladders from the roof. This suggests, perhaps, a need for defense in the greedier Neolithic world. Examples of art have survived, many of which deal with cows. Some rooms within buildings have been interpreted as shrines and contained female fertility figures and clay cow's heads and horns mounted on the walls.

Why a Revolution?

There are a number of theories about why the Neolithic revolution might have occurred, but there are as yet no firm conclusions. Some have suggested that perhaps it was an accident, a few wild wheat stalks dropping their seeds near camp and a surprised hunter/gatherer returning later to see plants growing near the site of his lunch. Or maybe it was an intentional invention encouraged by the changing environments after the Ice Age.

Some suggest that it could be the result of pressures from expanding populations. A rather fun (but seriously presented) idea is that the desire to produce beer was the incentive. For whatever reason, the revolution happened, and from that Neolithic foundation, great ancient civilizations would arise in several places in the world, beginning around 5,000 years ago.

Pitfalls and Pointers

Although we tend to look at an animal or plant as being domesticated or undomesticated, it's not that black or white. Domestication is not a single event but a process that takes place over time.

Let's Get Urban

What is a civilization? The actual word has its origins in the Latin word *civitas*, which means "city," and that term implies a densely populated and organized living center. The term seems inadequate, though, because what we mean by a civilization requires much more than an extra-large village or a city. Many scholars today prefer the term *complex society* to "civilization," and even then, it is much easier to describe than it is to define.

A complex society tends to have a ranked social, political, and religious system—that is, kings, bureaucrats, priests, merchants, slaves, peasants, generals, soldiers, and so forth. And there are lots of artisans, craftspeople, and occupational specialists. Contrast that to the hunters and gathers and perhaps even many of the early agricultural societies, where people could probably do each other's jobs without too much trouble.

Complex societies tend to build large religious or political structures, such as temples and palaces, and most had some sort of writing system. All these signs of a complex society are evidenced in the things that archaeologists dig up. In an ancient city, one can expect to find the sophisticated homes of the wealthy and the decrepit little shacks of the poor. Burials will likewise tend to show a difference in wealth, and you might find many kinds of workshops belonging to a variety of crafts specialists. The temples and palaces speak for themselves, especially if there is writing on the walls.

Just as the change to agriculture is of great interest to archaeologists, the origins of civilization, or complex societies, pose another huge problem to solve. Let's take a look at some of the older theories, and a few more recent ones.

Jargon Unearthed

A *complex society* is characterized by such features as class, wealth, and status differences, political, economic, and religious elites, craft specialists, relatively large populations, monumental architecture, and writing.

Mean Theories from the Privileged Few

The apparent "progression" from hunter/gatherer societies to civilization by way of agriculture has been recognized as far back as the Roman writer Lucretius (ca. 95–55 B.C.) and has fueled a good number of arrogant theories. In the 1800s and beyond, Westerners could propose that undeveloped groups of people were progressing through a series of cultural stages that would eventually bring them to the ultimate state, that of a European-like civilization. The most basic evolutionary scenarios involved a progression from savagery (hunters/gatherers) to barbarism (agriculturists) to civilization.

More elaborate versions subdivided these categories and provided criteria for membership into one group or another. For example, Upper Savagery was triumphantly attained when the bow and arrow were available, but Lower Barbarism required pottery. Civilization is finally achieved with the alphabet and writing. Other theorists were far less kind, and proposed that certain races or groups by nature or geographical region would never have the capacity to achieve civilized greatness.

The theorists, of course, always saw themselves at the top of the scale, and from that lofty pinnacle, they could look down at the "less sophisticated" and invent grand schemes. From a modern standpoint, however, one could argue that in an over-populated world full of violence and weapons, we have greatly regressed. Continuing upward progress is certainly not guaranteed. The so-called great civilizations of the past have disappeared or have been transformed, and with modern nuclear weapons we could, as callously projected by one general, be bombed back into the Stone Age.

Civilizations come and they go.

But Seriously, Folks...

Around 5,000 years ago, complex societies developed from agricultural foundations in several places around the world, including Mesopotamia and Egypt in the Near East and the Indus Valley and China in Asia. The same thing happened later in Central America and Peru in the New World. But complex societies didn't develop everywhere, and the timing of those that did is interesting. There are a number of theories that try to explain it.

One of the most famous ideas is that of Karl Wittfogel, who noticed that most early civilizations practiced intensive irrigation. In his book *Oriental Despotism: A Comparative Study of Total Power* (1957), Wittfogel proposed that the practice of organized irrigation would stimulate the creation of cultural complexity by the need for decisionmakers and a variety of different jobs. Writing might develop for record-keeping and communication, and differences in wealth might arise as some irrigated lands flourished more than others.

Others have suggested that population growth inspired cultural complexity, but could not the converse be argued as well? Another interesting theory involves warfare and population. As populations increase and resources become limited, a group might choose to conquer its neighbor. In doing so, status and wealth differences are created between the two, and the characteristics of complex societies develop as a result.

In short, we don't really know how the ancient civilizations came about. In some cases, they seem to appear almost "instantly," a phenomenon which has given rise to all manner of exotic explanations. One scholar, G. Elliot Smith, was impressed by similarities in ancient civilizations in diverse corners of the world and advocated a single origin for all civilizations: Egypt. And from there it all spread, far and wide. Others have called upon visitors from outer space. (We'll deal with that silliness in Chapter 24.)

As I mentioned above, it's easier to describe a civilization than to define it. We know that the classical Mayan society was far more technologically sophisticated than that of the Kalahari Bushmen, but who is to say that the Bushmen aren't or weren't more sophisticated in other aspects of their hunting and gathering lives? And at least one great civilization, the Incas, didn't have a writing system as such, although they had other clever means of communication, along with monumental architecture and other "civilized" characteristics.

Although most of us would consider ourselves to be "civilized," we're still uncertain as to exactly how we got that way. And if history is our laboratory, "civilization" is both a blessing and a curse. Our technology and information glut often complicate our lives, especially when we have become dependent upon such things as computers which can fail. And few could claim that being civilized has necessarily made us kinder to others or more responsible to the earth. But here we are. What comes after "civilization"?

Pitfalls and Pointers

Although in some instances it looks as if civilizations "instantly appear," we shouldn't forget that one inch of dirt separating a buried Neolithic village from a city built on top might represent a couple hundred years of change and development. We should likewise remember that certain important things, like the unwritten exchange of ideas, do not leave direct traces for the archaeologist to examine.

Lost and Found

Maybe at our core we are still hunters and gatherers, and these primal instincts manifest themselves in modern society by a fascination with the unknown and the seeking of lost information. Archaeologists, for instance.

> ### The Least You Need to Know
>
> ➤ Early humans got around, reaching East Asia from Africa perhaps 1.8 million years ago.
>
> ➤ Sometime near the end of the Ice Age, some groups began to domesticate plants and animals, engage in agriculture, and form permanent settlements.
>
> ➤ Out of an agricultural foundation, complex societies, or civilizations, began to appear just over 5,000 years ago.
>
> ➤ The explanations for these changes continue to challenge archaeologists.

Chapter 10

The Mud-Brick Civilizations of Mesopotamia

In This Chapter

➤ The land and history of Mesopotamia

➤ The ever-so-creative Sumerians

➤ The invention of writing

➤ Archaeological discoveries in Sumer, Babylonia, and Assyria

---

In the last chapter we saw how agriculture provided a foundation from which complex civilizations might develop. Now let's take a look at where the earliest known civilization arose: Mesopotamia!

Land Between the Rivers

Mesopotamia has often been called the cradle of civilization. In the area which encompasses much of modern-day Iraq and stretches to the Persian Gulf, we have some of the earliest evidence of the first domestication of plants and animals. Early on, small villages there developed into large towns and eventually cities.

The word Mesopotamia means "the land between the rivers," and the rivers in question are the Tigris and Euphrates, which flow south to drain into the Persian Gulf. Irrigation and the rich soil of the rivers' flood plains provided the basis for the population growth that fueled the growth of big cities.

Map of Mesopotamia.

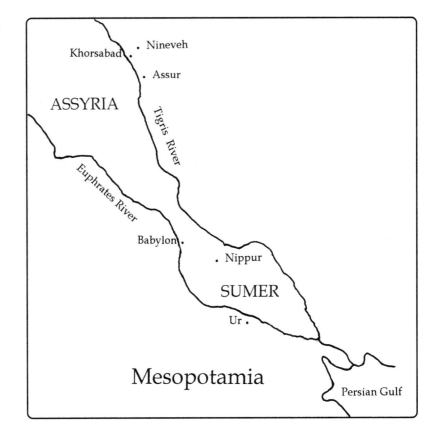

Who Was Who

The history of Mesopotamia is an interesting one, and before going into some specifics about its various civilizations, let's take a brief look at who came and went, to help keep things in order. No one group ruled in Mesopotamia indefinitely. Its history is more a matter of one bunch in charge, followed by another. What follows is the basic scenario.

The first major civilization in the area was the Sumerian, which later came under the control of the Akkadians. The Sumerians later made a brief comeback, and were eventually absorbed by the Old Babylonians, who in turn became subject to the Kassites and then the Assyrians. The latter succumbed to the Neo-Babylonians, who were conquered by the Persians, who were vanquished by the Greeks, to be eventually incorporated into the Roman Empire. That's not the end of it, but it's enough for our purposes.

Pitfalls and Pointers

Did you ever wonder why a minute is divided into 60 seconds? Or why a circle has 360 degrees? Couldn't we have 100 shorter seconds or 500 degrees in a circle? Blame it on our Mesopotamian friends, who established the base-sixty system in use today.

Palaces of Mud

Unlike some other civilizations in the region, Mesopotamia generally lacked stone, and there wasn't a huge supply of wood to be had. Living along the two rivers, however, they were assured of plenty of one thing—mud—which could be used to build not only houses, but also elaborate palaces and temples.

Unfortunately, mud brick doesn't have the lasting power of stone, and many of Mesopotamia's mightiest monuments now are ruined and melted piles of dirt. Many are now stranded out in the middle of the desert, abandoned after they were pillaged, or perhaps when the rivers changed course or the surrounding agricultural soil became poor.

Lost and Found

The study of ancient Mesopotamia is called *Assyriology,* practiced by *Assyriologists* (after one of the dominant groups, the Assyrians). They are interested in all aspects of the civilizations of the region and are usually trained in reading its difficult ancient scripts. A specialist in ancient Sumer is called a *Sumerologist* (or "unemployed," as the not-so-nice old joke goes).

The Sumerians: Creative Types

By 3500 B.C., there were large towns in much of Mesopotamia, and not long after, we find the first evidence of the Sumerians. Determining the origins of these people is problematic. Some say that they came into Mesopotamia from elsewhere and became the dominant culture; others suggest that perhaps they were indigenous to the region. It really is a puzzle, especially since their language is like no other known, ancient or modern. Surrounded by groups who speak languages belonging to either the Semitic or Indo-European families, Sumerian is an isolated orphan with no known relatives.

The achievements of the Sumerians are outstanding. There were so many, in fact, that it prompted the eminent Sumerologist Samuel Noah Kramer to write a book called *History Begins at Sumer* (1959). Since Sumer is the first known civilization, it's not surprising that we find in it early evidence for all sorts of new things, including the wheel, metal casting, and architectural innovations such as the arch and dome.

Diggers

American scholar Samuel Noah Kramer (1897–1990) was perhaps the world's foremost expert on ancient Sumer. His careful translations of difficult Sumerian texts are widely known, and his autobiography, *In the World of Sumer* (1986), gives a fascinating glimpse of the amazing career of a professional Sumerologist.

Writing It Down

Perhaps the greatest invention of all time first appears among the Sumerians—writing. The implications of writing are truly profound. For one thing, with it one can preserve information for the short and long terms—a nice bonus for archaeologists. Given the importance of writing as a whole, and since it is the source of most of what we know about ancient Mesopotamia, I think it's worth spending a little time on the subject.

Writing was not invented all at once, but rather was an evolving process. We don't know exactly what happened, of course, but here's the currently favored theory. In early Mesopotamia, little clay tokens were apparently used to keep track of how many of something people might possess. For example, an ox might be represented by a token in the shape of an ox. These tokens could be sealed in a ball of clay for accounting purposes.

Later, it became more common to draw a picture of the object, let's say an ox, on a flat piece of clay with some sort of tally marks next to it: three marks, three oxen. At this point, we could call this drawing a pictograph; not yet real writing.

The next big step to writing would be when that ox picture stands not just for an ox, but becomes a sound symbol that can be used to construct other words. So if the Sumerian word for ox is "gu," then the ox symbol might be used as a syllable and combined with other symbols to spell other words that have the "gu" sound in it, including those in other languages such as Akkadian, which borrowed the script, and have a completely different word for ox.

The classic example often used to describe this are the two words "bee" and "leaf." If we want to express those two things, we can draw a bee and a leaf and, providing that the drawing is good, we can convey a message. The symbols really become writing, though, when they stand for sounds and can be combined to write other words (such as "belief"), or be used in any other word containing those sounds. In fact, the ancient Sumerian script was written in such syllables, with additional symbolic signs to aid in understanding.

Love Those Wedgies!

Over the next couple of thousand years, the original pictographs behind the sound signs evolved until they were barely recognizable. It became standard in Mesopotamia to write on little tablets of clay, and a reed

Pitfalls and Pointers

When we are dealing with the distant past, attributing the "first" this or that to any individual group of people should be qualified as "the first known." Given our spotty knowledge of the archaeological record, and the uneven survival of the evidence, it's difficult to say with absolute assurance that any one thing was first.

Jargon Unearthed

Cuneiform is the wedged-shaped script, typically impressed into clay, which was used to write such languages as Sumerian, Akkadian, Elamite, and Old Persian.

stylus was used to produce wedge-shaped impressions in the tablets. This type of script is known as *cuneiform,* which means, literally, "wedge-shaped."

The Sumerian cuneiform script was adopted for the writing of Akkadian and other languages in the region, including Old Persian. Just as we have adapted the Latin alphabet to write such languages as English, German, Spanish, and even Hawaiian, so could the wedges be used for non-Sumerian.

Speaking of Akkadian, this would become the dominant language of Mesopotamia. It is a Semitic language and is in the same family as Hebrew and Arabic. The Akkadians lived in an area north of Sumer, and when Sargon of Akkad conquered his southern neighbor around 2370 B.C., he adopted much of their culture and borrowed their script to write his own language. Later rulers of Mesopotamia, such as the Babylonians and the Assyrians, would likewise speak dialects of Akkadian.

Deciphering Cuneiform

The decipherment of cuneiform script and the Akkadian language was an interesting process. Around 1802, Georg Grotefend (1775–1853) studied drawings that had been made of ancient Persian inscriptions using the script—inscriptions which were apparently written in three languages. Using some shrewd deductions, he was able to figure out that one of the scripts was Old Persian, and so was able to read some of the words, which proved to be royal inscriptions.

The key to translating Akkadian would ultimately be found primarily through the dogged efforts of a bold man, Henry Rawlinson (1810–1895), an English military officer and diplomat. While posted in Persia, Rawlinson heard of inscriptions carved into a huge rock cliff near the town of Behistun. There he found over 1,000 lines of cuneiform inscriptions, written in three languages and located over 300 feet above the ground.

Over the next several years, Rawlinson risked his life many times to make copies of the texts. After much comparative study, he published his translations in 1846. He concluded that apart from Old Persian, one of the languages was Babylonian (Akkadian), and thus the door was open to further study the many thousands of texts that would be recovered from Mesopotamia.

Lost and Found

A Semite is someone who speaks a *Semitic language* as their native tongue, including Akkadian, Arabic, and Hebrew. It is a common misconception among Westerners that everyone in the Near East is Semitic. But Iranians (Persians) are not Semites, and neither are the Turks. Their languages belong to the Indo-European family.

Pitfalls and Pointers

The pillaging of an ancient Mesopotamian town was no doubt an unpleasant experience for its inhabitants, especially when fire was used. For the archaeologist, however, a little fire in the right places brings a happy result: It bakes clay cuneiform tablets hard, so their chance of survival is much greater.

An example of cuneiform script: a Babylonian (Akkadian) text including the name of Nebuchadrezzar II. (After C. B. F. Walker, Cuneiform [London: British Museum, 1987], p. 58, fig. 37)

At this point, the existence of the Sumerians was still a mystery. Although the Babylonians and the Assyrians were known from the Bible, the older civilization was long forgotten. But the idiosyncrasies of the Akkadian script suggested that it had been borrowed, and the discovery of cuneiform inscriptions in a language other than Akkadian gave a clue that some other group was involved. Bilingual inscriptions, Sumerian words borrowed by Akkadian, and a study of the origins of the signs eventually allowed this unique language to be likewise translated.

Life in Ancient Sumer

A good deal of our knowledge about ancient Sumer and other Mesopotamian civilizations comes directly from the surviving cuneiform texts. There are thousands of economic, legal, religious and personal documents on clay tablets that provide an interesting picture of daily life. Archaeology, though, has done much to fill in the blanks or to verify the accuracy of some of the texts.

When we talk about the Sumerian culture, we can't think of it as if it were a modern country or nation. The Sumerians organized themselves into city-states. Each city had its own government and/or ruler and maintained a population of up to 50,000 people, and sometimes more. At the heart of each city was a temple dedicated to a favorite deity. These temples were often situated on raised platforms that would develop into one of the characteristic components of ancient Mesopotamian civilization: the ziggurat.

Land of Ziggurats

Ziggurats were built with up to seven stacked platforms, with a temple area on top. They shouldn't be confused with the early Egyptian step pyramids. Ziggurats were not tombs, and pyramids did not have stairs leading to a religious structure on top. Unfortunately, most unrestored ziggurats today look like dirty mountains in the sand. Some were quite huge, and those which have been studied show a tremendous amount of creativity with the use of mud bricks. Buttresses and recesses could be added for architectural interest, and walls could be decorated with friezes and colored tiles or cones.

The Death Pits of Ur

The most spectacular discovery from ancient Sumer occurred during the excavations of Leonard Woolley at the ancient city of Ur in the 1920s and '30s. There he uncovered around 2,500 graves of various sorts, including sixteen royal burials. They showed that the elite of Ur not only were buried with an impressive quantity of precious goods, but also took along members of their household.

In one "death pit," Woolley uncovered 6 male and 68 female servants, many dressed up for the big day. They probably killed themselves or were sacrificed to be buried with the boss. Although the whole concept is disturbing to us today, to archaeologists, the whole ghastly scenario, with its many artifacts and human remains, has provided an incredible wealth of information about the ancient Sumerians.

Diggers

Sir Leonard Woolley (1880–1960) excavated in many lands, including Nubia, Syria, Palestine, and Egypt. He is best known for his work at the Mesopotamian site of Ur. Woolley published a number of archaeological reports and some popular books as well, including *Digging Up the Past* (1930) and *Dead Towns and Living Men* (1920).

From Akkad to Babylon

You might think that with a common culture and language, the Sumerians could get along peacefully. Not always. The city-states used to battle with one another from time to time. This lack of unity didn't always work in their favor, and in fact probably weakened them for the likes of mighty Sargon of Akkad.

Sargon was perhaps the first warlord in ancient history, who around 2370 B.C. conquered Sumer and parts thereabouts. He and his Akkadian-speaking colleagues ruled the Sumerians for the next 150 years, after which time the Akkadians' power waned, and the Sumerians reestablished themselves in the Third Dynasty of Ur, named for their principal city.

This brief and creative period would not last long. Around 2000 B.C., a group of Akkadian-speaking people known as the Amorites invaded Sumer and established their own capital at Babylon, becoming known as the Babylonians. One of best-known individuals from this period was the sixth king of Babylon, Hammurabi (r. 1792–1750 B.C.), who unified much of Mesopotamia.

Hammurabi was known for his outstanding administrative skills. Most famous of all is his code of law, which has survived for us to study. The 282 laws are typically in two parts: a set of conditions and the resulting penalties. Here are some examples:

➤ If a man accuses another of murder and cannot prove it, the accuser dies.

➤ If a man passes a burning house and loots it, he will be thrown into the fire.

➤ If a son strikes his father, the son's hand shall be cut off.

➤ If a noble puts out the eye of another noble, he shall lose one of his own eyes. However, if he puts out the eye of a commoner, he shall pay a set penalty; and if it is a slave who is injured, the noble will pay the owner half his value.

➤ If a builder constructs a house and it collapses and kills the owner, the builder will be killed. If the house kills the son of the owner, the builder's son will be killed.

Lost and Found

The law code of Hammurabi was carved on a pillar of black diorite about seven feet tall, which was later (probably around 1200 B.C.) carried off from Babylon by the Elamites as a war trophy. In the winter of 1901–02, French archaeologists discovered the pillar at Susa, the ancient capital of the Elamites and later the Persians. It can now be seen at the Louvre in Paris.

There are plenty of harsh penalties, and responsibility for the quality of workmanship and services is emphasized. I imagine that there probably wasn't a lot of crime or too many shoddy goods after those laws were issued! The laws not only give us numerous important insights into ancient Babylonian society, but also show the characteristics of a complex society. The laws mention lots of different occupations and differences between the classes, and they didn't apply evenly to everyone.

The Old Babylonians eventually succumbed to outsiders and were taken over by a group called the Kassites. Meanwhile, a province way up in northern Mesopotamia was beginning to stir, and the ancient Near East was in for a bad surprise.

The Assyrians: Bad Boys of Mesopotamia

The Akkadian-speaking Assyrians had been up in the north for a long time, and were usually dominated by someone else. They get their name from their chief god, Ashur. Beginning around 1300 B.C., they started to secure their borders and then made forays to the south. They even managed to temporarily capture Babylon around 1100 B.C. Two hundred years later, they really struck out and began to conquer the Near East.

Assyrian king Tiglath-pilaser III became ruler of Babylon in 728 B.C., and his successor Sargon II defeated the Hittite army, captured Palestine, and deported the ten tribes of Israel (more on this later), extending Assyrian dominance all the way to the border of Egypt. His successor, Sennacherib, would continue the conquests, and the next king, Essarhadon, managed to conquer Egypt in 671 B.C.

Under his son and successor, Ashurbanipal, the Assyrian empire reached its greatest extent, and not long after began to fall apart. Egypt was lost in 660 B.C. It then took the combined forces of several different Near Eastern groups, including the Medes and the Babylonians, to shut down the Assyrian war machine. Their capital, Nineveh, was destroyed in 612 B.C.

The War Machine

Speaking of the Assyrian war machine, it was an amazingly well-organized force, complete with iron weapons, cavalry, and chariots. The army traveled with a variety of specialists, including interpreters, spies, engineers, and even accountants to tally the booty. The Assyrians had a reputation as real terrorists, and word that they were coming was probably sufficient to send many a village fleeing.

Big walled cities were apparently not much of an obstacle either, as the Assyrians used their engineers to build large siege machines that could attack the walls while diggers tunneled underneath. Needless to say, the homeland received the benefits of the conquest, and lots of fine goods and captured people were sent back to Assyria.

Lost and Found

In the year 1855, Mesopotamian archaeology was dealt a great blow. Rafts carrying around 300 cases of excavated Assyrian palace sculptures were capsized by river pirates. The antiquities, which were on their way to European museums, sunk to the bottom of the Tigris and were never seen again.

Digging Up the Assyrians

Major excavations of ancient Assyrian sites began with the French diplomat Paul Emile Botta (1802–1870), who excavated Sargon II's palace at Khorsabad in 1843. The site would produce an amazing quantity of carved stone reliefs that would prove typical of Assyrian palaces.

Most striking were the huge sculptures of human-headed winged lions and bulls. Tons of sculptures from the site were loaded up on rafts to be floated down the Tigris, where they would eventually be loaded onto ships for the long journey to France. They are now displayed in the Louvre.

The most famous excavator of Assyrian sites was Austen Henry Layard (1817–1894), who most notably dug up the Assyrian capital of Nineveh, which was well-known from the Bible. Layard estimated that he found almost two miles of sculptured reliefs. He also discovered the library of King Ashurbanipal, with well over 20,000 clay tablets. Many of his discoveries can today be seen in the British Museum in London.

A winged bull is discovered during excavations at Nineveh. (From A. H. Layard, Nineveh and Its Remains *[London, 1849])*

The New Babylonians

So back again to some history. When the Assyrians were effectively put out of action, part of the power vacuum was filled by a new dynasty of the Chaldeans, who took over the throne of Babylon. We call these folks the Neo-Babylonians so as not to confuse them with the Old Babylonians of Hammurabi's day. This new establishment would accomplish quite a bit in its short 70 years or so, but would never achieve the extent of the Assyrian empire.

Nebuchadrezzar, of Biblical Fame

Nebuchadrezzar II (r. 604–562 B.C.) is the most famous king of the Neo-Babylonians. He is notorious in the Bible for capturing Jerusalem in 586 B.C. and exiling many of the Jews to Babylon. Back at home, Nebuchadrezzar engaged in spectacular building projects that would amaze the German excavator, Robert Koldeway (1855–1925), who between 1899 and 1917 uncovered Babylon's huge walls and city gates and its temples and palaces. Many were beautifully decorated with glazed tiles.

The Hanging Gardens

The Babylon of this time is also known as the site of one of the Seven Wonders of the Ancient World, the famous Hanging Gardens of Babylon. The Gardens were rumored to be a magnificent tiered structure built by Nebuchadrezzar for the pleasure of his foreign wife, who missed her forested homeland. Koldeway thought he might have found the actual site of the Gardens, but it's quite hard to prove.

The successor of Nebuchadrezzar, Nabonidus, was unpopular with his own people. This made it even easier for the Persians under Cyrus the Great to conquer Babylon in 539 B.C. (We'll meet the Persians in Chapter 13.) From there on, the people of Mesopotamia would be under the thumb of various foreign powers until the twentieth century A.D.

Lost and Found

Perhaps the most famous example of ancient Mesopotamian literature is *The Epic of Gilgamesh.* The story tells the dramatic adventures of Gilgamesh, who was half-man and half-god. Although of Sumerian origin, its popularity is demonstrated by copies written in Akkadian. Some scholars now believe that the cuneiform sign which represents the sound "gil" should be read "bil," thus changing our hero's name to the seemingly less poetic "Bilgamesh" (or perhaps "Bill Gamesh" to those who wish to write the modern version).

The Least You Need to Know

➤ Complex societies, a.k.a. civilizations, probably first emerged in the region of Mesopotamia.

➤ We find the first evidence of writing in the ancient civilization of the Sumerians, among other innovations.

➤ The history of Mesopotamia is the story of a succession of groups dominating each other.

➤ We have learned a lot about ancient Mesopotamia from the many thousands of cuneiform clay tablets that have survived.

Chapter 11

Land of the Pharaohs

In This Chapter

➤ The land and history of Egypt

➤ The beginnings of Egyptology and the decipherment of the hieroglyphs

➤ King Tut and other pharaohs

➤ Temples, tombs, and archaeological discoveries

Of all of the places in the ancient world, Egypt seems to be the popular favorite. This is not surprising. There alongside the romantic Nile are the remains of a civilization that dates back to before the classical Greeks. In fact, the old Greeks and the Romans used to marvel at Egypt's antiquities just as we do now. When the ancient Greek historian Herodotus was writing about the pyramids around 450 B.C., they were already two thousand years old!

Apart from the numerous temples, tombs, and other spectacular monuments, there are hieroglyphs and mummies to surprise and delight us. And then there is the long history of wonderful archaeological discoveries, which continue to be made. Egypt seems to have something for everyone. This chapter will give you an overview of some of the most fascinating features, and also, I hope, spark your interest in some of the less glamorous, but equally important, studies that make up archaeology today.

Egypt: The Gift of the Nile

Herodotus poetically referred to Egypt as "the gift of the Nile." He was right! It's the Nile River, which flows north from sub-Saharan Africa to the Mediterranean, that was the lifeblood of Egyptian civilization.

Pitfalls and Pointers

Don't be fooled! The northern part of Egypt is called Lower Egypt, and the southern part is called Upper Egypt. That's because the Nile River flows north, so south is upstream.

Before the construction of the Aswan Dam in modern times, the natural cycle of the Nile included an annual flood, "the inundation," that would deposit rich nutrients on the productive fields each year. The river also served as a highway, with the currents taking you north and the winds taking you south.

The borders of ancient Egypt should not be confused with those of the modern country. Most of the ancient Egyptians lived on narrow strips of agricultural land along the banks of the Nile Valley (Upper Egypt) or in the broad Delta area (Lower Egypt) where the river divided into several branches before emptying into the Mediterranean.

Map of ancient Egypt.

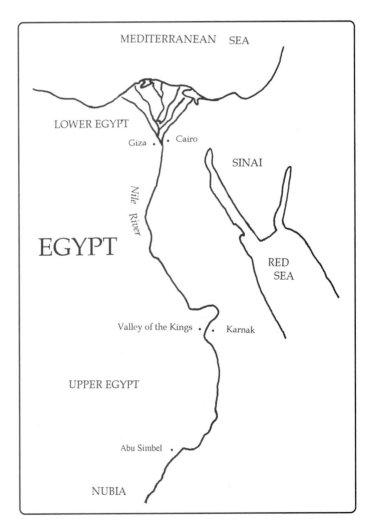

Ancient History

Ready for a little history? People have been living in the Nile Valley and adjacent territory for tens of thousands of years. Egypt achieved the Neolithic lifestyle relatively early, and numerous villages sprang up among the fertile agricultural lands. The Nile Valley and the Delta were apparently two political units in those early days, and each was divided into districts we call "nomes."

Traditional history claims that the political unification of Upper and Lower Egypt around 3100 B.C. was the beginning of civilization there. Thereafter, the land of Egypt would be ruled by a king who was considered the living embodiment of the god Horus. Among his typical titles were Lord of the Two Lands and King of Upper and Lower Egypt, both of which emphasize the importance of Egypt's new unity.

Manetho (ca. 280 B.C.), a priest and historian, divided Egypt's history into 30 dynasties or groups of ruling families. The system more or less works, and is a mainstay of Egyptology. The first three dynasties, which make up Egypt's Archaic Period (2920–2575 B.C.), show evidence of the growth of some components of a complex society, including monumental architecture, a centralized government, and the development of the ancient hieroglyphic script.

The Age of the Pyramids

The Archaic Period was followed by the Old Kingdom (2575–2134 B.C.), Dynasties 4–6. You can remember this as the Pyramid Age, as this is the time when many of the big stone pyramids, including the famous ones at Giza, were built. There's plenty of evidence of a gigantic bureaucracy at that time, and obviously a lot of command and control was necessary to carry out those incredible building projects.

Things started to fall apart politically near the end of the Sixth Dynasty, and the Old Kingdom gave way to what is called the First Intermediate Period (2134–2040 B.C.), a confusing period of history indeed. At that time, rival claims to Egypt's throne appeared, but eventually things settled down. The unity of Egypt was restored, and the civilization went on to prosper during the Middle Kingdom (2040–1640 B.C.).

Pitfalls and Pointers

Many of the Egyptian pharaohs are known by two names. The builder of the Great Pyramid, Khufu, is also called Cheops. The latter name is actually Greek, and was used prior to the decipherment of the hieroglyphs. When the hieroglyphs could be read, we could see that the name is more like "Khufu" than "Cheops."

Shifting Sands

Ever since the Old Kingdom, Egypt had been striking out in different directions to keep the neighbors in line and to secure exotic goods. This practice continued during the

Middle Kingdom, until the Hyksos took over during what is called the Second Intermediate Period (1640–1550 B.C.).

Exactly who they were still isn't clearly known. The Egyptians certainly didn't like them, and it took a while to kick them out. The Egyptians eventually did, thus beginning the New Kingdom (Dynasties 18–20, 1550–1070 B.C.). The Egyptians learned a thing or two from the Hyksos, however, including how to use chariots and iron weapons. The New Kingdom is known for its aggressive expansion of the Egyptian empire both south and east.

Many of the most familiar kings of Egypt ruled during the New Kingdom, including Hatshepsut, the female pharaoh; Akhenaten, known as the "religious fanatic" for his worship of a new god; Tutankhamun, the golden boy-king; and mighty Rameses II, the warrior and temple-builder. Egypt was strong and did well during the Eighteenth and Nineteenth dynasties, but things began to slip again during the Twentieth.

Thereafter, during the Third Intermediate Period (1070–712 B.C.) and Late Period (712–332 B.C.), Egypt was now and again ruled by a series of foreigners, including the Nubians, the Assyrians, the Persians, and the Greeks. When Alexander the Great conquered Egypt in 332 B.C., he was made pharaoh, and thereafter, much of the land was colonized by Greeks, who set up agricultural estates and businesses. It was a Greek ruler, the famed Cleopatra VII, who eventually succumbed to the Romans.

Lost and Found

Perhaps the most famous queen of ancient Egypt wasn't even an Egyptian. Cleopatra was a Greek, a member of the royal Ptolemy family, who were descendants of one of Alexander the Great's generals.

Jargon Unearthed

Egyptology is the study of ancient Egypt.

Napoleon and the Birth of Egyptology

Ancient Egypt was known to Westerners from the Bible and from classical writers such as Herodotus. It wasn't a particularly hospitable place to travel during the Middle Ages, but an occasional European journeyed up the Nile to gain firsthand knowledge of Egypt and its antiquities. In a curious twist of history, the birth of *Egyptology*, the study of ancient Egypt, would be a by-product of a military invasion.

In 1798, Napoleon invaded Egypt and brought not only his soldiers, but also a team of scholars, who were entrusted with the task of learning all there was to know about Egypt—from the local customs to the plant and animal life to the antiquities. The scholars did a fine job, and talented artists made detailed sketches in an era before photography. In 1801, the British routed the French from Egypt and confiscated some of the antiquities that the French had collected, including the famous Rosetta Stone. While Napoleon's campaign was nothing less than a military fiasco, his expedition to Egypt resulted in the publication in the early 19th century of the magnificent *Description de l'Égypte*, which to this day remains an important Egyptological work.

Deciphering the Hieroglyphs

For centuries, one feature of Egypt that had many people baffled was the ancient *hieroglyphic* script that seemed to be everywhere on Egyptian monuments. The language of Egypt had long before been replaced by Arabic, and knowledge of the hieroglyphs was completely lost. There were a number of theories about them, though, including that they were a form of picture writing or were wise and mystical philosophical metaphors.

The real answer would come through the work of a Frenchman, Jean François Champollion, and the Rosetta Stone would provide the key. The stone was found by French soldiers in 1799 and was inscribed with the same message in three scripts: Egyptian hieroglyphs, a cursive form of Egyptian known as demotic, and ancient Greek.

Pitfalls and Pointers

Everyone seems to call them "hieroglyphics," but the proper term for this ancient Egyptian script is *hieroglyphs*. The word *hieroglyphic* is actually an adjective used to describe such writing.

Glyph by Glyph

Since the knowledge of Greek was never lost, Champollion was able to compare the scripts, and discovered that the hieroglyphs were actually mostly phonetic. That is, individual glyphs stood for individual sounds or syllables in the ancient language. The discovery was proclaimed in 1822 and progress in translating ancient Egyptian came quickly. Many thousands of Egyptian texts today form the foundation of much of our knowledge of ancient Egypt, and there are plenty of Egyptologists who specialize exclusively in the study of such texts.

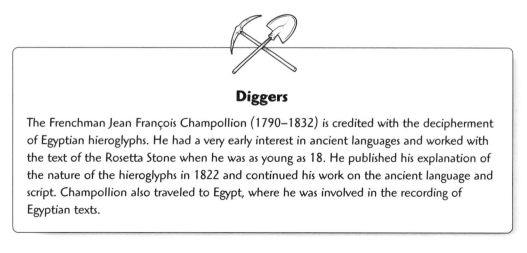

Diggers

The Frenchman Jean François Champollion (1790–1832) is credited with the decipherment of Egyptian hieroglyphs. He had a very early interest in ancient languages and worked with the text of the Rosetta Stone when he was as young as 18. He published his explanation of the nature of the hieroglyphs in 1822 and continued his work on the ancient language and script. Champollion also traveled to Egypt, where he was involved in the recording of Egyptian texts.

123

Egyptian texts come in many forms. The walls of temples and palaces were routinely carved with religious texts or accounts of the mighty or virtuous deeds of the pharaohs. Many funerary inscriptions and biographies survive on stone tablets, statues of the deceased, or on the walls of tombs. Documents written on papyrus paper have survived as have notes written on scraps of stone or pottery, and even ancient graffiti. We also have examples of genuine literature in the form of a variety of interesting adventure and morality stories and mythological tales.

An Egyptian hieroglyphic text. It talks about how King Thutmosis III ordered the dredging of a clogged canal. His name is found in the oval.

The Pyramids: Making Mountains for Their Majesties

When most people think of Egypt, the first image that comes to mind is the pyramids. It's not just how they were built that amazes people—it's also why. The famed smooth-sided classic pyramids seem to have evolved from rectangular tombs, called mastabas. When six of them were stacked atop each other, during the third dynasty, the result was a step-pyramid. Soon, the process evolved, and a true pyramid would be built, with four smooth inclined sides.

The biggest pyramids of them all were built during the Fourth Dynasty, including the Great Pyramid at Giza, which is considered one of the Seven Wonders of the Ancient World. It is estimated that it took at least 23 years to build the Great Pyramid, which is 481 feet tall and composed of approximately 2.3 million stone blocks.

The Great Pyramid is attributed to King Khufu (r. 2589–2566 B.C.), also known as Cheops. Another pyramid at Giza, that of Khafre (r. 2558–2532 B.C.), is nearly as huge. Not far away sits the Great Sphinx: a massive

Lost and Found

After visiting the Giza pyramids, the French general Napoleon calculated that the quantity of stone in these monuments was sufficient to build a wall ten feet high around all of France.

124

statue carved out of natural rock with the body of a lion and the head of Khafre. A third Giza pyramid, that of Menkaure (r. 2532--2503 B.C.) is much smaller than the other two but is nonetheless very impressive.

Most pyramids are basically solid except for a few passageways leading to a burial chamber containing a stone sarcophagus to hold the mummy of the deceased king. The interior structure of the Great Pyramid is more elaborate than most, with a great ascending gallery, two finished chambers, and some curious small "airshafts" and an uncompleted subterranean room. The outside of the big pyramids at Giza were fitted with smooth outer casing stones of limestone and granite.

Public Works

After the Fourth Dynasty the pyramids got smaller, but hieroglyphic religious texts began to be carved on the walls. In the Middle Kingdom, the pyramids were mostly of mud-brick with stone chambers and outer surfaces, a lot cheaper and easier to produce. There are dozens of pyramids in Egypt and they tend to be concentrated in groups on the western side of the river, the ones at Giza and Sakkara being the most famous. The West is where the sun sets each evening to descend into the Underworld where the dead dwell, so it's no wonder most Egyptian cemeteries were located in that direction.

The details of pyramid construction are still not clear, but they must have involved a huge workforce. The remains of bakeries and other support services for the workers have recently been excavated at Giza, giving a picture of the people behind the monuments.

Despite what Hollywood might suggest, there is no evidence that the pyramids were built by slave labor. They were probably massive public work projects that could keep a lot of people busy during the agricultural off-season when the Nile was flooded. The flooding might also have assisted the builders by allowing stones quarried elsewhere to be moved by barge closer to the building site.

The Great Sphinx with the Great Pyramid in the background. (From E. F. Jomard, ed., Description de l'Égypte *[Paris, ca.1812])*

A Big Wooden Surprise

While working on a road near the base of the Great Pyramid in 1954, a work crew discovered some unusual limestone slabs. When they lifted them up, it was found that they covered a large pit containing the incredibly well-preserved pieces of a dismantled boat made of cedar.

It took Egyptian restorer Ahmed Youssef many years to put the thing back together, like a puzzle, but the result is astounding: a beautiful ship 142 feet long with upturned prows. The boat is associated with the pyramid of Khufu and dates to ca. 2600 B.C. It is possible that the purpose of the ship is related to theological notions dealing with the deceased sailing across the sky with the sun.

A second boat pit was found next to the first. When a camera was sent down to investigate its contents in 1985, it was seen that it was in very poor condition, not having been sealed tightly through the ages like the first.

The Valley of the Kings

As secure burial chambers, the pyramids were big failures. They were like beacons visible from miles around that effectively said "Rob me!" During the New Kingdom, a different strategy was adopted for royal burials. An isolated mountain canyon beneath a big pyramid-shaped mountain would be used as the burial place of the god-kings, the Valley of the Kings. Despite their remoteness, most of these tombs, too, were big failures when it came to protecting the royal mummies and their contents. The vast majority were robbed or dismantled in ancient times.

There are about sixty tombs in the Valley of the Kings. About half belong to the pharaohs and the rest are small burials of royal relatives and special friends. Some of the royal tombs are quite huge and beautifully decorated with religious texts. As in the pyramids, a stone sarcophagus was placed in the burial chamber of each royal tomb.

The Italian circus performer and explorer Giovanni Belzoni was the first known European to excavate in the Valley of the Kings, beginning in 1816. He discovered several important tombs, and the Valley thereafter was explored by a number of diggers of varying ability. Although a few small tombs were found relatively intact, the ultimate goal of many excavators was to find an undisturbed royal burial. This would not happen until the year 1922.

Lost and Found

The Egyptians made paper from papyrus, a plant that once grew in great quantities along the Nile. Overlapping strips were pressed together to form sheets or joined to produce scrolls. With the changing climate over the last couple thousand years, papyrus no longer grows in Egypt, but it can still be found in huge swamps in central Africa.

King Tut's Tomb—One in a Million

In November 1922, English archaeologist Howard Carter discovered what many would argue is still the greatest archaeological discovery ever: the virtually intact tomb of an Egyptian pharaoh, that of Tutankhamun. Although there was evidence of light pilfering, the majority of the tomb's contents appeared to be intact and splendidly preserved.

The tiny tomb was packed with grave goods, including chariots, chests full of clothing, jewelry, food, and other afterlife provisions, gold-gilded furniture and shrines, and the intact mummy of Tutankhamun himself, enclosed in three nesting coffins. An exquisite golden mask covered the poorly-preserved mummy's head.

The tomb in the Valley of the Kings in which Tut was found was very likely not intended for him. A larger king-size tomb was probably being prepared for him elsewhere, but the boy-king Tutankhamun died young and was put into a tomb that had probably been built for a non-royal individual. Even so, it took nearly ten years to finish the archaeological work in the tomb, with each object carefully photographed and conserved. Fortunately, Carter had some of the best people available to help.

Pitfalls and Pointers

Although King Tut is a household name, he is actually one of the more obscure of the pharaohs. He became pharaoh around age eight and died when he was about eighteen. Historically, he was sort of a transition figure, but his tomb full of golden artifacts means all the world knows of Tutankhamun.

Diggers

Howard Carter (1874–1939) began his Egyptological career as a young artist who was hired to make accurate drawings of tomb and temple art for archaeological expeditions. Beginning in 1917, Carter worked in the Valley of the Kings under the sponsorship of George Herbert, Lord Carnarvon (1866–1923). After several years of limited results, the tomb of Tutankhamun was discovered in November of 1922.

The Working Class

The temples and tombs of Egypt were meant to last through the ages, and many were quite successful in that regard. Most ancient structures have not survived as well, since they were built of mud brick and the Nile floods annually. It's a happy thing for scholars that the Egyptians painted scenes of daily life on the walls of their tombs and buried their dead with household provisions, which give us a lot of information about how people lived. And one interesting village has survived to help fill in the gaps: a village of workmen involved in building the tombs in the Valley of the Kings.

Deir el-Medina, as it is called in Arabic today, is located at the foot of the mountains not far from the Valley of the Kings. It's a dry place and apparently was abandoned when the Valley was no longer being used for burials. Between 1917 and 1947, the Frenchman Bernard Bruyère (1879–1972) excavated there, recovering numerous artifacts and lots of *ostraca*, documents written on scraps of pottery and flakes of limestone.

These documents provide us with details of not only royal tomb construction, but also the affairs of the workers themselves. In their spare time, some of the residents worked on their own tombs. To be sure, Deir el-Medina is a bit of a fluke, a well-preserved specialized village, but there's no reason to believe that its inhabitants' basic daily lives were radically different from the majority of common people.

Jargon Unearthed

Ostraca (singular: "ostracon") are pieces of pottery or flakes of limestone which were used as writing surfaces.

Places of Worship

The ancient Egyptians worshiped many gods in many forms, and much has survived in the form of temples, art, and religious texts to give us a fairly good idea of the Egyptians' beliefs. Numerous temples, which served as houses for the gods, are found all over Egypt and from most time periods.

The focus of Egyptian religious belief was the maintenance of cosmic order and the prevention of chaos. This could be done by living in divine harmony with the universe, including the worship of appropriate household, local, or state gods. The Egyptians worshipped a huge number of gods, some of which were perceived in animal, human, and sometimes hybrid forms. Here are a few of the most famous:

➤ Osiris—husband and brother of Isis and ruler of the Underworld (the land of the dead). He is not only associated with death, but with resurrection and fertility as well.

➤ Isis—wife and sister of Osiris, and mother of Horus.

➤ Horus—the son of Isis and Osiris. A sky god in the form of a falcon, who, among other things, was identified with the ruling pharaoh.

➤ Amun—a popular and powerful god who, when combined with the sun god Ra, produced a powerful diety, Amun-Ra.

➤ Thoth—god of wisdom, knowledge, and writing, usually depicted as an ibis bird or a baboon.

➤ Anubis—jackal god of mummification and guardian of the cemeteries.

➤ Maat—goddess of truth and order.

Karnak

At the site of Karnak near Luxor in southern Egypt is an extraordinarily huge complex of temples. Beginning in the Middle Kingdom and continuing over the next couple thousand years, temples were continually being built or modified at the site, producing a truly impressive sprawl of pylons, obelisks, statues, columns, and even a sacred lake. A good bit of the temple is dedicated to the god Amun-Ra, who was prominent for much of the New Kingdom.

An old view of the Temple of Karnak. (From E. F. Jomard, ed., Description de l'Égypte *[Paris, ca.1812])*

The Drowning Temples of Abu Simbel

The Egyptian pharaoh Rameses II (1279–1213 B.C.), a.k.a. Rameses the Great, was rather fond of building big monuments in celebration of himself. One of the most spectacular temples in Egypt was carved into a mountainside in Egypt's deep south. Four seated colossal statues of the king serve as a facade, and a door leads to a network of halls and chambers, some of which feature more sculptures of the mighty one himself. A smaller temple dedicated to his wife Nefertari is carved into another mountain nearby.

When it was decided to build a modern dam to the north at Aswan to provide flood control and electricity for a growing nation, the temples of Abu Simbel and many other archaeological sites were threatened with destruction by the lake which would be formed. In an emergency salvage operation during the early 1960s, archaeologists and

Lost and Found

In appreciation for its significant efforts during the campaign to save the monuments that would have been drowned behind the Aswan Dam, the Egyptian government rewarded the United States with a small rescued ancient temple. The Temple of Dendur now stands in a special atrium in Metropolitan Museum of Art in New York City.

engineers from many countries went to work as the waters rose. The two huge temples at Abu Simbel were sawed in pieces and reassembled on higher ground nearby, where they are a popular tourist attraction today.

Archaeology Today

Beginning with Napoleon's invasion, a growing number of foreigners came to Egypt to explore the monuments and relieve the land of its antiquities. With the formal establishment of an antiquities service in 1857, archaeological work has been conducted with the permission of the government. In the early days the antiquities bureau was run primarily by Europeans, but the political revolution of 1952 put the business of caring for the monuments of Egypt firmly in the control of Egyptians, where it remains to this day.

Hundreds of expeditions, both Egyptian and foreign, have conducted projects on everything from prehistoric sites to old Islamic towns and monuments. Today, conservation work is emphasized, and exploration for new tombs and the like is discouraged, because there are plenty of things already discovered that require attention. Some of the best and most important archaeological work in Egypt today is being done by those who are there to make records of the existing monuments.

Researchers from the University of Chicago, for example, has been working for decades in the Luxor area, where they have been documenting several of the temples found there. As time and nature (not to mention air pollution) take their toll, these published drawings may serve as the only records of the fantastic texts and decorations that have survived for thousands of years, and are now gradually eroding away.

Lost and Found

Egyptology actually has fan clubs. There are a growing number of Egyptology societies, most of which are composed of enthusiastic amateurs. Go to a conference dealing with the subject and it wouldn't be a surprise if the amateurs outnumber the professionals. Many of these amateurs are extremely well-informed on the subject, and some have made valuable contributions to the field.

The Least You Need to Know

➤ Despite its unusual origins with the invasion of Egypt by Napoleon, Egyptology has bloomed into one of the most popular areas of archaeology.

➤ Ancient Egyptian temples, tombs, and inscriptions have provided us with an excellent view of the details of one the world's great ancient civilizations.

➤ The discovery of the tomb of King Tutankhamun remains one of the most spectacular archaeological discoveries of all time.

➤ Many archaeologists are active in Egypt today, where conservation and recording of the monuments is a priority.

Chapter 12

Digging Up
the Bible

In This Chapter

➤ The controversial field of Biblical archaeology

➤ The Bible as history

➤ The Dead Sea Scrolls and other big discoveries

➤ Lost arks and more

The Bible has been a source of inspiration, speculation, and controversy for many centuries. As a religious document, it serves as a foundation for three of the world's great religions: Judaism, Christianity, and Islam. These religions in turn have provided cultural values that stand at the core of many modern cultures. As a historical document, the Bible has provided a valuable source of information about ancient times in the Near East, including the civilizations of the Mesopotamians, Egyptians, Hebrews, and many others.

Given its importance, it is no surprise that various scholars have attempted to examine the contents of the Bible from many different angles. Theologians attempt to discern its meaning while others seek to see the text as literature to be compared with that of other ancient cultures in the region. Archaeologists, with their special skills in examining the remains of the past, have been very active in the lands mentioned in the Bible. In this chapter, we'll take a little look at how our subject fits in, or at least tries to.

What Is Biblical Archaeology?

There's an incredible amount of variety in the Bible. The first book, Genesis, talks about creation, and other books describe Jewish history, laws, and philosophy. Opinions regarding the accuracy of this great book vary widely. There are those who feel that every word found within it is the inspired word of God: If science or archaeological findings do not match the Biblical text, then it is due to the inaccuracy of our own flawed human abilities.

On the other hand, there are those who look at the Bible as just another collection of myths, stories, and propaganda pieces that serve as cultural reinforcement. And there are a hundred opinions in between, including views that parts of the Bible are borrowed Near Eastern myths and traditions, while other parts contain clear historical value.

Given such debate, it's not surprising that attempts to use archaeology to "test" the truth of the Bible have led to great controversy. Ask two archaeologists working on the subject, and you'll probably get three opinions.

The Books of the Bible

To begin, we need first of all to sort out what we mean by "the Bible." The early compilation of books is often simply referred to as the Hebrew Bible, since it is written predominantly in Hebrew. This is often referred to by Christians as the *Old Testament,* as opposed to the *New Testament*, which contains other books describing the life and teachings of Jesus of Nazareth and some of his immediate followers.

The Old Testament is called the Tanack in Hebrew and is divided into three sections: the Torah (law), the Prophets, and the Writings. The first four books of the New Testament are called the Gospels, and contain the sayings and activities of Jesus, whom Christians believe fulfilled Old Testament prophecies. Other New Testament books include the writings of Paul, a convert to Christianity who spread the word to the Greek and Roman world of his day.

Lost and Found

The movable-type printing press was one of the most significant of all human inventions. The usual method of copying all books and documents by hand was a tedious process, but the press allowed for numerous copies to be quickly produced for dissemination. The first book printed by its European inventor, Johann Gutenberg (ca. 1400–1468), was the Latin translation of the Bible around the year 1455. Since that time, untold millions of copies of the Bible have been printed in thousands of languages.

Lost and Found

The Hebrew Bible, or *Tanack,* is often referred to as the *Old Testament.* The *New Testament,* written in Greek, is composed of additional books emphasizing the life and teachings of Jesus of Nazareth. The Koran, the holy book of Islam written in Arabic, is built upon both testaments, and Muslims consider both Christians and Jews "peoples of the Book."

How the Bible was composed, and when and by whom, is a subject of great controversy. The earliest material was probably passed on orally through the generations. Tradition holds that it was the scribe Ezra who gathered many Old Testament books into their standardized form around the fifth century B.C. The Hebrew Bible was thereafter translated into Greek and then into Latin, and today can be found in literally hundreds of different languages.

Define Your Territory

The notion of "Biblical archaeology" at face value doesn't appear to be a difficult one. Biblical archaeologists are interested in what archaeology can tell us about the Bible. But there are others who prefer other terms. Since the majority of the story involves the life and history of the Jews in the area of modern-day Israel, there are some who prefer to call it the archaeology of the land of Israel.

Others find that term politically charged, and these people might prefer the term Syro-Palestinian archaeology, or Palestinian archaeology. Still others see that term as too restrictive, given that the Bible includes tales of Egypt, Mesopotamia, and other places in the region, and refer to themselves as archaeologists of the lands of the Bible or the Near East.

Modern-day Israel seems to be one big archaeological site. Interest in archaeology is a matter of national pride, and numerous excavations take place there every year. Biblical archaeology is popular in much of the world. Several glossy magazines cater to a public thirst for more information, and many scholarly journals address the subject, under various names. To keep things simple, let's just use the term "Biblical archaeology" to refer to any archaeology that relates to the Bible and its peoples in both the Old and New Testaments.

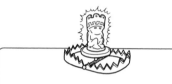

Pitfalls and Pointers

Although many of the Arab population of the Palestine region of modern Israel refer to themselves today as Palestinians, the geographical term by itself is politically neutral. The area was, in fact, known by that name until the state of Israel was created in 1948.

Map of Palestine.

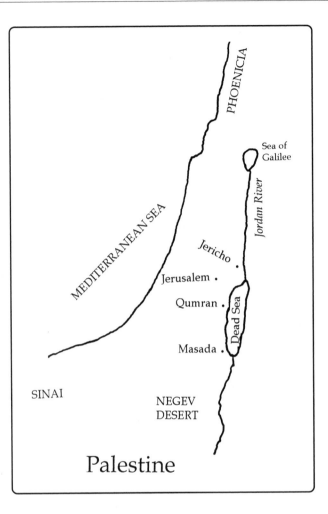

Palestine

The Land of the Bible

The term *Palestine* refers to a geographical region which more or less incorporates the area of the modern state of Israel and the territory east to the Jordan River. The word has its roots in the word *Philistine*, which was the name for a group of people who lived along the coast. The name was in general use to describe the region until the modern state of Israel was formed in 1948.

Palestine, where much of the Biblical story takes place, is located at a wonderful crossroads between Egypt and a good number of ancient civilizations to its north and east. Located on the Mediterranean, it was accessible by sea, and the territory was also readily traversed by land. As a result, it was often overrun by other powers within the region, including the Egyptians, Babylonians, Assyrians, and Persians.

A History of Biblical Proportions

After the tale of creation, the Bible relates a number of stories involving the relationship of humans to a Supreme Being, divine plans for leading a good life, and human successes and failures. It doesn't take long for humans to disappoint God, and at one point, God is so disappointed in their behavior that he destroys most life on earth in a great flood. (More on this later.) Humans are so arrogant in their belief that they can reach heaven that they build a mighty tower (a ziggurat?), but God thwarts their project by causing them to speak mutually unintelligible languages, neatly explaining one of the more puzzling aspects of human society.

The Twelve Tribes

These sorts of stories aside, Jewish history begins with Abraham (ca. 1800 B.C.), a nomad from Mesopotamia who became the first known *monotheist* and whose descendants would be organized into the twelve tribes. Then comes a period of slavery in Egypt and the deliverance therefrom by a leader named Moses, who received the laws of God, including the Ten Commandments. The Bible then tells of the Hebrew tribes conquering

Jargon Unearthed

Monotheism is a belief in one god, as opposed to *polytheism*, a belief in many gods.

Palestine, the construction of a temple in Jerusalem, and the division of the tribes into two groups, the ten tribes of Israel in the north and the two tribes of Judah in the south.

Babylon and Back

When the Assyrians ran through Palestine in 721 B.C., the ten tribes disappeared, and when the Neo-Babylonians had their turn in 586 B.C., they destroyed the Hebrew temple in Jerusalem (built ca. 950 B.C.) and led many of the people into captivity in Babylon, where they would be released to return home by the Persians in 538 B.C. The temple was rebuilt, and Palestine came under the dominance of the Greeks after Alexander the Great routed the Persians in 332 B.C. A brief period of Jewish independence in Palestine (140–63 B.C.) came to an end when the Romans took control in 63 B.C. It is within the history and culture of Jewish Palestine under Roman rule that the story of Jesus takes place.

Romans Rule

There were rebellions against the Romans, all of which eventually failed, and in 70 A.D. the temple was once again destroyed, never to be rebuilt. The area ultimately became part of the Ottoman Empire and therefore generally Islamic, although populations of both Jews and Christians would continue to live there. Christian pilgrims and crusaders were interested in finding old Biblical sites and artifacts, and eventually, European adventurers and early archaeologists would visit with Bibles and shovels in hand.

So with that, the world's most abbreviated history of Biblical times, let's look at just a few of the many interesting sites in Palestine and a few of the topics that perpetually grab everyone's attention.

Tell Me an Old, Old Story

The archaeological history of Palestine is organized into the classic groupings of Paleolithic, Neolithic, Chalcolithic (Neolithic with copper), Bronze Age, and Iron Age. Many of these "ages" are subdivided into specific time periods. For example, Late Bronze Age IIb refers to the years 1750–1550 B.C., and Iron Age I is 1200–1000 B.C. (The dating is occasionally subject to dispute.)

People have been living in the area of Palestine for tens of thousands of years, and even Neanderthal remains have been found in Israel. Perhaps it was a route for *Homo erectus* and others as they spread from Africa into Europe and Asia. Many of the archaeological remains in Palestine survive in the form of big mounds, or *tells*, which are the accumulated debris of human occupation over the millennia.

Jargon Unearthed

A *tell* is a mound made up of the accumulated debris of human occupation. Tells are commonly found all over the Near East.

Just as in Mesopotamia, and here and there in Egypt, so too the mounds in Palestine tend to look like big hills, and the archaeologist who dares to excavate these places is bound to find an amazingly complex series of layers, features, artifacts, and structures. Trying to relate one part of a site to another can be complicated, and digging a tell can be like sorting out a massive three-dimensional puzzle.

Archaeologists and volunteers excavating a complex tell in Israel.

The Walls of Jericho

Many of the ancient sites mentioned in the Bible have been identified, some by surviving place names, and others by their Biblical descriptions. One of the most famous sites is that of Jericho, which, apart from its role in the Bible, has the reputation of being one of the world's oldest cities. People had been living there since at least around 8500 B.C. The city was walled during much of its history, and the evidence indicates that it was abandoned several times and later expanded and rebuilt several times.

Jericho is best known for the Biblical story of its conquest by the Hebrews under the leadership of Joshua. The story relates how the Hebrews marched around the city blowing horns until, by the hand of God, the walls collapsed. The site of Jericho was excavated most notably by John Garstang (1876–1956) in 1930–1936 and Dame Kathleen Kenyon in 1952–1958. They did find collapsed walls, although it's difficult to prove the details of that famous Biblical tale. The 12-foot-high perimeter walls predate the Hebrews by a long time.

Diggers

British archaeologist Dame Kathleen Kenyon (1906–1978) was one of the most prominent female excavators ever. Along with her mentor Sir Mortimer Wheeler, Kenyon devised methods of excavating difficult sites that would be adopted extensively in Near Eastern archaeology. She is best known for her excavations at the site of Jericho and in the city of Jerusalem. She was a tough and persistent leader, and apart from digging, she also served as a lecturer in Palestinian archaeology at University College in London.

The Siege of Lachish

There are other sites which relate directly to Biblical history. The fortified city of Lachish, for example, is mentioned several times in the Bible. When the Assyrian king Sennacherib attacked Palestine, fortified Lachish was one of the cities he assaulted, in 701 B.C. This is noted in the Old Testament (2 Kings 18), and most remarkably, the attack is featured on sculptured reliefs in the palace of Sennacherib in the Assyrian capital of Nineveh. The reliefs show the Assyrian use of siege machines against the city and the carrying away of booty. When the tell was excavated, archaeologists found plenty of evidence of this event.

Looking for Moses

One of the greatest Biblical stories is that of Moses, a Hebrew child raised in the court of an Egyptian pharaoh. Moses would leave Egypt, and later return under the orders and direction of God to free his people from slavery. It takes a series of horrible, miraculous plagues to convince the pharaoh to let the Hebrews go, and then more miracles take place when the Egyptians decide to pursue the emigrating tribes.

Pitfalls and Pointers

The Bible contains many stories of God's direct intervention in human affairs that we call miracles. Miracles, however, are very difficult to prove in the archaeological record. We can't see the handprints of God on the walls of Jericho, for example, but what does that prove? Mostly that if you're looking to dig up miracles, you're probably wasting your time.

Jargon Unearthed

The body of water known as the Red Sea is often identified with the story of Moses and the Exodus. In the original Hebrew text, however, the name given is the "Sea of Reeds," the location of which has not been clearly identified.

A body of water called the Sea of Reeds is parted to allow the Hebrews to cross, although it drowns the pursuing Egyptians. The migrants are guided by a pillar of smoke during the day and a pillar of light by night. Food and water are miraculously provided for this large group. Eventually they camp at the base of Mount Sinai, where God gives Moses the Ten Commandments prior to the Hebrews' invasion of Palestine, a land the Bible says is theirs for the conquering.

The Egyptian Connection

There has been a tremendous amount of interest in finding the historical details of this story. Who was the pharaoh of the Exodus? How did the miracles occur? Where is Mount Sinai? The Egyptian part of the story is often explored. The name "Moses" itself is not unusual for the Egyptian New Kingdom. The pharaoh of choice for the Exodus is mighty Rameses II (r. 1279–1213 B.C.), although a number of other Egyptian pharaohs from the New Kingdom have also been accused.

Curiously, there is only one mention of the Hebrew people in Egyptian texts. In a text dating to the time of Merneptah (r. 1213–1203 B.C.), the successor of Rameses II, a group of people called "Israel" are noted along with others in a list of people conquered in Palestine by the Egyptians.

The Bible says nothing of this Egyptian assault on the Hebrews, however, nor is the Egyptian defeat by drowning in the Sea of Reeds recorded. On the other hand, the Egyptians are not known to advertise their failures, so the most we can really say is that the name of Israel in an Egyptian text is evidence that the Egyptians knew of the existence of such a people.

The name of Israel in Egyptian hieroglyphs.

The Exodus

The miracles in the Exodus story also receive lots of attention. Various plagues have been explained by natural phenomena such as hail, locusts, or micro-organisms which might cause the Nile to turn red. One of the more interesting attempts to relate the Biblical story to regional events is the notion that the catastrophic eruption of a large volcano in the Mediterranean, Thera, could explain the pillars of smoke and fire.

A related earthquake with an accompanying tidal wave could have caused the Sea of Reeds to temporarily part to allow the Hebrews to cross and escape the pursuing Egyptians. Of course believers require none of these attempts at scientific explanation, unless they see God using the forces of nature to carry out miracles.

Lost and Found

The Jewish people are the spiritual descendants of the Biblical Hebrews and are thus, perhaps, the most vibrant and enduring legacy of the ancient Near East. Whereas the religions of the ancient Egyptians and the peoples of Mesopotamia have long ago fallen to the wayside, Judaism is alive and well in the modern world.

Searching for Milk and Honey

And what of Mount Sinai, where Moses received the laws of God while the Hebrew people waited below? There is a traditional site for Mount Sinai, in Egypt's Sinai peninsula, where a monastery, St. Catherine's, established in A.D. 330, is still manned by Greek Orthodox monks.

Others have speculated that the real Mount Sinai might be one mountain or another in the same region, or in Israel's Negev desert, or even in Arabia! There are few traces to provide a solid answer, and skeptics point out that thousands of wandering and camping Hebrews would leave quite an impact in the archaeological record—a record which has not yet been found.

When it comes to the Hebrews conquering Palestine, that too becomes a complex proposition to prove. There is evidence of the destruction of a site here and there at about the right time, but it is difficult, if not impossible, to determine who did the damage among the fallen walls and ashes. There are some skeptics who believe none of it ever happened at all: The Hebrews were never captive in Egypt, Moses didn't exist, and the Hebrews never conquered Palestine.

The archaeological record doesn't support these ideas, they say, and perhaps the Hebrew civilization evolved from within the indigenous Canaanite people of Palestine; the early heroic myths would eventually be replaced by genuine history in later chapters of the Bible. It's an extremely controversial subject, needless to say, and it tends to invoke both anger and smugness. (Who says history is dull?)

Pitfalls and Pointers

Is it appropriate to use archaeology to prove the details of a book such as the Bible? It really comes down to a matter of individual faith and expectation. Archaeology is merely a tool that can shed light on the past. It can't on its own impart spirituality or define miracles or the nature of God.

Pitfalls and Pointers

There are large gaps in our knowledge of the life of Jesus of Nazareth. The New Testament provides information about the first two years of his life, age twelve, and then the last three years of his life when he was actively preaching his message. What was he doing in the meanwhile? Various speculators have him learning wisdom in India or elsewhere, traveling extensively, living with the Essenes in Qumran, and so forth. The fact is, we really don't know what he was doing during these "missing" years.

The Dead Sea Scrolls Come Alive

Who hasn't heard of the Dead Sea Scrolls? Bedouins looking for a lost goat throw a rock in a cave and hear pots breaking. The pots are found to contain ancient scrolls, and the story of the wheeling and dealing between the Bedouins, antiquities dealers, and Jewish archaeologists to obtain the scrolls is something right out of a spy novel.

The cave in which the scrolls were found is located not far from the Dead Sea at an area known as Qumran, which at the time of the scrolls' discovery in 1947 was located in TransJordan. As archaeologists searched several caves in the vicinity, they found the remains of over 800 documents, including some of the oldest examples of the books of the Bible. Who wrote these documents, and why are they hidden in caves?

Essenes and Other Theories

In the early 1950s, the attention of archaeologists turned to the ruins of an ancient settlement found directly below the cliffs containing the caves. The excavators concluded that it was an isolated settlement inhabited by a Jewish sect called the Essenes, who lived apart from mainstream society in this relatively remote desert location. There they copied books of the Hebrew Bible along with their own peculiar spiritual documents. Perhaps they hid the scrolls in the caves to protect them during the Roman battles with the Jews in the first century A.D.

Other scholars are not so sure. Some argue that the remains at Qumran have nothing to do with the Essenes, who themselves are an obscure group not even mentioned in the Bible. Perhaps the remains are those of a desert retreat for wealthy inhabitants of Jerusalem. Perhaps the scrolls themselves are from Jerusalem and were hidden in the caves for safe-keeping. Others have even suggested that Jesus was an Essene who lived out at Qumran prior to his preaching days.

Studying the Scrolls

Apart from the archaeology of the site itself, the scrolls are starting to reveal interesting information. A nearly complete Biblical book of Isaiah has demonstrated that most of the modern Biblical text has been transmitted through the ages with a great degree of accuracy. The texts as a whole have contributed greatly to our knowledge of Judaism and the culture from which Christianity arose. It is easy to count the discovery of the Dead Sea Scrolls as one of the all-time great archaeological discoveries.

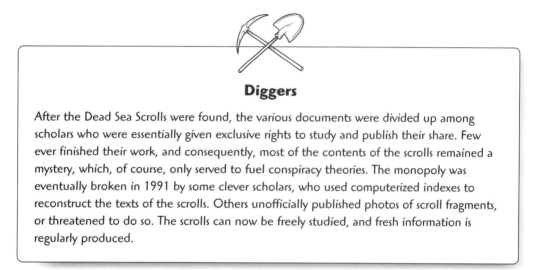

Diggers

After the Dead Sea Scrolls were found, the various documents were divided up among scholars who were essentially given exclusive rights to study and publish their share. Few ever finished their work, and consequently, most of the contents of the scrolls remained a mystery, which, of course, only served to fuel conspiracy theories. The monopoly was eventually broken in 1991 by some clever scholars, who used computerized indexes to reconstruct the texts of the scrolls. Others unofficially published photos of scroll fragments, or threatened to do so. The scrolls can now be freely studied, and fresh information is regularly produced.

Masada and the Hilltop Defenders

One of the most important archaeological sites in Palestine is that of Masada, King Herod's mountaintop palace and fortress not far from the Dead Sea in southern Israel. The story of Masada is not recorded in the Bible, but is told by a Jewish historian named Josephus (ca. A.D. 37–100). Josephus relates how Masada served as a stronghold for Jewish rebels during the wars with the Romans in A.D. 66–73.

According to the story, the rebels held out on top of the mountain while the Romans built a huge ramp up its side. When they eventually broke through the walls on top in A.D. 73, they found that everyone had committed suicide rather than succumb to Roman domination. The story has become a very important symbol for the modern state of Israel, which proclaims the motto that Masada shall never fall again.

Israeli archaeologist Yigael Yadin excavated Masada from 1963 to 1965. A beautiful three-tiered palace perched on the very edge of the cliff was uncovered, as were huge cisterns for collecting water, a Roman-style bath complex, numerous storerooms, and a synagogue.

There was plenty of evidence of the Roman siege, too, with several camps built around the base of the mountain and the huge earthen ramp still reaching up one side. There are some archaeologists, however, who dispute the details of the heroics on top of Masada. The mass suicide of the 960 rebels as reported by Josephus remains unverified archaeologically. The remains of fewer than 30 individuals were found in excavations and the precise cause of death remains unclear. It is possible that the rebels involved were killed or captured in the Roman seige operation, which has been documented by the archaeological evidence. Nonetheless, anyone who has been there can attest to the stark beauty of the location and the perseverance that must have been necessary to hold on in such a place while the enemy slowly crawled upward.

Lost and Found

In the late nineteenth century, European Jews began to immigrate to Palestine to settle in the land of the Bible. One immigrant, Eliezer Ben Yehuda (1858–1922), argued that Jews living in a Jewish homeland should speak the language of their ancestors. Today, modern Hebrew, which was once only a Biblical and liturgical language, is spoken by the approximately six million citizens of Israel, and many others.

Diggers

The multi-talented Israeli archaeologist Yigael Yadin (1917–1984) was the son of a famous Jewish archaeologist, E. L. Sukenik. Yadin's many prominent exploits included digging at the site of Hazor, big discoveries in caves near the Dead Sea, and the excavation of the site of Masada. He was involved in the acquisition of some of the Dead Sea Scrolls and published on the subject. Yadin was also a great military man, and was Chief of Staff of the Israeli army. He served in the Israeli parliament and at one time was Deputy Prime Minister.

Raiders of the Lost Arks

Plenty of archaeologists out there might think it inappropriate for me to discuss the next couple of topics in an archaeology book. Too bad! These topics are widely known by the public and quite worthy of attention: the lost arks! English translations of the Bible use the same word, "ark," to describe two very different objects. One, Noah's ark, is a boat, and the other, the Ark of the Covenant, is a box. Although both are technically receptacles, the Hebrew words for each are different. Let's look a little at each.

Noah's Ark

In the book of Genesis, God gets tired of evil humans and decides to destroy the life on Earth and start over. He selects a rare good man, Noah, and instructs him to build a big boat, or ark, on which he and his family, along with pairs of all the animals, would survive the flood. The waters came, the waters receded, the ark came to rest on a mountaintop, and the world was repopulated.

A mountain named Ararat on the border of Turkey and Armenia has been traditionally identified as the spot on which the ark came to rest. Many expeditions have traveled to Ararat in search of the boat. Some have returned with small pieces of wood, but it seems that every time someone claims to have found the ark, the photographs can't be produced or the images depict rocks or other natural formations. Various parts of the mountain have been explored, and there are competing ideas about where the boat might lie.

Many of the ark-hunters seem to have more enthusiasm than mountaineering skills. To make things worse, the Bible does not specify one mountain, but refers to the "Mountains of Ararat" as the ark's resting place. And pieces of wood? It would not surprise me if people have been building little shrines and such on this sacred mountain for a good number of years.

So is the ark up there? Again, this is a matter of faith. The skeptics might say the flood never happened or that it was a local event. Recent research has produced some convincing geological evidence for a massive flood in the Black Sea area around 5600 B.C. It seems that as world sea levels began to rise following the Ice Age, the waters in the Mediterranean began to rise, and eventually poured into the Black Sea, which was at that time a freshwater lake. Ancient tales of floods from many cultures around the world might describe similar sea level rises. No matter what the evidence, there will always be those who maintain an abiding faith that the ark is out there somewhere, and that its discovery will vindicate the Bible for all who don't believe.

Pitfalls and Pointers

Many Bible stories are similar to stories from other places in the Near East, especially Mesopotamia. There is a similar flood story from Sumer, and some Hebrew texts are found in nearly identical form in ancient Egyptian literature. So what's going on here? The material might be borrowed, or maybe the stories are independent accounts of the same events in a shared cultural milieu.

The Ark of the Covenant

A lot of people were exposed to the subject of the Ark of the Covenant by way of the first Indiana Jones movie, "Raiders of the Lost Ark," during which Professor Jones competes with Nazis to recover this powerful and elusive artifact. So what exactly is it?

In the Biblical book of Exodus, God instructs Moses to build a special box constructed of acacia wood, which would be carried along by the Hebrew tribes as they wandered through the desert, and set up in their tabernacle. The box was gilded and had figures of two angels on top, and served as a sort of throne of God. Inside were the stone tablets bearing the Ten Commandments, and perhaps some other precious artifacts.

The Hebrews were said to have taken the Ark along with them into battle, where it would often assure success. When a permanent temple was built in Jerusalem, the Ark took its special place in the Holy of Holies. It is never heard of again after the destruction of the temple by the Babylonians in 586 B.C.

So where is this lost ark? Some say it was destroyed during the destruction of the temple. Others say it is hidden in a chamber at the site of the temple in Jerusalem, and just a few years ago a rabbi claimed to have caught a glimpse of it before his excavations at the site were interrupted. Someone else claimed to have seen it in a cave in Jordan, and a book has been recently written which argues that the Ark is actually kept in Ethiopia. As with Noah's ark, the proof is with the artifact. Let's see it and examine it, and we'll talk about it from there.

Where Jesus Walked

No matter what you might think of Jesus, there is good evidence that he walked the earth. Whether or not you think he was the Son of God, a great wandering philosopher, or otherwise is your own business. Unlike the Old Testament stories of the Creation and the Exodus and so forth, the events of the New Testament take place in relatively recent times, and written commentary on the subject was quickly forthcoming by those close to the action.

Lost and Found

The Shroud of Turin is one of the most controversial artifacts around— a sheet of cloth bearing the likeness of a crucified man which some claim is Jesus. Radiocarbon dating places the shroud in the Middle Ages, but true believers still hope that the shroud is nonetheless authentic. The shroud is housed in a church in Turin, Italy.

Interest in artifacts and places related to the story of Jesus began early on, and pilgrims began to visit Palestine. Around A.D. 330, Helena, mother of the Christian Roman emperor Constantine, visited the region looking for authentic Biblical locations. The Crusades during the Middle Ages were in part fought to protect these sacred sites. Today, churches abound in various places identified as important throughout the Palestine region, and pilgrims continue to visit by the millions.

To understand Jesus and what he was saying and doing, you really need to understand the historical and cultural context of the times. Jesus was a Jew living in Palestine under Roman occupation. The more you know about the dynamics of that past situation, the clearer the texts become: yet another good reason for studying archaeology and history, no matter what your spiritual viewpoint.

The Least You Need to Know

➤ The archaeology of Palestine and the Bible is a wonderful and controversial subject.

➤ Apart from its spiritual value, the Bible also contains a good bit of history.

➤ Archaeology can assist in the understanding of Biblical times and places, but can't be expected to prove miracles or their divine origins.

➤ You can expect lots of interesting discoveries and insights from the dynamic field of Biblical archaeology.

Chapter 13

A Near Eastern Grab-Bag

In This Chapter

➤ The power-playing Hittites and Persians

➤ The truth about the Philistines

➤ Those travelin' and tradin' Phoenicians

➤ Lost cities and lesser-known groups

When it comes to the ancient Near East, Mesopotamia, Egypt, and the Bible seem to get the majority of the attention. The fact remains, however, that there were dozens of other cultures, both big and small, who came and went—each playing its own role in the grand history of the region. Some groups, such as the Persians and the Hittites, were truly mighty in their day, while there are others who were less prominent, and some who have only recently been discovered. Let's take a look at just a few of the many fascinating ancient Near Eastern groups, who may very well deserve more appreciation than they ordinarily get.

Ugaritic, Anyone?

In 1928, a farmer working a field near the Syrian coast came across a buried chambered tomb. The interesting pottery found within attracted the attention of French archaeologists, who began to explore the nearby tell of Ras Shamra the following year. Excavations continued for decades. The site has been identified as the ancient city of Ugarit, which was occupied beginning around 6000 B.C. By the Late Bronze Age (ca. 1500–1200 B.C.), Ugarit had developed into a small, prosperous kingdom that from time to time was under the dominance of foreign powers such as the Egyptians and the Hittites.

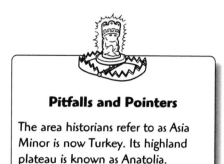

The most famous discoveries at the site were thousands of clay tablets written not only in Akkadian cuneiform, but also in an alphabetic script using cuneiform symbols. The language of the tablets, Ugaritic, is similar to Biblical Hebrew, and was deciphered in short order. The texts are especially important to Biblical scholars, who have found that they shed a lot of light on Old Testament times and practices.

Another Syrian site, that of Ebla, was excavated beginning in 1964, and has also turned up thousands of clay tablets. These are written in Sumerian and a Semitic language called Eblaite. Like Ugarit, this prosperous trading city is of interest to those who study the Old Testament and the Near East.

Don't Mess with the Hittites

Although a group of people named the Hittites is mentioned in the Bible, very little was known about them until about a hundred years ago. And what a group they were! The capital of the Hittites was called Hattusha, and was located in Asia Minor at the site of Bogazkoy, in what is now central Turkey.

Unlike many of the other groups residing in the Near East, the Hittites spoke an Indo-European language and used a cuneiform script. Indo-European groups such as the Hittites probably entered Anatolia by about 2300 B.C., and the first recorded Hittite king is known from around 1680 B.C. The Hittites and their "Kingdom of Hatti" became serious players in the Near East. They established their own moderate-size empire and even vigorously competed with the Egyptians for influence in the Syro-Palestinian area.

They actually fought and essentially defeated the Egyptians during a battle for control at Kadesh in Syria around 1274 B.C. (The Egyptians bragged about how they themselves were victorious, but that's to be expected.) After the battle of Kadesh, a peace treaty was made between the Hittites and the Egyptians, and pharaoh Rameses II took two Hittite princesses as wives.

The Hittite kings were hard bargainers and included rulers with great names like Suppiluliuma and Hattusili III. Eventually the Hittites had to fight off the Assyrians in the East and were weakened. The capital of Hattusa was burned by invaders around 1200 B.C, effectively putting an end to the great Hittite civilization.

Meet the Philistines!

When, according to the Bible, the Hebrew tribes set out to conquer Palestine, they not only had the various Canaanite people to deal with, but also a group called the

Philistines. The Philistines first appear in the area around 1100 B.C., and were apparently one of the Sea Peoples, a little-known group that came from the Aegean area and caused problems all over the Mediterranean around that time.

The Bible mentions five big Philistine cities near the Palestine coast, including Ashkelon, Ashdod, and Gaza. They were prominent in the area until about 600 B.C. Goliath, the big bully slain by David the shepherd boy in the Biblical story, was an extra-large example of a Philistine.

The modern cliché of the Philistines as brutes is probably undeserved. They were city dwellers and farmers, and if you looked at their pottery, you might conclude that they were quite artistic. So the next time someone calls you a Philistine, say "thank you very much." Living where they were, the Philistines were subject to the usual beatings and demands by various Near Eastern rivals, and Philistia ceases to be prominent around 600 B.C.

Lost and Found

In 1887, a woman digging for fertilizer in the ruins of el-Amarna in Egypt discovered the first of several hundred clay cuneiform tablets. They are mainly correspondence with the Egyptians written by Babylonians, Assyrians, Hittites, and others. Most seem to date to the time of pharaoh Akhenaten (1353–1335 B.C.) and shed much light on diplomatic relationships and trade at that time.

The Phoenicians: Traders Extraordinaire

The people we refer to as the Phoenicians occupied the coast of what is now Lebanon. Several of their port cities are quite famous, including Tyre, Sidon, Byblos, and Berytus (Beirut). From these cities they engaged in trade throughout the Mediterranean. Although sharing a common culture, the major Phoenician cities were independent political entities.

Phoenicia as a recognizable force begins around 1200 B.C. Its position at both sea and land crossroads between Egypt and Palestine, the eastern Mediterranean, and parts east such as Arabia, Mesopotamia, and Persia made Phoenicia an ideal location for regional trade and also left it subject to the Near Eastern invader du jour. The Assyrians were quite happy to dominate the area, and the Neo-Babylonians would likewise take their turn, followed by the Persians.

Jargon Unearthed

The Phoenician city of Byblos was well-known as an export center for papyrus paper, which the Greeks referred to as *byblos*. The word "Bible" was derived from this word, which means book.

Among the Phoenicians' most famous exports was cedar from the mountains of Lebanon, which was highly prized, even by the Egyptians. Dyed purple cloth, the color derived from the Murex sea snail, was also quite popular. They also specialized in the production of small objects such as jewelry and things made of glass, and were experts at obtaining and working silver and gold.

The great Phoenician traders expanded their commercial routes by establishing colonies in the western Mediterranean, including southern Spain, and in North Africa. The most famous of these was Carthage, which was founded around 800 B.C. and is located on the coast of modern-day Tunisia.

As Phoenicia itself weakened because of invasions, Carthage thrived and became a power in its own right. The Carthaginians set up trading posts far and wide, and came to control much of the western Mediterranean. When the Romans began to build their empire, they had to face the Carthaginians, which they did in a series of conflicts known as the Punic (from "Phoenician") Wars. The Carthaginians were eventually routed from the west, and Carthage itself was burned.

Alphabetically Speaking...

Perhaps the most famous contribution of the Phoenicians is the transmission of the *alphabet* to the Greeks around 800 B.C. From there it spread to the Etruscans and then to the Romans, and evolved into many of the modern scripts in use today, including English.

The alphabet provides a real departure from the generally cumbersome Near Eastern scripts of the day, such as cuneiform and hieroglyphs. The script consisted of 22 letters representing consonants only, as is the common practice with Semitic languages. The Greeks added vowels and eventually fixed the direction of their writing from left to right, as opposed to the Semitic right to left.

Phoenician and Greek alphabets. (After Pierre Swiggers, "Transmission of the Phoenician Script to the West." In Peter T. Daniels and William Bright, The World's Writing Systems *[New York: Oxford University Press, 1996], p. 262, Table 21.1)*

THE ALPHABET: FROM PHOENICIA TO GREECE

1 = PHOENICIAN C.900 BC
2 = GREEK C.700 BC
3 = CLASSICAL GREEK C.400 BC

Early Explorers

The Phoenicians and Carthaginians were also known as great explorers, venturing out to sea along the Atlantic coasts of both Europe and Africa. The Greek historian Herodotus reports that a Phoenician ship was commissioned by an Egyptian pharaoh he calls Necho (Nekau II?) to navigate around the African continent around 600 B.C.

Apparently, the explorers were successful, and accomplished the trip from the Red Sea around Africa to the Mediterranean in a period of three years. Another explorer, a Carthaginian named Hanno, traveled down the west coast of Africa around 500 B.C., and his narrative of the journey survives for us to study today. His expedition predates European exploration of the same area by almost 2,000 years.

Pitfalls and Pointers

An alphabet is a system of writing in which (ideally) a single symbol stands for a single sound. Even though we technically use an alphabet, the English language has (sadly) strayed from the simple concept of one symbol for one sound, partly because English contains far more sounds than the 26 letters we have for spelling it.

Those Well-Spoken Arameans

Another familiar name from the Near East region is the Arameans. They were made up of a group of tribes and a few small states around the area of Syria and Mesopotamia. Although little is known about the people themselves, their Semitic language—Aramaic—is quite famous. Aramaic achieved widespread use as an international language in lands of the Assyrian empire, and was used as such for centuries.

Aramaic's fame is primarily due to its use in Biblical manuscripts and as the common language of Palestine during the time of Jesus. Jesus probably spoke both Aramaic and Hebrew, and perhaps Greek as well, which was also commonplace in the region at that time. A form of the Aramaic writing would replace the old Hebrew script, and is the form used today in the Hebrew Bible and modern Hebrew.

Lost and Found

The world's most famous Carthaginian was probably Hannibal (ca. 247–183 B.C.), a great general who fought the Romans in the Second Punic War (218–201 B.C.). While the Romans were busy, Hannibal marched his mighty army, including war elephants, across the Alps to attack Italy from the north. He eventually failed, but his reputation as one of the great military men of ancient history remains.

Empire-Building with the Persians

Ancient Persia, one of the best-known of the ancient Near Eastern states, was located in the area presently occupied by the state of Iran. The Persian civilization reached its height during the *Achaemenid* Dynasty, under which the Persians would truly make an international impact. The first king of this dynasty, Cyrus II, or Cyrus the Great (r. 559–530 B.C.), conquered his neighbors, including the Medes and the Lydians, and began to build a huge empire, the size of which had hitherto not been seen in the Near East.

Jargon Unearthed

The *Achaemenid Dynasty* (559–331 B.C.) refers to a succession of Persian rulers who presided over the building of the mighty Persian Empire, beginning with Cyrus the Great and ending with Darius III.

Cyrus next turned his attention to Babylon, which he successfully conquered in 539 B.C. The Biblical book of Ezra records the Cyrus's edict sending the Jews held in captivity by the Babylonians back to their home in Palestine. Before his death, Cyrus managed to put the Persians in control of much of Asia Minor and Afghanistan, and took over the territory of the Babylonian empire.

His successor, Cambyses II (r. 530–522 B.C.), added Egypt and parts of North Africa to the Persian pie. The expansion of the Empire continued under Darius I (521–486 B.C.), who conquered parts of India and a number of Greek colonies and islands along the coast of Asia Minor.

Troubles with the Greeks

With a widespread empire made up of a large number of people of different cultures, it's not surprising that the Persians would often be called upon to quell various rebellions here and there. Their squashing of such an uprising in the Greek colonies resulted in some of the most famous episodes of Persian history. To punish the Greek city-state of Athens for assisting in the uprising, Darius decided to invade Greece in 490 B.C. He lost.

His son, Xerxes (r. 486–465 B.C.), however, put together a massive land and sea force and invaded Greece again in 480/479 B.C. Despite initial successes, the Persians were again defeated, but not until they had inflicted significant damage, including the burning of Athens. The Empire continued to prosper despite this defeat, until it was finally conquered by Alexander the Great, who battled the forces of Darius III (r. 336–331 B.C.) between 334 and 331 B.C.

Empire Maintenance

The Persians were quite clever in their attempts to maintain their empire. They divided their territory into regions that were connected with a massive system of roads to facilitate communication and the movement of troops, trade, and booty. Compared to some of the other empire-builders in the region, the Persians were relatively gentle to the peoples they conquered, allowing them to retain much of their cultural independence.

Darius I moved the Persian capital of Susa to Persepolis, where he built an utterly spectacular city. Despite the fact that it was destroyed in 330 B.C. by a vengeful Alexander the Great, many of its incredible columned buildings and carved stone reliefs have survived, and Persepolis today is truly a beautiful archaeological site.

Yet Another Wonder

Maussollos was the ruler of Caria in western Asia Minor, and a governor of the area for the King of Persia between the years 377 and 353 B.C. At Hallicarnassus on the Mediterranean coast (at what is now the town of Bodrum, Turkey), a tomb was built for him that was sufficiently spectacular to make the list of the Seven Wonders of the Ancient World.

Descriptions of the monument tell of a structure rich in marble sculpture and topped by a stepped pyramidal structure with a sculptured horse and chariot at its summit. Unfortunately, very little survives today; its stone was carried away for other uses in later days. A few of the beautiful sculptures have been salvaged from the ruins, some of which can now be seen in the British Museum in London. By the way, we get our word "mausoleum" from this man and his tomb.

The Nabateans and the Lost City of Petra

One of the most unforgettable images among the Near Eastern ruins can be found in southern Jordan. There, you can ride a horse through an incredibly narrow canyon with high walls. Suddenly, the canyon opens up, revealing a massive carved-stone facade known as The Treasury. Welcome to Petra, "the rose red city half as old as time," immortalized by the poet John Burgon. Petra was the home base of the Nabateans, who may have originated in northeast Arabia. The Nabateans had a reputation as merchants, trading in exotic goods such as perfumes and spices.

The Nabateans may have been in Petra by about 300 B.C., when they apparently drove out the

Pitfalls and Pointers

One intriguing aspect of old Persian culture is the appearance of a prophet by the name of Zoroaster around 600 B.C. A monotheistic religion called Zoroastrianism grew up around his teachings, which promoted a belief in a conflict between good and evil. The one god of the religion is named Ahura Mazda.

Lost and Found

John William Burgon (1813–1888) immortalized Petra in his famous poem entitled "Petra." Here's an excerpt: "It seems no work of Man's creative hand, By labor wrought as wavering fancy planned; But from the rock as if by magic grown, Eternal, silent, beautiful, alone!" The poem goes on: "Match me such a marvel save in Eastern clime, A rose-red city half as old as time."

Edomites, a group of Semites mentioned in the Bible. The Romans conquered Petra in 106 A.D. and incorporated the area into their Arabian province. The famous "treasury" one encounters is merely the prelude to another canyon containing more carved facades, which eventually opens up into a vast area that was the heart of Petra. Clever irrigation schemes assured that this dramatically sited city had plenty of water.

The rose-red city of Petra, here in black and white.

Diggers

John Burkhardt (1784–1817) was a bold Swiss explorer who traveled extensively in the Near East, often disguised in Arabic dress and using the name Sheikh Ibrahim. He explored far up the Nile Valley, brought the site of Petra to the world's attention, and even visited Mecca and other restricted Islamic holy sites. Burkhardt had hoped to find a route from North Africa to the Niger River but never accomplished the task, dying of dysentery in Cairo. He was a great inspiration to Giovanni Belzoni, who himself later died of dysentery exploring the Niger.

Ubar: A Lost City Found

The ancient fortress city of Ubar was known as a trading post for frankincense, a valuable sweet-smelling substance produced from the sap of Boswellia trees. An Islamic legend tells that the city was destroyed by God on account of its great evil, and its location afterwards became lost. Modern searches for the fabled city proved fruitless, although its general location was thought to be somewhere in the vast deserts of southern Arabia, in the so-called "Empty Quarter."

In the early 1980s, the amateur American archaeologist Nicholas Clapp began an effort to find Ubar, and approached NASA's Jet Propulsion Laboratory for help. He scrutinized the area using radar images from the space shuttle, and although there were no direct indications of an actual city, camel tracks visible on the images converged on one particular area, located in modern day Oman.

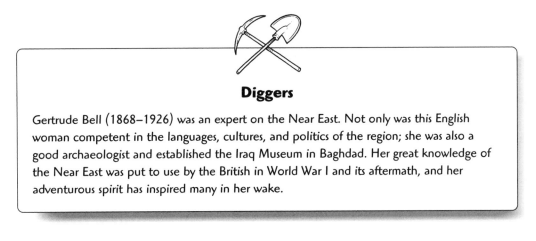

Diggers

Gertrude Bell (1868–1926) was an expert on the Near East. Not only was this English woman competent in the languages, cultures, and politics of the region; she was also a good archaeologist and established the Iraq Museum in Baghdad. Her great knowledge of the Near East was put to use by the British in World War I and its aftermath, and her adventurous spirit has inspired many in her wake.

When Clapp and British adventurer Sir Ranulph Fiennes explored the site in the early 1990s, a fortress was found, sunken beneath the surface. Apparently, the city had indeed met a catastrophic end, when the limestone cavern on which the fortress was built collapsed. The rediscovery of what is probably Ubar is a great tale of library research, space-age technology, and good old-fashioned archaeological exploration!

The Least You Need to Know

➤ The ancient Near East was a wonderfully complex mosaic of cultures great and small.

➤ Indo-European groups such as the Hittites and the Persians played a big role in the history and culture of the region.

➤ The Phoenicians were international traders and explorers and are credited with introducing the alphabet to the Greeks.

➤ Some of the lesser known Near Eastern groups, such as those at Ugarit, Ebla, and Ubar, are the source of a number of the most interesting and dramatic archaeological discoveries of recent times.

Part 4
The Old World

In the next few chapters, we're going to be dealing with "the Old World." The term "Old World" dates back to around the time of Columbus and refers to lands known to the Europeans before they became aware of the American continents. The Old World, therefore, consists of Europe, Africa, and Asia. The Near East is certainly included in the definition as well, but since we've given them plenty of attention in the last several chapters, we're now going to examine the rest.

Asia was the home of two of the earliest civilizations, in the Indus Valley and China, and many more on the continent were to follow. In Africa, the remains of some of the earliest humans have been found and the whole continent played host to a myriad of great cultures over a period of perhaps two million years! In the northeast corner is Egypt, which has always garnered the majority of the attention, but to the South, East, and West were great kingdoms in such places as Nubia, Ethiopia, and Mali. People have been living in Europe for eons and along its southern Mediterranean borders we find such ancient civilizations as Greece and Rome, which continue to have a profound effect on modern society.

The "Old World" is bursting with the remains of lost civilizations and I think that you'll find the archaeology of all three of these continents to be equally fascinating. There is still a lot left to explore so we can certainly look forward to a long future of new discoveries that will no doubt transform our ideas about the ancient people who lived in these great territories.

Chapter 14

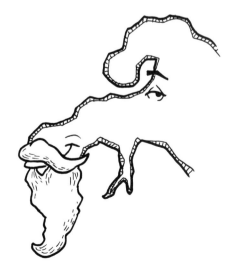

Europe Before There Were Airports

There are loads of archaeological sites in Europe, including the remains of some of the earliest inhabitants, their tools, and beautiful representations of Paleolithic art. Big stone monuments, ancient villages, and a lot of surprising artifacts are abundant. Europe is well-excavated and interest in the subject remains high.

And why not? This was essentially the nursery for the development of the field of archaeology, and it was Europeans who first explored the ancient remains of not only their own continent, but the Near East and other regions as well. In this chapter we'll take a look at some of the interesting things found in Europe, and we can expect a lot more to be uncovered in the future!

Europe in the Ice Age

Humans of sorts have been running around Europe for at least 700,000 years. Homo erectus and early Homo sapiens established themselves there, as did the Neanderthals. This human settlement occurred during the Ice Age, at which time much of northern Europe was glaciated or otherwise brutally cold.

In the places where it was livable, humans shared their turf with a whole variety of fascinating creatures you won't find there now. As the Pleistocene came to an end, the glaciers began to melt, the environment began to change, and new lands became available for human colonization.

Europe Through the Ages

The archaeology of Europe is organized by a more developed version of the Three Age System we talked about in Chapter 2. There is the Paleolithic, or Old Stone Age, divided into Lower, Middle, and Upper periods; the Mesolithic, which represents a transition to the Neolithic, or New Stone Age; and then the Bronze Age and the Iron Age.

These, of course, are convenient categories for organization but can't with any degree of precision be applied simultaneously to a whole continent. Nonetheless, we see agriculture creeping into southeastern Europe around 7000 B.C. and making its way west to Britain by about 4000 B.C. Bronze makes its appearance in Europe around 2300 B.C, and iron becomes widely known there by around 700 B.C.

Pitfalls and Pointers

In between the major periods of glaciation during the Ice Age, there were warming periods, and some scientists have suggested that we might be in such a stage right now. In other words, another Ice Age is on its way! Others, though, argue that human industrial activities are causing global warming and sea-levels might continue to rise with the further melting of glacial ice.

The Tribes of Europe

Apart from southern Europe, which was dominated by the likes of the Greeks, Romans, and Carthaginians, much of central and western Europe would become the domain of Celtic and Germanic tribes. The Romans would encounter and battle with a lot of these people as they attempted to expand their empire, but the tribes persisted.

They were often migratory, and eventually we find Angles, Saxons, and Jutes moving into the British Isles, Ostragoths dominating Italy with the fall of Rome, Franks in France, and Visigoths in Spain. And let's not forget the Vikings up north, who went on rampages far and wide, and even visited the New World before Columbus got there. (More on that in Chapter 25.) From groups such as these emerged the kingdoms that would form the foundation of modern Europe.

Diggers

The famed Julius Caesar can add "early anthropologist" to his long list of accomplishments. While battling the European tribes who seemed to constantly threaten Rome's expanding borders, Caesar took note of the lifeways of the "barbarian" cultures he fought. His book *De Bello Gallico,* The Gallic War, contains lots of useful information about people like the Gauls. The Roman historian Tacitus (55–117 A.D.) also left us valuable observations about some of the Germanic tribes in his *Germania.*

Cavemen Draw

Apart from bones and stone tools, there aren't a lot of surviving artifacts from the oldest days of humans in Europe. But there is one startling exception. Some of our prehistoric comrades engaged in a little artistic expression, and when they chose to do so in the protective confines of natural caves, some of their artwork survived the ages for us to ponder and admire.

Some of the art is in the form of scratched sketches; some is painted in magnificent colors. Animals are a common theme, and they provide a wonderful snapshot of the wildlife of Ice Age Europe, which included bison, rhinoceros, elephants, bears, horses, and lions. In some caves, there are curious stencils of human hands, some of which appear to be missing parts of fingers.

So what does this all mean? Explanations run the gamut, from the idea that they were drawing for fun to deep psychological interpretations. Others attribute magical purposes to the art, where the artist believes that drawing scenes depicting a successful hunt will help bring about a real one. Still others suspect religious or mythological meaning.

Pitfalls and Pointers

Science has yet to devise a method for reading the minds of living people, let alone dead ones. But that hasn't stopped scholars from guessing at the meaning of cave art, sometimes with great self-confidence. Call me a skeptic, but maybe some of those animal drawings have nothing to do with spirituality. Maybe those Paleolithic folks just liked to draw!

A sketch of a Paleolithic painting from the cave at Lascaux, France. (After H. Breuil, Four Hundred Centuries of Cave Art *[New York, Hacker, 1979], p. 127)*

161

Here are some of the more famous caves:

➤ **Altamira, Spain.** Altamira was first noticed by a hunter in 1868. The cave contains many depictions of bison which were drawn or painted between 14000 and 12000 B.C. The first excavations in this cave were carried out in 1879 by a local landowner named Don Marcelino Danz de Sautuola. Altamira was instrumental in stimulating an interest in ancient cave art.

Lost and Found

After its discovery, the cave of Lascaux became an international sensation and attracted hundreds of thousands of visitors—so many, in fact, that the paintings were beginning to deteriorate. After the cave was closed to tourists in 1963, an excellent reproduction of the original, called Lascaux II, was opened. It allows the public to view "the cave" without threatening the original.

➤ **Lascaux, France.** This cave, perhaps the most famous of all, was found in 1940 by four schoolboys who discovered a hole in the woods. The cave art generally dates to around 17,000 years ago and contains many hundreds of drawings and paintings. Some consider this site to be a Paleolithic "Sistine Chapel" in terms of sheer artistry.

➤ **Chauvet Cave, France.** Amateur cavers were exploring this large cavern in 1994 when they came across a network of chambers and about 300 examples of ancient art on the walls. The Chauvet cave contains the oldest known examples of cave art, dating back about 31,000 years.

➤ **Grotte Cosquer, France.** Yet more Paleolithic rock art has been recently found in France by divers, in a cave whose entrance is today underwater. As sea levels rose at the end of the Ice Age, the entrance was submerged. The earliest art in the cave dates from around 27,000 years ago.

Diggers

Henri Breuil (1877–1961) was a modern caveman. He was a French priest and the foremost authority on the subject of Paleolithic art. An artist in his own right, he recorded numerous examples of Stone Age art, and claimed to have spent approximately 700 days of his life underground exploring and working in caves.

Otzi the Iceman: Feeling No Pain

On September 19, 1991, two hikers traversing a glacier at an elevation of over 10,000 feet on the Italian side of the Italian/Austrian border stumbled across a disturbing sight: a dead man was melting out of the ice. This is not a particularly unusual thing in the Alps; a good number of dead mountain climbers, some even a hundred years old, thaw out from time to time. However, this was no ordinary dead mountain climber, but a hunter who had died 5,000 years ago. Though he is affectionately known as Otzi the Iceman after his discovery in the Otzal Alps, scientists refer to him as Similaun Man after the glacier in which he was found.

The Iceman survived quite well in the ice, although some of the methods used to remove him caused a little damage. He was just over five feet tall and probably in his forties. Not unlike some modern youth, he had a shaved head, tattoos, and perhaps even an earring. He might have died from exposure or exhaustion in a storm that quickly buried him in snow, thus saving him the indignity of being chewed up by scavengers. His teeth were worn, he had smoke-blackened lungs, hardening of the arteries, and several recently broken ribs. In short, he wasn't in the best of health.

Along with the body were found about 70 artifacts of equal interest. Our friend was carrying a copper ax with a wooden handle, a wooden bow with a deerskin quiver containing fourteen arrows, a flint dagger with wooden handle, a backpack and some maintenance tools, and various and sundry small objects. Many of his clothes were missing when he was found, but he at least had his boots and leggings, which were stuffed with insulating straw. We can assume that he was probably wearing some sort of pants in the mountains and perhaps a leather jacket and hat, and maybe also a grass rain cloak.

What was he doing up there? Was he a shepherd, a hunter, or a miner? Was he working or just crossing the mountains? Only the Iceman knows for sure. What we can say is that the Iceman is a fine specimen of a dead man of his day, unceremoniously frozen in his tracks—a human time capsule that captures a regular guy going about his business.

Pitfalls and Pointers

The Iceman was found extremely close to the Austrian/Italian border and the body was taken to Innsbruck, Austria, for examination. Soon afterward, surveyors discovered and learned that the body had actually been found in Italy. The Italians claimed that the Iceman was theirs, and ultimately a happy compromise was reached. The body was studied and conserved in Austria and then returned to Italy, where it is now on exhibit in Bolzano.

Stonehenge: Circle in Stone

Perhaps the most recognizable monument from ancient Europe is an amazing circular group of stone pillars standing out on Salisbury Plain in the south of England. Apart from being an impressive engineering feat, it has also inspired a good deal of mysterious lore.

The site of Stonehenge is actually much more complicated than it first appears. The site was developed in several stages, the first being around 3100 B.C. At that time, a huge circular ditch about 330 feet in diameter was constructed, with the excavated earth forming banks on either side. Inside was a circular series of 56 holes. It's possible that a couple of the smaller standing stones might have also been placed at that time.

Circles Within Circles

Around 2000 B.C., the famous circle of standing blocks was erected in the center of the original area outlined by the ditch. The 30 blocks and their lintels were made of sandstone and stand about thirteen feet high to form a circle about 108 feet in diameter. Later on, five more pairs of blocks with lintels were added within the larger group. Still later, around 1100 B.C., more smaller stones were positioned within and between the circles to complete the whole arrangement.

Needless to say, there was a tremendous amount of work involved in all of this. The big sandstone blocks were quarried from a site almost twenty miles away and weigh up to 50 tons each. Some of the other stones were imported from as far away as Wales.

So what is Stonehenge? There are a good number of ideas. Legends relate it to mischief with the devil, the work of Merlin the magician, or hand-holding giants doing a dance and then becoming petrified. It's been attributed to all sorts of groups, including outer space visitors, Phoenicians, and most notably the Druids.

Despite the speculation, there's no need to attribute its building to anybody other than the ancient inhabitants of Britain, who may have used it ritualistically. Interestingly, the monument seems to be astronomically aligned. During the summer solstice, the sun rises directly over one of the prominent stones, the "Heel Stone." As such, it might have served as some sort of early calendar.

Lost and Found

As it has become clear that many ancient people had a serious and knowledgeable interest in astronomy, one field of archaeological inquiry has become increasingly legitimized. It's called *archaeoastronomy:* the study of how people in the past used astronomy. Related sites are being recognized regularly.

Jargon Unearthed

Megalithic literally means "large stone," and refers to ancient constructions involving the use of large stones.

Stonehenge.

More Megaliths

A site such as Stonehenge is referred to as "megalithic," and it's by no means the only such site in England or Europe. There are thousands of sites with standing or arranged stones to be found in the region.

At Avebury in southern England are groupings of ditches and stones that rival Stonehenge in complexity, and at the site of Carnac in France, over 3,000 stones can be found arranged in various configurations. At Newgrange in Ireland, a shaft of light penetrates to the interior of a megalithic tomb around the time of the winter solstice.

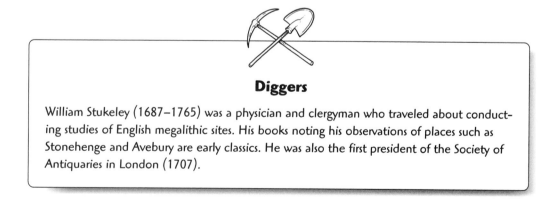

Diggers

William Stukeley (1687–1765) was a physician and clergyman who traveled about conducting studies of English megalithic sites. His books noting his observations of places such as Stonehenge and Avebury are early classics. He was also the first president of the Society of Antiquaries in London (1707).

Roll Out the Barrows

Ancient Megalithic tombs are commonly found throughout Europe, especially in Britain. Most consist of two components, the burial chamber and the covering earthen mound, the "barrow." Many have passageways leading to the burial chamber. The earliest of the megalithic tombs dates to around 4800 B.C., and the practice continued until around 2500 B.C. in Ireland and France.

The predominant practice in megalithic tombs was collective burial, in which the remains of up to 350 people were placed in a single tomb. Grave goods were few and most of the bones appear to be disarticulated, as if the corpses were defleshed or bones were shuffled well after the bodies had decomposed, probably to make room for the more recently deceased. Some barrow tombs have bones sorted by type, such as long bones and skulls, suggesting not only repeated entry into the tomb but also that selected bones had been removed, possibly for use in religious ceremonies.

The early days of proto-archaeology in Europe can be seen in the sport of barrow-digging in the early 1700s. Wealthy gentlemen could spend an afternoon digging up one or more of the hundreds of mounds for the sheer pleasure of scrutinizing its contents.

Although such activity was initially crude and destructive, some fledgling roots of scientific archaeology can occasionally be found. General Pitt-Rivers (see Chapter 2) honed his skills on barrows and produced some of the finest examples of systematic archaeological technique.

Ruins of Runes

Although symbolic art and artistic expression abound in early Europe, there is little evidence of writing among most of the tribal groups, with one exception: the "runes" found in some of the Germanic tribes, including the Vikings. Examples have survived carved on stones or other non-perishable objects, although it is likely that wood was used as a regular writing surface.

Not many long inscriptions survive, but any example is of interest. Many small object with runes bear the name of the owner and there are runic tombstones and historical tributes. There were several different rune alphabets, or "futharks" as they are called (after the first seven letters); they seem to have been somewhat inspired by the Roman alphabet. They appear around the second century A.D.

Jargon Unearthed

A *runologist* is someone who studies runes.

It's likely that their use was primarily functional, although their reputation today is often one of mystery and divination. This often happens when knowledge is lost and the unusual is explained by superstition. It didn't help when J. R. Tolkein's Hobbits used runes, thus adding another layer of unreality to the whole subject.

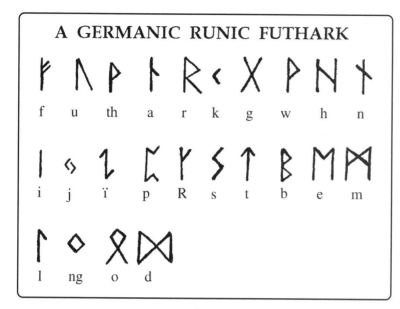

A GERMANIC RUNIC FUTHARK

f u th a r k g w h n

i j ï p R s t b e m

l ng o d

A Germanic runic futhark. (After R. I. Page, Runes *[London: British Museum, 1987], p. 8, fig. 1)*

Another type of script, called "ogham," can also be found here and there in Ireland. This writing consists of combinations of parallel strokes at different positions along a line. They can be a bit difficult to interpret, and the fact that they are lines has caused a lot of confusion. Plow marks on stones in farmers' fields in America, for example, have been mistaken by excited enthusiasts as clear evidence of contact between the continents prior to Columbus.

Permanent Dry Dock

Over the millennia, thousands of ships have met disaster at sea, and several have been painstakingly recovered by underwater archaeologists (see Chapter 8). But once in a rare while, a ship is actually recovered on land. You might recall the example of the boat found at the base of the Great Pyramid in Egypt, in Chapter 11. In Europe, a few extraordinary examples of landlocked ships have been discovered. Here are a couple of them.

Sutton Hoo—*Ghost Ship in the Sand*

In 1939, excavations of a mound at Sutton Hoo in Suffolk, England, revealed an amazing sight: an 89-foot-long boat buried in the sand, containing what might be a royal Anglo-Saxon burial. The conditions were such, however, that no organic materials were found, including the boat itself or a body. So what

Lost and Found

The term "Anglo-Saxon" is often used to describe people of British ancestry. The Anglo-Saxons, though, were late-coming immigrants from two northern European tribes, the Angles and the Saxons, who invaded Britain in the fifth century A.D.

am I talking about? Although the boat itself did not survive, it left an incredible impression and stains in the sand that revealed its appearance.

The ghostly ship contained a veritable treasure trove, including jewelry, objects of gold and silver, a sword, helmet, and shield, coins, and many other precious artifacts. The lack of a body might suggest that this wasn't a burial, but served some other purpose; then again, the same acidic conditions that dissolved the boat itself would likely have done the same to a human body and a wooden coffin. The burial dates between A.D. 620 and 650.

Viking Boat Burials

Between about A.D. 800 and 1100, Western Europe had much to fear from Viking marauders from Norway, Sweden, and Denmark. Tough, sea-hardy, and with swift boats, the Vikings traveled as far south as North Africa and east to Russia to terrify whomever they encountered. To the west, they settled in Iceland and Greenland and visited North America almost 500 years before Columbus.

Several magnificent Viking boat burials have been found in Norway. Unlike the "ghost" impressions of the Sutton Hoo boat, these ships survived in excellent shape, with their wood and much of their contents intact, thus giving us a remarkable look at these rambunctious seafarers.

Lost and Found

In 1957, the remains of five Viking ships dating to the 11th century A.D. were found in a narrow fjord channel at Skuldelev, Denmark. The ships were apparently sunk as part of a defensive blockade to protect the old Danish capital of Roskilde. During the 1960's, the ships were excavated after a cofferdam was built which allowed archaeologists to document and salvage the remains without resorting to underwater tactics.

One of the most famous burials was found in a mound at Gokstad in 1880. The ship is approximately 78.5 feet long and about 17 feet wide, and dates to about A.D. 900. A grave chamber found on board contained the burial of an arthritic man about 60 years old, along with a number of artifacts. Three small boats were also found with the ship.

In 1903, another ship was found preserved in a deposit of blue clay overlaid with peat. The Oseberg ship, dated at A.D. 834, is 70.5 feet long with a breadth of 17 feet and included a mast, 30 oars, and a rudder. The bodies of a young woman and an old lady were found in a grave chamber set up in the boat. Although the burial had been robbed, the ship contained many artifacts, including a wagon, chests, clothing, and kitchen gear. Also present were the sacrificed remains of two oxen, twelve horses, and four dogs. Oak seems to have been the wood of choice for these ships, and both can now be seen in the Viking Ship Museum in Oslo, Norway.

Bog Bodies

Like the Iceman mentioned earlier, a well-preserved ancient body is always a welcome discovery for the archaeologist. In Western Europe, several hundred have been found in relatively good shape in peat bogs, where the conditions are such that much of the body is preserved. Some date back as far as 800 B.C.

How'd they get in the bog? Although a few might be simple burials, most seem to have sinister aspects to them that suggest murder, suicide, execution, or human sacrifice. They are typically found by peat-cutters who mine the bogs for fuel. Here's a trio of the most famous:

➤ **Tollund Man.** Found in Denmark in 1950, he's probably the most famous and dates to ca. 200 B.C. His head is remarkably well-preserved, and it looks as if the fellow is merely taking a nap. Unfortunately, the noose around his neck suggests he wasn't just out taking a snooze in the bog.

➤ **Grauballe Man.** Also from Denmark, this fellow was found in 1952 with a cut throat and head injuries. He's not as handsome as the Tollund Man, but he's got great looking hands and feet! He dates to ca. 55 B.C.

➤ **Lindow Man.** This one, from England, was discovered in 1984 and dates to ca. 300 B.C. His head had been knocked, his throat was cut, and he had been asphyxiated.

Don't get the idea that it's just men turning up in the bog. There have been plenty of women, too.

As you can see, European archaeology has a little of everything: cave art, big monuments, old boats, ancient writing, and well-preserved dead people to examine. Archaeology tends to be well-appreciated in many of the countries on the continent where there are thousands of museums and many organizations which promote the study of the past. And we're not through with Europe yet. The Greeks and Romans are coming up next!

Lost and Found

A British man admitted to killing his wife when a woman's head was discovered in the Lindow bog. Unfortunately for him, the head turned out to be about 2,000 years old. He was convicted of murder anyway, based on his confession.

The Least You Need to Know

➤ Europe was populated by early humans as they spread out of Africa during the Pleistocene.

➤ There is ample evidence of prehistoric human creativity in cave art and other archaeological discoveries of ancient Europe.

➤ While the great civilizations of the Near East were flourishing, some European groups were erecting their own impressive monuments in stone.

➤ A complex history of migrations, conflicts, and interminglings of European groups established the foundations for the peoples and nations of modern Europe.

Chapter 15

Those Classy, Classic Greeks

In This Chapter

➤ Fast and furious Greek history

➤ The original Homer

➤ Mycenaeans and Minoans

➤ Alexander the Great kicks butt

➤ The Seven Wonders of the Ancient World

Since I've made sure that you're well aware that the ancient Near East was an important source of "civilized influence," let's take a little look at those Greeks who get so much attention. Yes, people (in Western society, at least) have a lot to credit to or blame on the Greeks, whose philosophy, literature, art, architecture, mythology, history, and so forth continue to be actively studied today as they have been for centuries.

Although they benefited greatly from certain Near Eastern inventions such as writing, the Greeks themselves were great innovators. For Western civilization, at least, much of how we think, conduct politics and look at art and beauty, for example, has its roots in ancient Greek culture. In this chapter, we're going to skim the surface of a very detailed subject, but in doing so, perhaps you'll become intrigued with the Greeks, as have many in numerous generations before you.

The Land of the Greeks

The area known as Greece is essentially a big peninsula that juts out of eastern Europe into the north Mediterranean. In Greece itself, a peninsula called the Peloponnese splits off to the south. To its east, between the Greek mainland and Asia Minor, is the Aegean Sea, in which are found many islands that were inhabited by the ancient

Greeks. And further to the south, in the Mediterranean, lies a linear island, Crete, which was home to a truly unique civilization.

Jargon Unearthed

The study of ancient Greece and Rome is called *Classics,* and its practitioners are *classicists.*

The geography of Greece in many ways shaped the nature of its civilization. Areas like Mesopotamia were broad and relatively accessible and thus conducive to control and invasion. Large kingdoms and empires could be established by invading armies. Greece, on the other hand, is mostly composed of narrow valleys and small plains, and much of the region is bordered or surrounded by water. Here in these little pockets would develop independent Greek city-states that, although sharing much of a common culture, were mostly independent political entities.

Map of Greece.

History Fast and Furious

You want some fast history? Hang on, here it comes. Agriculture spread to Greece about 7000 B.C., and bronze appears around 2800 B.C. Around 2000 B.C., Greek-speaking people moved into the area and began to dominate. A rich civilization called the Mycenaeans (after its biggest city, Mycenae) developed and flourished, especially between 1600 and 1100 B.C., after which the area seems to have been overrun by a new people, traditionally by a group of Greek-speakers called the Dorians—but who knows for sure?

The next 300 or 400 years are referred to as the Dark Ages, because little is known of them, but then the lights came on. Around 700 B.C., Greek colonies started appearing around the borders of the Mediterranean, and Greek city-states, including Athens and Sparta, began to develop and bloom.

What might be called the Classical Age begins around 500 B.C. This is the era most people probably think about in connection with ancient Greece. It is a time when the arts flourished and many of the city-states thrived. It was also a time of wars.

The Persians invaded Greece twice: Darius in 490 B.C. and Xerxes in 480/479 B.C. (see Chapter 13.). Alliances of city-states fought each other during the series of skirmishes known as the Peloponnesian Wars (431–404 B.C.), which essentially pitted Sparta and its allies against Athens and its allies.

All of this discord weakened the Greek city-states, thus preparing them to be invaded, beginning in the fourth century B.C., by an old Greek kingdom in the north, Macedon, featuring King Phillip II and his son, popularly known as Alexander the Great.

Alexander created an immense empire, the likes of which the world had never seen. Upon his death, the empire was divided up among Alexander's generals, who would rule until the Romans took over in the first century B.C. Is your head spinning? Let's back up a bit and talk about some of the specifics!

Pitfalls and Pointers

The Dark Ages, so called by historians, may tell us more about ourselves than about the people we're trying to describe. It is mostly we who are in the dark, since we don't know much about the era because there are few texts from that time for us to read.

Homer and the Search for Troy

One of the most enduring and still widely read pieces of classical literature is called the *Iliad*, said to have been written by a Greek named Homer. The *Iliad* is an epic tale about a war between certain Greeks (called the Aecheans) and the Trojans, who seem to have lived on the coast of Asia Minor. Memorable characters abound, including King Agamemnon, Achilles, Paris, Helen of Troy, and the Trojan king Priam. And let's

Lost and Found

The poet Homer (ca. 750 B.C.?) has been credited with writing those two great literary works, the *Iliad* and the *Odyssey*. There's been plenty of discussion about who he might have been, whether he himself composed one or both or any of the books, and when they might have been written down. Some say he was blind. In any case, he's still a popular author today.

Lost and Found

Schliemann's treasures from Hissarlik/Troy were housed in a museum in Berlin, from which they disappeared at the end of World War II. In 1991 they were rediscovered in Moscow, having been taken as war booty by the Red Army in 1945.

not forget the Trojan horse, a hollow wooden horse full of enemy soldiers left by the Greeks as a parting gift to the Trojans. According to the Iliad, the Greeks attacked the great walled city of Troy over a period of ten years. The soldiers hidden in the wooden horse were able to open the city's gates, allowing the Greek army to utterly destroy the place and its citizens.

Schliemann Finds Gold

As a small boy, a German named Heinrich Schliemann (1822–1890) was intrigued by the stories of the *Iliad*. After achieving financial success as a businessman, he went out to look for archaeological evidence of the Trojan Wars. Using the *Iliad* as a guidebook, he searched the coast of Asia Minor for an area that he felt best matched the geographical descriptions in Homer's work.

Schliemann located a mound called Hissarlik, which he identified as Troy, and began digging there in 1870. In 1873 he made his biggest discovery: a hoard of artifacts manufactured from precious metals, including golden cups and crowns, silver vases, dozens of gold earrings, and over 8,000 gold buttons and rings. He claimed he had found the treasure of King Priam. As the treasure actually appears to be a collection of finds from various dates, there is a debate as to their relationship, if any, to the events and period of the Trojan War.

Believing now that he had found the home of the Trojans, Schliemann next turned his attention to the other half of the equation, the home of the Greeks who fought in the war. He chose to excavate at a site known as Mycenae, an ancient stronghold in the Peloponnese that contained a number of impressive tombs.

In 1876, Schliemann dug up several of these and found some bodies buried with gold funerary objects, including some impressive golden death masks. (One of these, the most famous one, is thought by some to be a fake.) He was now convinced that he had found the graves of King Agamemnon and other Greek royalty mentioned in the *Iliad*. Afterwards, he returned to Hissarlik and other sites and continued digging, though he made no more such spectacular finds.

Diggers

Heinrich Schliemann (1822–1890) was a German businessman and student of the Classics, adept at both making money and learning languages. His fascination with the works of Homer led him to excavate the site of Hissarlik in Asia Minor (which he thought was Troy), tombs at Mycenae, and elsewhere in Greece, including Ithaca, Marathon, and Tiryns. Although Schliemann's name survives among the greats in the history of archaeology, most modern scholars agree that several of his interpretations are the result of his enthusiasm, and a few others suggest that he was less than truthful as an individual and in his writings.

Myth and Reality

Schliemann's work, which is described in his very popular books, has made him one of the best known archaeologists of all time. He certainly still has a lot of fans today, including many whose interest in archaeology was fueled by his romantic tales of a quest to find the lost civilizations described in one of the world's most famous books. So did he really find what he thought he did?

First of all, we have to consider whether there is any truth whatsoever to the *Iliad*, or whether it's just a folk story concocted by Homer or embellished from oral traditions. The events allegedly took place centuries before Homer, so he certainly wasn't there.

And Hissarlik? It's the one site that best matches Homer's description in the region, but there's no "Welcome to Troy" sign at the city limits. As for the so-called bodies of Agamemnon and company, there was nothing that provided a name for these bodies other than Schliemann's fertile imagination.

Pitfalls and Pointers

Just because Homer's *Iliad* is full of supernatural interventions by Greek gods doesn't mean there isn't some historical truth there. Even if the events took place 500 years before Homer, could there not be real history behind the embellishments added through time? It's a difficult task for the historian to sort out the myth from the reality!

The Myceneans

Enough of Schliemann! Let's turn our attention to the Greeks we know existed—the Bronze Age residents we call the Mycenaeans. Mycenae was the most powerful of a group of powerful cities, including Pylos and Tiryns, that formed in southern Greece during what is called the Mycenaean Period (ca. 1600–1100 B.C.). Their thick-walled

Jargon Unearthed

Linear B is a script written in a form of archaic Greek. Clay tablets with inscriptions in this script have been found on both the Greek mainland and the island of Crete.

fortifications, weapons, and other artifacts suggest that conflict was not unusual among these peoples. The presence of gold in some of the elaborate burials indicate both wealth and the presence of elites.

There was apparently a good deal of interaction with the island of Crete, which the Mycenaeans might have invaded around 1450 B.C. The discovery of clay tablets in Mycenaean palaces written in a script called *Linear B* has provided interesting economic information about the times, and reveals the craft specializations and social diversity (including slaves) characteristic of a complex society.

The Minoans

Out in the Mediterranean, south of Greece, is the island of Crete, about 160 miles long and 35 miles wide. The island is well-situated between Greece, North Africa, and the Near East to serve as a fine base for the interregional exchange of goods and ideas. Here developed a civilization like no other, one that has been given the name "Minoan" after King Minos, a legendary ruler of Crete from Greek mythology. The Minoan civilization flourished from about 2200 B.C. to about 1450 B.C.

Land of the Minotaur

The Minoans were a sea-going people who exchanged goods and ideas with others. Egyptian goods have been found on Crete and vice-versa, and recently a Minoan settlement has been found on the coast of Egypt. Their influence on Mycenaean culture was great, and they appear to have had an influence in some of the Aegean islands, as well.

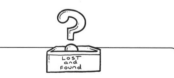

Lost and Found

The bull seems to have played a special role in Minoan culture. The horns of bulls are depicted symbolically, and paintings exist of an odd sport in which athletes vault over the horns of running bulls. Add to this the Minotaur tales, and there's definitely something going on here.

By looking at the remains of Minoan culture, we can get a reasonable idea of what these people were about. The surviving art often depicts sea themes. The towns and elaborate palaces seem to be placed in pleasant areas rather than at sites that are defensible. In fact, there is a profound lack of defenses in any of their settlements, which suggests that they weren't particularly worried about being attacked.

The ancient capital of the Minoans, Knossos, was excavated by the Englishman Sir Arthur Evans beginning in 1900. Evans was thoroughly entranced with the Greek legends of King Minos, as is obvious when one studies his excavations and reconstruction of the site. A large complex of rooms, for example, was named "the labyrinth" after the gruesome story of the son of King

Minos, half-man and half-bull (the Minotaur), who was kept locked up in a basement maze, where he was occasionally fed tasty Greek youngsters.

The palace of Knossos is more like a villa than a castle and was beautifully decorated with colorful frescoes. Huge storage jars were found in the palace complex containing grain, wine, and olive oil, attesting to a wealth verified by many of the written records found at the site. Bathrooms connected to a sophisticated plumbing system added a nice touch to what was probably a very comfortable lifestyle.

The ancient Minoan Palace at Knossos. (Courtesy of Sharon Nelson)

Diggers

Englishman Sir Arthur Evans (1851–1941) is best known for his excavations at the site of Knossos in Crete. He actually bought the site in 1896, and excavated there over a 30-year period beginning in 1900. Evans, who coined the name "Minoan" for the civilization, brought ancient Crete prominently to the attention of the archaeological world.

Let's Get Linear

Thousands of clay tablets bearing texts have been found on Crete, written in at least three different scripts. A pictographic type of writing and a script called *Linear A* have yet to be deciphered. The most common, and later, script, called *Linear B*, was deciphered in 1952 by a young British architect named Michael Ventris (1922–1956). He discovered that the texts were written in a form of early Greek, although the Minoans are not believed to be Greek speakers. The script was apparently adopted by the mainland Mycenaeans. Most of the texts are lists of goods, and seem to be primarily economic or administrative.

The End of an Era

Around 1450 B.C., the Minoan palaces were burned, and Minoan civilization seems to have come to an end. What happened? It has been suggested that the Mycenaeans might be responsible, since a lot of their stuff starts appearing on the island at that time, replacing or altering the characteristic Minoan styles.

Lost and Found

Apart from *Linear A* and *B*, another type of writing has been found on Crete. A single disk of clay found at Phaistos is called "The Phaistos Disk" and bears stamped hieroglyphs on both sides. It has yet to be convincingly deciphered.

On the other hand, some suggest that the downfall of the Minoans might have been the eruption of a long-dormant volcano on the island of Thera (now called Santorini) to the east of Crete. The explosion was apparently massive and may have produced tidal waves and had other dangerous effects, such as earthquakes (apart from blowing apart most of the island). The story is still unclear, but recent research seems to indicate that the eruption actually took place during the year 1628 B.C, thus occurring much too early to be responsible for the major changes on the island of Crete.

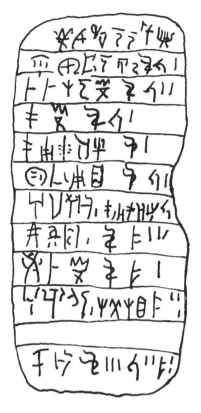

An example of Linear B script. (After John Chadwick, Linear B and Related Scripts [London: British Museum, 1987], p. 14, fig. 3)

The Classical Life

After the Bronze Age, Mycenaean civilization diminished around 1100 B.C., followed by those few hundred years of historical obscurity known as the Dark Ages; then the Greeks started to prosper again. City-states, or *poleis*, developed, and colonies were established all over the Mediterranean, including on the coast of Asia Minor, in southern Italy and Sicily, Libya, and along the Black Sea to the north.

A Tale of Two Cities

Many of the Greek city-states during Classical times took on their own special character and, though Greek, showed a wide variety of differences. A classic contrast, if you will, is that between the city-states of Athens and Sparta. The wealthy and powerful city of Athens was located near the sea and heavily involved in trade. Not surprisingly, it had a well developed navy. The concept of democracy was developed here, as were many of the things we often consider to be the height of Greek culture, such as philosophy and drama.

Jargon Unearthed

A *polis* (pl. *poleis*) is a Greek city-state. A city-state is an independent political entity with a city at its core.

179

Pitfalls and Pointers

Some of Athens's greatest architectural achievements were accomplished during their so-called Golden Age (ca. 450–430 B.C.). The Athenians were greatly aided by their looting of the war-chest established by a group of city-states to finance any future wars with the Persians.

Sparta, on the other hand, was almost the opposite. Located inland on the Peloponnesian peninsula, Sparta strove to be self-sufficient and austere (hence the term "Spartan"). From a very early age, Spartan boys were harshly raised to be warriors. Neighboring *poleis* and others might be conquered in time of need, and slaves could be put to work on Spartan land.

Trade was minimal, and they weren't noted for their arts. Apparently they were quite musical, though, and put on some good dances in the form of mock fights. The Spartans were ruled by two kings, and they practiced a whole host of interesting things that whole books have been written about, and we don't have space to go into here. You'll just have to go out and read about them on your own.

War and Peace

Despite being polar opposites, the Spartans and the Athenians actually got along in times of great mutual need, such as when the Persians invaded Greece. On the other hand, though, it was ultimately to neither's advantage to engage in the long protracted feud known as the Peloponnesian War, which the Spartans finally won after some thirty exhausting years of fighting had weakened them both.

The Athenian acropolis with its temple serves as a symbol of Greece's ancient splendor. (Courtesy of Sharon Nelson)

While the Greek city-states fought in the South, the kingdom of Macedon watched in the North, and finally made a move. King Phillip II (382–336 B.C.) began a campaign to conquer the Greek city-states, a project that was only temporarily cut short by his assassination, because his successor and son, Alexander III (356–323 B.C.), would finish the job and then some! But before we talk about that, let's take a look at a truly remarkable discovery made in Macedon a few years ago.

The Tomb of Phillip II?

In 1977, Greek archaeologist Manolis Andronikos was excavating at Vergina in northern Greece when he found what is apparently an intact royal Macedonian tomb. The remains of body armor, a gold case for bow and arrows, and a shield, sword, and helmet indicated that this might be the tomb of a great warrior.

When a marble sarcophagus was opened, it was found to contain a box of solid gold with the embossed royal Macedonian symbol of a sunburst. Inside were the partially burned bones of a man between 35 and 55 years of age. An adjacent chamber contained another sarcophagus with a golden box containing the remains of a woman in her twenties.

Although many are convinced that the tomb belongs to none other than the great King Phillip II, father of Alexander III, there were no inscriptions to indicate specifically whose tomb this might be. All the objects found in the tomb, though, can be stylistically dated to the fourth century B.C., and a reconstruction of the male skull shows a major traumatic injury to the side of the face. King Phillip II was known to have suffered a battle injury to his eye. In any case, Phillip II's or otherwise, the tomb is one of the great discoveries of archaeology.

Pitfalls and Pointers

Whenever you catch yourself feeling a little superior, pick up one of the Greek classics and have a read. It can be pretty humbling to realize that people have been smart, literate, and articulate for thousands of years. And you might even learn something new!

Alexander the Great Spreads the Word

With the death of Phillip II, his son Alexander III was not content merely to consolidate the Greek city-states within his domain—he first and foremost wanted to go after the Persians, who had over a hundred years before invaded Greece and burned Athens, and who still posed a threat. Alexander attacked Persia with a vengeance, burned Persepolis, and took over the mighty Persian Empire, including Egypt. In Egypt he was made pharaoh and established a city named after himself, Alexandria. He was more than happy to accept the various ruling titles as he pressed east all the way to India over a period of a dozen years.

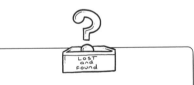

Lost and Found

Alexander III had quite an upbringing. The Greek philosopher Aristotle was his personal tutor, and when his father Phillip went to war, Alexander was left in charge of Macedon at the tender age of 16.

Alexander wanted to keep going, but his troops were tired and wanted to go home. On the way back, the mighty Alexander died of a fever, and his vast empire was divided among a few of his generals, who set up ruling dynasties in their various territories. The most important among them were Seleucus, who took over the territory of the old Persian Empire, and Ptolemy, whose prize was Egypt.

In each conquered land, Greek culture was introduced as colonists flocked to set up colonies and towns. Greek became the universal language in these regions, and the arts would again flourish, often in new ways influenced by local traditions. This time is known as the *Hellenistic* period—from the Greek word "Hellas," which is Greek for Greece. Alexandria in Egypt became an international capital of this Hellenistic world, and a major economic and cultural center.

Jargon Unearthed

Hellenic is an adjective meaning "Greek," from the word "Hellas," meaning "Greece" in Greek. The term Hellenistic usually refers to the widespread world of Greek culture that resulted from Alexander's conquests.

A World-Class Tragedy: The Library of Alexandria

One of the most important monuments ever created in ancient times was founded by Ptolemy I, the general who established the dynasty of Greek rulers in Egypt. At the capital of Alexandria, Ptolemy established a great library that would eventually hold most of the written works of the Greek world. The library grew through time into a huge facility with perhaps over half a million papyrus documents. A professional staff of librarians and copyists were employed, and scholars were put to work editing such texts as the works of Homer. The Hebrew Bible was even translated into Greek there!

One of the greatest losses to civilization of all times was the destruction of this valuable archive. Part of the library was accidentally burned in 48 B.C. during a Roman military campaign. A mob of religious fanatics might have burned a bit more in A.D. 391, but the complete torching of the facility apparently occurred in A.D. 646. It has been traditionally blamed on Arab invaders, but the facts are not clear. Whatever happened, it's gone, and with it went much of the accumulated knowledge and literature of ancient Greek civilization.

Pitfalls and Pointers

We know about many more written works of the ancient Greeks than we have actual copies. The Greeks would often quote from or mention the works of other writers, so we have bits and pieces or names of books, plays, studies, etc. And occasionally, some of these lost works are actually rediscovered.

Diggers

The Greeks established numerous towns in Egypt, and beginning in the late 1800s, archaeologists began digging around the fringes of these towns, in their ancient garbage dumps. They worked with the specific purpose of finding documents written on papyrus paper, and they were quite successful.

Two Oxford gentlemen, Bernard Grenfell (1869–1926) and Arthur Hunt (1871–1934), were successful in retrieving a huge number of scraps and complete documents. Many of the papyri are just ordinary domestic subjects, letters, receipts, etc., but there have been some interesting surprises with the finding of some lost works of known authors. Since the towns were often occupied for centuries, the dumps also sometimes contained Roman and Christian documents of equal interest.

The Seven Wonders

Seven has been considered a special number in several ancient cultures, and so too in the Classical world. Lists of this and that might be composed in sevens; the seven greatest, worst, biggest, smallest, loudest, etc. And thus we have a list of the Seven Wonders of the Ancient World. The elements of the list were debated in ancient times, but the definitive choices seem to have been established sometime during the European Renaissance. And here they are:

➤ The **Great Pyramid of Giza** in Egypt, built by Egyptian king Khufu around 2550 B.C. as a royal tomb.

➤ The **Pharos Lighthouse at Alexandria** in Egypt, which served as a beacon for ships at sea. It was built around 280 B.C. and destroyed in an earthquake in A.D. 796.

➤ The **Hanging Gardens of Babylon**, built by Nebuchadrezzar around 600 B.C. to please his foreign wife.

➤ The **Mausoleum at Halicarnassus**, built about 360 B.C. as a tomb for the Persian governor Mausolos.

➤ The **Colossus of Rhodes**, a massive bronze statue of the god Helios on the Greek island of Rhodes. It was built around 290 B.C., and an earthquake brought it down less than a century later.

➤ The beautiful **Temple of Artemis** at the Greek city of Ephesus (in modern Turkey), built by King Croesus around 560 B.C. It burned down, was rebuilt, and was finally destroyed by the Goths in A.D. 262.

➤ The giant **Statue of Zeus** at his temple in Olympia, Greece. It was sculpted from wood and gilded in gold, and dates from about 430 B.C.

Of the seven, only the Great Pyramid remains, although pieces of the Mausoleum have been retrieved and can now be seen in the British Museum in London.

Like the Seven Wonders, Alexander's empire didn't last forever. Another great power was growing in the region—the Romans—and over a couple of hundred years, they would chip away at the Greek world until much of it was firmly under their control.

Although we've emphasized archaeology and history in this chapter, we needn't forget the many contributions of the Greeks in such areas as drama, philosophy, politics, and medicine. The Romans valued this stuff, because they borrowed and modified much of it to suit their own civilization, and they are the subject of our next chapter.

Lost and Found

Greek and Roman tourists would visit the pyramids and other monuments of Egypt to marvel at the antiquities. And like some tourists of today, many left a record of their visits in the form of graffiti. Although modern graffiti is presently condemned as vandalism, ironically, similar scribblings from ancient times provide valuable historical information.

The Least You Need to Know

➤ Legends, old texts, and modern archaeology have helped untangle the earliest history of the ancient Greek world.

➤ The Mycenaeans and the Minoans were two distinct early civilizations, and we still have much to learn about these fascinating cultures.

➤ What we call ancient Greece was a group of culturally linked city-states, often with very different personalities.

➤ Alexander the Great created the largest empire in the ancient world and spread Greek culture far and wide.

Chapter 16

The Romans: Conquering the World for Fun and Profit

If there were an award for the most surviving antiquities from an ancient civilization, the Romans might win. With its great empire and skilled builders, and a wealth of surviving artifacts, structures, and documents, Rome left remains that are found widely in Europe and the Mediterranean region. We know a good deal about these folks. And compared to say, the Hittites and the Sumerians, they're a relatively recent civilization. For an Egyptologist like me, these Romans happened the day before yesterday.

The Romans heavily influenced the development of Western culture and their impact is still felt today. What did modern civilization inherit from the Romans? A bit of government and law, architectural and engineering skills, and some fine literature. The language of old Rome—Latin—was standard for both science and the Roman Catholic Church until relatively recently.

Geography and History in a Nutshell

The Italian peninsula where Rome would arise is quite a bit different from Greece, with its geographically separated city-states. In Italy, especially in the north, there are large fertile areas. This can be good and bad. The Po River valley, for example, was not only good land for agriculture, but also made a great entryway for the various marauding tribes who would dash in from time to time and sack Rome.

Italy wasn't all populated by the Romans, or even by the region's numerous local tribes. The Greeks, with their fondness for setting up colonies, were prominent in southern Italy. There were so many Greek settlements there, in fact, that the territory was known as Grecia Magna, or Greater Greece. Greeks could also be found on much of the island of Sicily. Okay, that's the territory. Now it's speedy history time! There were a lot of tribes in north-central Italy in the first several millennia B.C., and one significant urban society, the Etruscans, provided the first kings of the growing city of Rome. Eventually the Romans dominated the Etruscans, as well as the rest of Italy, and conquered both the western Mediterranean and the surviving empire of Alexander.

Over the years, a representative form of Roman government would be transformed into an imperial dictatorship as the Romans worked hard to maintain control over a massive empire. The empire was eventually split in two, and the western half, including Rome itself, would fall away while the eastern half would survive for another thousand years as the Byzantine Empire. Whew. Now let's go back and take a look at some details.

The Mysterious Etruscans

I mentioned above that there were plenty of other people in Italy besides the Romans. Tribes such as the Umbrians, Latins, Sabines, and Samnites held sway over various parts of the Italian peninsula. One group, though, the Etruscans, maintained a highly sophisticated civilization in central Italy between about 700 B.C. and the first century B.C.

These people were organized into city-states and shared a mutual language, customs, and beliefs. In some ways they are a bit mysterious. Their language is neither Semitic nor Indo-European. From what we do know about them, they were sophisticated and somewhat cosmopolitan, artistic, and creative.

The Etruscans engaged in many commercial ventures with the other powers in the region, including the Phoenicians/Carthaginians, the Greeks, and the Italian tribes. The Etruscans adopted a good bit of Greek culture, including the alphabet, which would be inherited by the Romans.

Lost and Found

After Rome fell in the late fifth century A.D., many old books or documents deteriorated or were burned. Thanks to enlightened monks during the European Middle Ages, many of these writings were preserved and copied, and thus they survive to this day.

Pitfalls and Pointers

Although there are thousands of short inscriptions in the Etruscan language, they unfortunately don't tell us that much about the culture. No real literature has survived. A few bilingual inscriptions in Etruscan and Latin or Phoenician have helped us to better understand the grammar.

It was the complex culture of the Etruscans, with its literacy and monuments, that formed the foundation of Roman civilization. The Romans, however, continued to speak their native tongue of Latin. The Etruscans dominated Rome during the early years of that city, but eventually the Etruscans declined and were absorbed into a growing empire.

Trojans and Wolf-Babies

The Romans offered a couple of stories and one traditional date for the founding of their great city. The year is 753 B.C., and neither of the stories bear much credibility. The first story tells how Aeneas, a survivor of the Trojan Wars, made his epic way to Italy. After a series of intrigues with the local rulers, his descendants became the founders of the city.

The second and more famous story involves two twin brothers, Romulus and Remus, who were thrown into a river by their evil uncle and then taken in by a humane she-wolf until they were adopted by some shepherds. They grew up, fought, and Romulus killed his brother and became the founder of Rome, giving it its name.

Jargon Unearthed

The city of Rome gets its name from Romulus, one of the twin brothers rescued by a wolf as a baby. Or so the story goes.

Can we believe either of those stories? The Aeneas story is an epic in the manner of Homer and is in a sense the sequel to the *Iliad*, in this case brought to us by the poet Virgil. First of all, we don't even know if the Trojan War actually happened, and if it did, it probably occurred around 1200 B.C., not in the eighth century B.C.

As for the babies raised by wolves, well, what do *you* think? On the other hand, it is possible that Romulus could be an historical figure who was mythologized. In any case, the city of Rome probably grew up gradually as villages were combined and swamps were drained.

They've Been Hellenized!

Although the Romans had some culture and religion of their own, the Greeks had a profound effect on the Etruscan and Roman civilizations—so much so that some scholars say Roman culture is really just an extension of that of the Greeks. Those who are less kind might characterize it as a bastardization of their beloved Greek civilization.

Lost and Found

The Romans seemed to have had a real love/hate relationship with the Greeks. On the one hand, they borrowed, imitated, and adapted a great deal of Greek culture. Yet they were more than happy to thrash the place with their armies and loot the Greeks of their art. A Greek education was considered prestigious, even while it was fashionable to bad-mouth them.

The influence is not hard to see: Just look at the art, the architecture, and much of the culture and literature. Even the religion isn't immune. The Greek god Zeus can be found in the guise of the Roman Jupiter, and Athena lurks behind the Roman goddess Minerva. The rest of the Roman pantheon follows suit, although the Roman religion has some unique elements as well.

The First Republicans

Rome, so they say, was originally ruled by Etruscan kings. According to traditional history, the monarchy was overthrown because of a gross abuse of power by a member of the royal family. It could very well have been a coup on the part of wealthy nobles.

What replaced the system of kingship was a kind of representative government. Much of the history of Rome can be seen in the evolution of this government, which featured two senior executives called consuls, a Senate, and several assemblies made up of free citizens.

Jargon Unearthed

A *patrician* is a member of the aristocratic Roman upper class. A *plebeian* is a Roman commoner.

Pitfalls and Pointers

How do we know all of this detailed Roman history? Just as the Greeks had historians such as Herodotus, Thucydides, and Xenophon, the Romans had their Livy, Tacitus, and even Julius Caesar, who wrote down history as they collected or experienced it.

The Senate and the Roman People

Roman society was divided into at least three classes. The patricians were the wealthy upper class (probably no more than 10 percent of the population), the plebeians were the commoners, and then there were the slaves. The consuls and senators were typically patricians, and they held most of the power. A series of reforms gave the plebeians more of a say, including the appointment of two executive-level representatives called tribunes, and a tradition that one of the two consuls would be a plebe.

Good Idea Gone Bad

This nicely organized system of representative government and rule of law began to deteriorate as Rome began to expand its borders and the system was repeatedly abused. Then there were generals with loyal armies who, after a successful campaign, would turn around, march their armies toward Rome, and make demands.

One such commander, a fellow named Octavian, survived his rivals and was welcomed back at home, where immense powers were bestowed upon him by the Senate. He became the first emperor and was given the name Augustus, and the republican government thereafter would be mostly a charade, since the emperor essentially became a dictator over the Empire.

Building the Empire: Romans, Romans Everywhere!

So how did the vast Roman empire come about? Well, it was built in stages. The first step was to conquer the neighbors, which the Romans did early on, beginning with the civilized Etruscans and then the various tribes in Italy. The Greeks had to be dominated in the South in order to consolidate most of the peninsula. Way up in the North, the Gauls would present an annoying obstacle for most of Roman history.

Elephants over the Alps

With much of Italy proper taken care of, there were still two major competitors who had to be squashed in the Mediterranean: the Carthaginians and the Greeks. The Carthaginians were dealt with in a series of three conflicts known as the Punic Wars that took place between the years 264 and 146 B.C.

The Carthaginians put up a pretty good fight, too, especially when Hannibal, their most famous general, went on the offensive and invaded Italy by coming through the Alps, complete with war elephants. Alas for Carthage, the wars ended with the brutal destruction of that magnificent city itself, and the Carthaginians ceased to be a power in the region.

Lost and Found

On his way to invade Italy, Hannibal marched across the Alps with his army of forty thousand men, thousands of horses, and forty elephants. Perhaps as many as 25,000 soldiers were lost in the process after suffering many catastrophes due to the dangerous environment and attacks by marauders.

Conquering the Greeks

With much of the western Mediterranean cleared of those pesky Carthaginians, and the Greeks in that area no longer a real threat, the Romans turned east, where Alexander's mighty empire stood more or less intact. It was a Greek world out there, with the kingdoms established by Alexander's generals in control of vast territories, including Asia Minor, Persia, Egypt, and Palestine. The Romans sent armies out to thrash Greece itself while others gradually ate away at the Hellenistic world. The big finale finally came with the Roman acquisition of Egypt in 30 B.C., and the story that goes with it is almost too sappy to believe.

In a strange tale of love and betrayal, Marcus Antonius gives away Roman territory to his girlfriend Cleopatra VII, the Greek queen of Egypt. Mark's rival Octavian would have none of such nonsense, and the two battled. Octavian won and Cleopatra killed herself, as did Marcus, and Egypt became Rome's. It makes me ask the question: Can history really work that way?

Heading North

Now the Roman Empire was immense, and the Mediterranean was essentially a "Roman lake." In the meantime, there was the rest of Europe to take care of, and much of western Europe was touched by the Romans, including most of what would become modern France, Spain, Portugal, and Great Britain. The Romans certainly weren't unopposed, as they regularly fought the "barbarians" along their borders.

Lost and Found

The emperor Hadrian constructed a great wall across northern Britain (ca.122 A.D.). The wall, which stretches across 118 kilometers, was designed to control the movement of people into Roman territory and as a defense against unruly tribes. Much of the wall still stands today.

Lost and Found

Vindolanda is an old Roman outpost in Great Britain not far from Hadrian's Wall. When it was excavated in the 1960s, over a thousand writing tablets were found addressing a wide range of topics, including military business and personal correspondence. A variety of surviving small artifacts has likewise provided an unusual glimpse into the details of life at an outpost of Rome far from home.

Running the Empire: All Roads Led to Rome

But how to control such a vast area? The Romans were very clever. In the early days, a citizen of Rome was someone who lived in Rome or the immediate vicinity. As the Empire began to grow, citizenship was extended to the conquered peoples, but on a sort of probational basis. If they behaved and fully submitted, they could be granted full Roman citizenship, otherwise they could be entitled to more or less privilege based on their behavior. The empire was divided into provinces ruled by Roman governors or their local lackeys.

Like the Persians, the Romans set up vast networks of roads that allowed troops to take care of any of the uppity conquerees (such as the Jewish rebels in Palestine). Most importantly, they allowed taxes, tribute, booty, and a wide range of exotic goods to make it back to the homeland or to wealthy Romans everywhere. All this wealth helped those Romans who were so inclined to engage in the variety of vices for which Rome was noted. So dependent did Rome itself become on imports, that a disruption in shipping could cause a serious crisis, such as a food shortage.

Feats in Concrete

The Romans were great builders. You can find a Roman road just about anywhere they traveled. The same goes for aqueducts and bridges. Roman engineers designed and built marvelous systems that could bring water from mountains or rivers to wherever it was needed, even if that meant spanning large ravines. They were masters of the arch, and the Roman aqueducts and bridges were so solid that many are still in use today.

The Romans have also been credited with the first wide-scale use, if not invention, of concrete. Concrete has the great advantage of being relatively portable (before it is mixed) and can be formed into all manner of shapes, including domes. Some amazingly sturdy pieces of architecture survive today in Rome and elsewhere in the old empire, attesting to the durability of their buildings. Where Romans lived, it's not unusual to find the remains of theaters and public baths and, occasionally, elaborate luxury villas.

Life and Death: Vesuvius Erupts

On August 24, 79 A.D., a major catastrophe struck the Italian coast near Naples. The volcano Vesuvius erupted and buried two towns. Pompeii was covered in a suffocating layer of volcanic ash, while the nearby town of Herculaneum was entombed in a mud flow. Pompeii was discovered in 1594 during the construction of an irrigation channel. Herculaneum was first encountered a century later when locals excavating a well came across statues.

What we have in Pompeii and Herculaneum is another classic example of an archaeological time capsule, and once again, human tragedy has become a blessing to the archaeologist. The cities were buried quickly, so most everything is as it was left: dinner on the table, tools in the workshop, and so on. Unfortunately for the citizens, the rapidity of the destruction also meant that many of them weren't able to escape, and perhaps 2,000 people died.

Pitfalls and Pointers

Are you in the mood for love? Read the Roman poet Ovid's *Art of Love* for some sassy tips on how to pick up women, or how to avoid being picked up. Horace also provides some high-class romantic poetry.

Lost and Found

When excavator Giuseppe Fiorelli was in charge of excavations at Pompeii between the years 1860 and 1875, he noticed hollows where ash had solidified around decaying objects, creating molds. When he poured plaster into the molds, the result was casts of the victims themselves. Some were in the act of fleeing, while chained-up pets and a couple of manacled gladiators didn't stand a chance.

Diggers

Johann Winckelmann (1717–1768), who excavated at both Pompeii and Herculaneum, has been called "the father of classical archaeology." His *History of Ancient Art* (1764) was highly influential, with a fresh approach to studying antiquities.

A view of Pompeii. (From L.W. Yaggy and T. L. Haines, Museum of Antiquity *[Chicago: Law, King and Law, 1884])*

Those Wacky Roman Emperors!

Life seemed good in Rome in 27 B.C. when Octavian/ Augustus began his rule of the Empire. Augustus was quite popular and some consider these the best days for Rome, a creative and prosperous time. When Augustus died in A.D. 14, though, his adopted son Tiberius became emperor. Tiberius was not like his dad, and was a bit mean-spirited and power-hungry.

His son and successor, Caligula, was genuinely insane, and Caligula's successor, Claudius, was a flake. His son Nero was also crazy. A power struggle after the death of Nero caused a crisis, and four people claimed the throne. A politician and military commander by the name of Vespasian (r. A.D. 69–79) won out and thus started a new line of rulers.

Pitfalls and Pointers

Do you want the dirt on Caligula and Nero? Read Suetonius's *Lives of the Caesars,* a genuine collection of ancient gossip, rumor, and history. Some of it is outright disgusting, while other bits are quite funny.

The Five Good Emperors

When this little dynasty ended, with a cruel ruler without a successor, the generally impotent Senate appointed an elder respected statesman to be emperor, thus begin- ning the reign of the "Five Good Emperors." The new rule thereafter was that the emperor would adopt a worthy successor as his son, rather than let the office fall to his own potentially dubious genetic offspring.

Here are the five good emperors:

1. **Nerva** (A.D. 96–98). A good solid character. Just what Rome needed after a series of quirky rulers.

2. **Trajan** (98–117). A competent man. Monuments to his military triumphs still decorate the city of Rome.

3. **Hadrian** (117–138). Like his predecessor, Hadrian was quite the builder. The long wall he built at the Scottish frontier remains today as a legacy of his defense of the Empire at its remote edges.

4. **Antonius Pius** (138–161). A competent, peaceful man.

5. **Marcus Aurelius** (161–180). Presided over the last great days of Rome. He was also a poet and philosopher, as evidenced by his *Meditations*.

Unfortunately, Marcus really screwed up the system when he promoted his own despotic, cruel, and incompetent son Commodus as his successor.

Things went downhill fast, especially after the death of Commodus in 192. During the third century A.D., plenty of Roman emperors came and went. Many were murdered and replaced. Attempts at reform were short-lived, and Rome was getting so bad that even some of her own emperors wouldn't live there. One such emperor, Diocletian, conceded that the empire was simply too large for one man to control, and developed a system in which he would share his rule with three others. This idea was short-lived.

It should be mentioned that Christianity began in Palestine under Roman control during the first century A.D. The followers of Jesus enthusiastically spread their message and it soon reached Rome itself, where small communities of Christians were established. Refusing to worship the Roman gods, many Christians were put to death, some in the arenas for public entertainment. Ironically, Christianity would eventually become the official religion of the Roman Empire during the reign of the emperor Theodosius (A.D. 379–395).

Lost and Found

One of the most dangerous jobs in the Roman world was probably that of emperor. It's hard to find many emperors who didn't meet their end in some violent or suspicious manner. This makes for some great stories, and material for your next party trivia game.

Jargon Unearthed

The city of Byzantium would be renamed Constantinople, city of Constantine, in honor of the great emperor. Today it is known as the Turkish city of Istanbul, and as the old song goes, that's "nobody's business but the Turks."

Constantine Cleans House

Another emperor, Constantine, attempted to improve the situation by dividing the empire into numerous provinces and creating a huge bureaucracy to control it. In A.D. 330, he also formally moved the capital of the empire to the strategically located old Greek city of Byzantium at the westernmost juncture of Asia Minor and Europe proper. The city was renamed Constantinople in his honor.

The empire was eventually divided into western and eastern halves, with the dividing line just east of Italy. The western empire collapsed in A.D. 476, when a German warlord by the name of Odoacer dethroned the last Western emperor. The Eastern half, known as the Byzantine Empire, would continue for another thousand years until 1453, when the Ottoman Turks captured Constantinople.

Lost and Found

The emperor Constantine is a wonderfully interesting fellow. Apart from his moving of the Roman capital east and his efforts at reform, he converted to Christianity in A.D. 312 after experiencing a vision. His sponsorship of the Council of Nicaea in A.D. 325 resulted in the establishment of the official fundamental beliefs of Christianity.

Jargon Unearthed

Gladiators were slaves trained to fight for the entertainment of spectators. They often used real weapons, and the consequences could be fatal.

The Sporting Life

When some people think of Rome, it's not poetry they're thinking about—it's the wild stadium activities. The Romans were notorious for their special forms of public recreation. Especially during the time of the emperors, rough and often brutal events were staged for the masses to enjoy. Slaves, for example, were trained to fight in death matches for the delight of audiences. These gladiators might fight one-on-one or in multiple pairs.

Large arenas such as the massive Coliseum in Rome, built by Vespasian, could hold around 50,000 people. Is ground combat not sophisticated enough for you? Perhaps the stadium will be flooded for a sea battle between troops on little boats. Prisoners could be fed to hungry animals or otherwise executed. Wild animals could be pitted against each other, lions versus tigers, bears versus boars, and so forth.

There also seems to have been some competition to produce ever bigger shows. It's said that the emperor Augustus put on a spectacle with 625 pairs of gladiators and that 10,000 fighters were involved in a celebration for the emperor Trajan. Perhaps more "civilized," but still very dangerous, were chariot races. The racetrack in Rome, the Hippodrome, could accommodate over 200,000 spectators.

The Roman Coliseum today symbolizes both architectural excellence and human decadence. (From A. Stebastiani, Romanarum Plantarum [Rome, 1815])

The Fall of the Roman Empire

Where'd they go? The so-called "fall" of the Roman Empire was more of a steady decline. Even though the fall of Rome is often fixed at the year A.D. 476, when a barbarian warlord conquered the city, the end of the empire really can't be pinned to one factor. We need to look at why such a thing could occur. After all, the Romans fought off invaders from the north for hundreds of years. Here are just a few of the suggestions that have been offered:

➤ The vast Roman empire was simply too big to control; in short, the Romans were overextended.

➤ Too many holidays. Too many handouts. Laziness. Moral corruption. Overtaxation. Lack of incentives.

➤ Environmental causes, such as soil exhaustion and drought.

➤ Bad government: Some of the brightest people seem to have been regularly killed off by the opposition.

➤ And my favorite: Lead pipes in the plumbing of the wealthy contributed to the nuttiness of some of the emperors and their poor leadership.

The answer might lie in a combination of all of the above, and then some. Whatever the cause, the glory days of Rome were over, although certainly not forgotten. The influence of Rome is still felt today in the areas of law, government,

Lost and Found

It's possible that the Romans contributed to the extinction of certain species in parts of the Empire through their demand for beasts for their spectacles. Have you seen any lions running around Syria lately?

engineering, and architecture, and its literature is still widely read both in the original Latin and in modern translations.

What's in Store for Us?

It's been really popular for years for doomsayers to point to the conditions in the latter days of Rome and compare them to our modern culture. "Look! It's just like Rome and that's where we're heading, yes sir!" Various analogies are made, with an emphasis on decadence and moral and spiritual decline. Well, don't pack up to colonize Antarctica just yet.

Rome was Rome. What we have going today may retain some superficial parallels, but we have our own situation. There are as many things different as there are in common. Sure, it's possible that we might be in "decline," although such a thing is really difficult to measure. Others might in fact argue that we're on the edge of a "golden age."

History is interpreted in its aftermath, and we don't even have the Roman story quite figured out, much less can we claim to have the historical distance to assess our own culture fully and impartially. If there are lessons that can be derived from Roman history, let them have a positive effect. The very fact that people call attention to them suggests that history and the study of the past might actually have a practical purpose.

The Least You Need to Know

➤ Roman civilization borrowed heavily from the Greeks and the Etruscans.

➤ Although the Romans established a system of representative government, it was gradually transformed into an imperial dictatorship as laws were broken and power was abused.

➤ The Romans built a vast empire which especially benefited the Romans themselves, who were able to live a relatively luxurious existence.

➤ The influence of Rome is still felt today in the areas of government, law, engineering, and architecture, and its literature is still widely read.

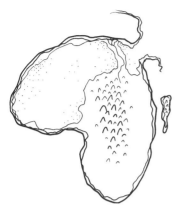

Chapter 17

Africa: Where They Say It All Began

In This Chapter

➤ Bones, tools, and some of the earliest humans

➤ Rock art in the desert

➤ The remains of some great civilizations

➤ An African Egypt?

Africa is the second largest continent on this planet and is about three times the size of Europe. Northern Africa is often referred to as Saharan Africa, because it is dominated by the vast Sahara desert, which stretches from coast to coast across this great continent. Ancient cities sit on the coast or inland along old trade routes. Below the great desert is the bulk of the rest of the continent, sub-Saharan Africa, with a variety of both arid and lush environments that support an incredible diversity of life.

Africa played a crucial role in the human story, being the place where humans are said to have ultimately evolved. And on that continent arose the well-known civilization of the Egyptians along with other great ancient cultures which have yet to receive the full attention they deserve. In this chapter, we're going to be taking a look at this remarkable continent and its rich history and culture.

Africa.

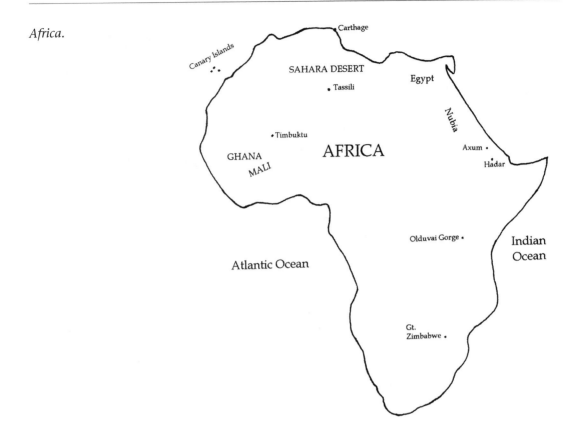

The African Connection

There's an amazing number of cultures and languages in Africa, along with a great deal of physical diversity. Members of African groups can be tall like the Masai or short like the Bambuti; very dark-skinned like the Nuba or fair and light-haired like the Berbers; speakers of Arabic or Hausa; Muslim, Christian, Jewish, animist, and everything in-between.

The overwhelming majority of the people in the north today are Islamic and Arabic-speaking, a result of the Arab invasions in the seventh and eighth centuries A.D.

Early Explorers

Africa was a mysterious continent to most Westerners, with the exception of the areas bordering the Mediterranean, which were certainly known to the seafaring cultures of the region. The Greeks and Phoenicians had colonies on the north coast, including Carthage, which

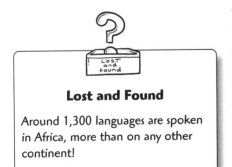

Lost and Found

Around 1,300 languages are spoken in Africa, more than on any other continent!

attracted the attention of the Romans. Few explorers (that we know of) ventured out into the Atlantic, although there are a handful of Phoenician, Carthaginian, and Roman sites on the upper northwest Atlantic coast of the continent in what is now Morocco.

We have the stories of the Phoenician Hanno sailing down the coast of West Africa around 500 B.C., and the tale of the expedition commissioned by the Egyptian pharaoh Necho II, which allegedly spent three years doing a complete traverse around the African continent, around 600 B.C. Apart from these expeditions, the European civilizations to the north generally seem to have been ignorant of the African interior.

We do know that Egypt, on the very northeastern-most edge of the continent, conducted expeditions out of the Red Sea toward Somalia, trading, and occasionally battling, with the kingdoms to the south. On the Mediterranean coast, Africans traded with Arabs and groups from the Persian Gulf and the Indian Ocean region for millennia.

The Europeans Arrive

The European exploration of Africa began with the desire to find a sea route to India. After a number of tries, an expedition led by the Portuguese Vasco da Gama in 1497/ 1498 was successful in following the African coasts to India and back, opening the way for exploration and exploitation along the coasts. As the Americas were colonized, the slave trade became a big industry on the west coast, but few Europeans ventured inland.

The European age of African exploration included great efforts to find the sources of some of the great African rivers, including the Nile and the Niger. Many perished in the process. While Europeans were worried about geography, the Africans went about their normal routines.

Once the vast resources of the continent were known, however, Africa would never again be the same. Artificial borders were drawn up in Europe that rarely took into account the distribution or desires of the African people. Given this cultural and geographical ignorance, it's no wonder that African archaeology got off to a relatively late start.

Pitfalls and Pointers

One of the great goals of nineteenth century exploration was to find the source of the Nile, the river that supported the ancient Egyptian civilization and empties into the Mediterranean. It wasn't until the mid-nineteenth century that Europeans became aware of the source of the Nile, in an arduous competition of rival explorers.

The Hunt for Early Humans

Physical anthropologists tell us that the earliest humans developed in Africa. According to the scenario, humans evolved from early primates known as the australopithecines, developing a larger brain and the ability to walk on two legs in the process. The ability to adapt and the use of tools were paramount. And where do they find the fossils that seem to point to all of this? Africa, of course. And from there a form of early human, *Homo erectus*, quickly dispersed through much of the Old World.

Although virtually all evolutionary scientists agree that early humans originated in Africa (see Chapter 9), two main theories are debated regarding the origins of modern *Homo sapiens*:

➤ *Homo sapiens* evolved from *Homo erectus*, who had spread out of Africa all the way to Southeast Asia by about 1.8 million years ago.

➤ *Homo sapiens* evolved in Africa and essentially replaced *Homo erectus*, who became extinct.

Lost and Found

Remember when we talked about mtDNA, the maternally transmitted DNA, in Chapter 6? A controversial research study called "the Eve Hypothesis" claims that the mother of all modern humans can be traced back to the Africa of about 140,000–290,000 years ago.

Much of the hunt for the earliest humans has taken place in East Africa, in places like Ethiopia and Tanzania. In certain places there, the geology is conducive to the discovery of fossils from long ago. Instead of being buried under tons of sediments, layers of the earth have been exposed due to erosion or faulting. The Great Rift Valley in particular, which splits 1,200 miles north to south through eastern Africa, has proven to be such a place.

As an added bonus, ancient volcanic activity in the region has allowed the use of such methods as potassium-argon dating to determine the age of the really old stuff, which is well beyond the limits of radiocarbon dating. We're going to look at just a couple of these important early African sites because, as the chapter title says, it's where they say it all began.

Hadar, Ethiopia

In an area of northeast Ethiopia in what's called the Afar Triangle, extraordinary fossils of alleged human ancestors have been found. Thousands of fragments have been discovered representing dozens of individuals. Most famous is the nearly complete skeleton of a 3.2 million year old creature called "Lucy," discovered in 1974. Known scientifically as *Australopithecus afarensis*, Lucy was the first of her kind ever found. Since then the fossilized remains of still more of her species dating back some 3.4 million years have been discovered in East Africa, and a 3.6 million year old relative from South Africa has just come to light.

The following year, the remains of at least 13 individual hominids were found in the same vicinity, suggesting that they all died at the same time. Apart from the bones, stone tools have been found that could be as old as 2.5 million years. In southern Ethiopia, the sites of Omo and Turkana have likewise provided a wealth of fossils related to the early human story.

Olduvai Gorge

The world-famous Olduvai Gorge is a big ravine located in the Serengeti Plain of northern Tanzania. In many ways the Gorge resembles Arizona's Grand Canyon, with layer after layer of its geological history exposed in its walls. It became quite famous after the discoveries made by Louis and Mary Leakey in the late 1950s and 1960s.

The earliest hominid layers at Olduvai date to 1.8 million years ago and include the remains of both australopithecines and a kind of early human known as *Homo habilis* (the handy man). Known as the first tool maker, *Homo habilis* was found at Olduvai along with simple tools created by flaking river cobbles. Known as the "Oldowan" toolmaking, this method of manufacture was practiced from about 1.8 million to 800,000 years ago.

Homo erectus appeared on the scene at Olduvai at about 1.4 million years ago, bringing into fashion a newer and more useful tool-making tradition. These tools, the most common of which is a hand ax with a two-sided blade, were in use from about 1.4 million years ago to about 100,000 years ago. More importantly, however, a stone hut structure was discovered at Olduvai, showing human alteration of the site, along with the bones of animals that had been butchered with the use of tools.

Aside from a large quantity of truly old stone tools and early hominid bones, the fossils of numerous species of extinct animals have been found in the area; these give an excellent impression of the type of environment in which humans developed.

Footprints in the Ash

Bones are always welcome finds, of course, and so are stone tools, but once in a while, something really different is discovered. In 1978, Mary Leakey found solidified tracks in a volcanic ash deposit dating to more than 3.5 million years ago.

Included in the tracks were those of two little hominids with human-like feet. The size of the feet and the stride indicate that they were considerably less than five feet tall, but most importantly, the footprints indicated that these creatures were apparently walking upright on two legs, as do we.

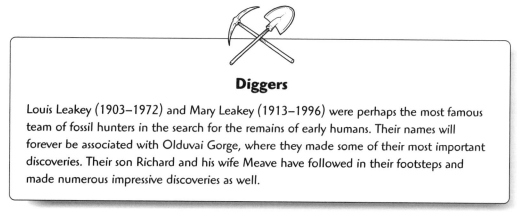

Diggers

Louis Leakey (1903–1972) and Mary Leakey (1913–1996) were perhaps the most famous team of fossil hunters in the search for the remains of early humans. Their names will forever be associated with Olduvai Gorge, where they made some of their most important discoveries. Their son Richard and his wife Meave have followed in their footsteps and made numerous impressive discoveries as well.

The Sahara Never Looked So Good

Africa as we know it today didn't always look that way. We've already talked about how environmental change may have affected human cultures after the Ice Age and about the situation in Egypt, where the hippos depicted on tomb walls no longer frolic in the papyrus swamps that likewise no longer exist there.

Elsewhere in Africa, there's ample evidence of different environments long ago. In North Africa in particular, art in the form of drawings and paintings on rock show a different land: a tropical land where giraffes and other beasts of the savanna roamed in an area that is now a hot, rugged desert.

An assortment of images from Tassili rock art. (After B. Davidson, African Kingdoms *[New York: Time, 1966], p. 44 ; A. M. Josephy,* The Horizon History of Africa *[New York: American Heritage, 1971], p. 35; A. Muzzolini, L' art rupestre prèhistorique des massifs centraux sahariens [Cambridge, 1986], p. 166, fig. 28)*

Tassili in southern Algeria is one of the most famous of these African prehistoric rock art sites. Here one can see the Sahara like never before. The rock art was first brought to archaeological attention in the 1920s and studied in the decades that followed. It's very hard to date art of this sort, but one can almost follow along through time with a long progression of hunters, herders, civilized folk with chariots, and the era of the camel, a creature highly suited to a land transformed into desert.

Much of the art has been attributed to the Neolithic, beginning about 6000 B.C. It includes lots of antelopes and elephants, along with what appear to be domesticated sheep, goats, and cattle. Many difficult to interpret motifs, such as masked figures, could provide some insight into ancient views of the world or religion if only they could be understood.

Nubia: Egypt's Southern Neighbor

When it comes to civilizations on the continent of Africa, Egypt gets most of the attention. Sure, the Egyptians spent a few thousand years building big things out of stone, but travel a little further south and you'll be in for a big surprise. Just south of Egypt, in a land now generally consumed by the desert, existed a great African civilization that competed with, fought with, and even at one time conquered their powerful northern neighbor. I'm talking about Nubia.

The area of Nubia is located in the southernmost reaches of modern Egypt south of Aswan and the area of Sudan north of Khartoum. The Nile passes through this area and a series of six cataracts, or rapids, interrupt navigation and serve as natural borders. Although the river provided many advantages to its neighbors, as it did in Egypt, fertile land along its banks was generally narrower and more sporadic in Nubia.

The Land of the Bow

As in Egypt, Nubia was inhabited by hunters and gathers for eons before agricultural practices came to the region. The Nubians were the beneficiaries of a wealth of desirable natural resources, including copper, gold, and other precious materials. Cattle herding was also big. And most importantly, Nubia was situated right in the middle of the corridor that served as the commercial land route between sub-Saharan Africa to the south and Egypt and others to the north. Through here passed such goods as ebony and ivory, wild animals, slaves, incense, and all manner of exotic products.

With their rich resources and control over the trade corridor, the Nubians lived a pretty good life—a life envied by the Egyptians, who sought to control Nubia over and over again. The Nubians were by no means passive, and the Egyptians built forts on their southern frontier. At one point, the Nubians actually conquered Egypt during what is called the 25th Dynasty (747–656 B.C.). Two of the Egyptian names for Nubia were "Kush" and "the land of the bow," the latter referring to the Nubians' favorite weapon.

Pitfalls and Pointers

I said it elsewhere and I'll say it again: it's very difficult to accurately interpret ancient rock art. There is often a tendency to assign religious or ritual meaning to such art when the possibility remains that it was art for art's sake or a way of recording events. At Tassili, strange bubble-headed humanoids drawn on the rock have been interpreted as masked individuals, mythological creatures, and even aliens, by those so inclined.

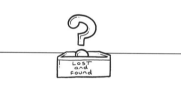

Lost and Found

As early as the Old Kingdom, Egyptians were making trips to the land of "Punt" and returning with exotic goods. On her temple at Deir el-Bahri, Egyptian pharaoh Hatshepsut vividly recorded an expedition by sea which, among other things, brought back living trees to be replanted in Egypt. Most scholars agree that Punt was located on the Red Sea coast of Sudan, Somalia, or Ethiopia.

Pyramids and Hieroglyphs

Nubian civilization possessed an interesting mix of African and Egyptian styles. The later rulers built small steep-sided pyramids by the dozens at such places as Nuri and Meroe, and many of their religious concepts and structures, too, were hybrid. Egyptian hieroglyphs and language were borrowed for writing. From the second century B.C., though, a script using 23 hieroglyphs and another used as a form of cursive were used to write the Nubian language.

These scripts are known as "Meroitic," after the Nubian capital of the time, Meroe. The language is not very well understood, and it might be unrelated to any now known. The Nubian civilization flourished for over 1,000 years, from about 700 B.C. to about 400 A.D. Nubia's decline was in part due to the Romans, who began to acquire their exotic goods by sea from another African kingdom, Axum, located on the Red Sea in Ethiopia.

Nubian pyramids. (From F. Calliaud, Voyage à Mèroè *[1826])*

The Sturdy Stele of Axum

The city of Axum, located on a high fertile plateau in northern Ethiopia, was home to another prosperous group who had great sources of raw material, such as ivory, and who were part of the great trade network connecting India, Africa, and the Roman Empire. The city was the result of the mingling of Ethiopian farmers and immigrants from southern Arabia. Axum was especially prominent during the first centuries A.D.

The cemetery at Axum is famous for its gigantic, beautifully carved granite *stele*, or standing stone slabs, which seem to have served as royal tombstones. There are nearly 120 of these monuments, and the largest one still standing is 71 feet tall and weighs numerous tons. Another stele, now broken, is over 100 feet tall, and was one of the largest standing pieces of stone ever carved in ancient times.

Great Zimbabwe

South of Axsum and Nubia, in the south-central part of the country of Zimbabwe, lie perhaps the greatest surviving ancient ruins in sub-Saharan Africa: Great Zimbabwe. There are found immense walled structures of dry stone granite masonry, some of the walls being up to 17 feet thick! The largest structure at the site is called the Great Enclosure and features a high wall hundreds of feet in length.

Great Zimbabwe served as the center of a prosperous little Iron Age state, which flourished primarily between about 1100 and 1500 A.D. At its height, perhaps as many as 20,000 people lived inside or in the vicinity of the site. Apart from herding and agriculture, Great Zimbabwe was involved in the control of an extensive trade network in the area. Even Chinese goods have been found there, though they may have passed through many hands before arriving in Africa.

It's not known exactly why Great Zimbabwe was abandoned. It doesn't seem to have been attacked. Some suggest that maybe the soil was exhausted or the people ran short of trade resources. Although it was known by a few Europeans as early as the 1500s, it wasn't until the German geologist Carl Mauch visited the site in 1871 that the world became aware of this impressive place.

Jargon Unearthed

A *stele* (pl. *stelae*) is a standing stone slab, often with carved decorations and/or an inscription.

Jargon Unearthed

Zimbabwe is a Shona word meaning "houses of stone." The name lends itself not only to the famous ruins, but also to the modern country of Zimbabwe, which was known as Rhodesia until 1980.

Diggers

Gertrude Caton-Thompson (1888–1985) was a prominent archaeologist who worked in a variety of areas, including Egypt, Arabia, and sub-Saharan Africa. It was her excavations at Great Zimbabwe in 1929 that definitely concluded that the magnificent constructions there were of indigenous African origin.

Some speculated that it was the home of the Biblical Queen of Sheba or associated with King Solomon's gold mines. Many who came to see the site refused to believe that Africans were capable of building such a great site, attributing the remains to Phoenicians or some other foreign civilization. These racist views were shattered when archaeological excavations revealed the truth: Great Zimbabwe had indeed been built and occupied by African people.

The conical tower at the ruins of Great Zimbabwe.

Kingdoms of Gold

Now let's take a look at the other side of the continent. In West Africa, several great kingdoms arose during the first dozen centuries A.D. Ghana (ca. 400–1200 A.D.), for example, developed a reputation as a supplier of gold. The Ghanans were sophisticated traders, and the monarch and his kingdom were protected by a huge loyal army. For reasons not totally clear, the kingdom of Ghana declined around the thirteenth century. But others would follow. Mali came to the forefront for about two centuries beginning around A.D. 1250, and was able to organize its great trade network from the famous city of Timbuktu.

Pyramids in the Atlantic

Off the coast of what is now Morocco in North Africa are a group of volcanic islands known as the Canaries. Columbus stopped there for supplies on his way to the New World. When the Spanish decided to conquer these islands during the 1400s, they were inhabited by a group of people called the Guanches, who put up fierce resistance. The Guanches were a fascinating culture resembling few others in that part of the world. They were cave dwellers who maintained goats and crops and mummified their dead. Their language is hardly known, and their origins are the subject of controversy.

The Guanches first came to the Canaries perhaps three thousand years ago. They must have had some sort of boats to colonize the various islands, although none were in use when the Spanish began to conquer the islands in the 1400s. The nearest land mass is northwest Africa, less than a hundred miles away, and it's altogether likely that the Guanches originated there, perhaps from the Berbers. Like the Berbers, many of the Guanches were described as fair-skinned.

In the lovely town of Guimar on the island of Tenerife, some controversial structures have recently been brought to the attention of archaeologists. You can't really say that they were recently discovered, because they sit on a piece of property right in the middle of the town! The structures appear to be several little step pyramids, with stairs leading up to their tops, oriented to the summer solstice.

The site has been set aside for protection, and a museum has been built there, but many questions have yet to be answered. Who built the pyramids of Guimar, and when? And very importantly, why? It is hoped that ongoing excavations will be able to answer some of these questions.

Jargon Unearthed

The name of the Canary Islands has nothing to do with little squeaky yellow birds. They are actually named after the dogs (*canids*) found living there.

Lost and Found

A few skeptics have claimed that the Guimar pyramids are of recent manufacture and are just piles of rocks created by farmers clearing their fields. The pyramids, though, seem to be filled with rubble, and the stones in their walls are trimmed. There are also other pyramids in the Canaries, including one near the edge of a cliff, which detracts from the stone-pile theory.

Black Athena

What color were the ancient Egyptians? Was ancient Egyptian civilization a black African culture? Did this black Egyptian culture have a profound effect on other great civilizations of the ancient world, such as Greece? Has racism suppressed evidence of

Pitfalls and Pointers

I was once asked if I've performed melanin tests on the mummies I've discovered in order to determine their race. No, I haven't. The Egyptians could be green as far as I'm concerned. But I'm glad that someone else is looking into it.

Jargon Unearthed

Afrocentrism is a perspective on a given subject from an African point of view, as opposed to *Eurocentrism*, which features a European perspective.

the African nature of ancient Egypt? These questions and others of a similar sort have been asked by several black scholars in the latter decades of the twentieth century. The focus is on Egypt, and the perspective is called *Afrocentrism*.

The whole matter of the race of the Egyptians is a difficult one to discuss, especially in these days of race sensitivity and political correctness. Many black people, especially in America, look to Africa as a great and splendid cultural homeland and seek pride in the accomplishments of their ancestors. Given Egypt's indisputable prominence in the world of great ancient civilizations, it's easy to understand why any group would want to claim it as their own.

There are certainly African characteristics in the Egyptian civilization, especially in aspects of ancient cattle culture and religion. The ancient Egyptian language itself has been classified as Afro-Asiatic, meaning that it has characteristics of both African and Semitic languages. Afrocentric scholars are quick to point out other similarities to African cultures, including examples of Egyptian art in which "typically Negroid" physical features seem to be apparent.

So what color were the ancient Egyptians? Well, I'm going to have to say "Egyptian-colored." It's altogether likely, especially during the later periods when a lot of Greeks and other foreigners were involved, that there was quite a bit of physical diversity, much as you find there today. Egyptian art often depicted men with brown skin, women with yellow, Semitic foreigners with light skin, and other Africans with black skin.

The ancient Egyptians don't really seem to have cared much about what color people were, and to tell you the truth, neither do I. Is it possible that some scholars have ignored the "blackness" of Egyptian civilization? Perhaps. We all approach the study of the past with our own set of lenses. But I can guarantee you that there are many scholars of all colors who have no personal agenda other than discovering the truth. End of story.

The Least You Need to Know

➤ Evolutionary scientists believe that humans first evolved on the African continent, where lots of early fossil evidence has been found.

➤ The African continent has played host to a wide variety of people, animals, and environments over the millennia.

➤ Old African civilizations thrived in such places as Nubia and Zimbabwe in East Africa and Ghana and Mali in West Africa.

➤ Archaeology has helped uncover the ancient history and many achievements of African peoples and their cultures.

Chapter 18

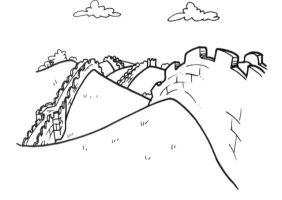

Big Things Going On in Asia

In This Chapter

➤ An early civilization in the Indus Valley

➤ Royal Chinese tombs

➤ Mystery mummies!

➤ Frozen tombs in Siberia

➤ "Lost" cities in the Cambodian jungle

Along with Egypt and Mesopotamia, the Indus River Valley and China, both in Asia, are the homes of early civilizations in the Old World. It's difficult to describe Asia geographically. Nearly every sort of climate and landform can be found in its immense continental territory, including extreme cold, deserts, jungles, and the highest mountains on earth. In this chapter, we're going to concentrate on a few of the centers of ancient Asian civilizations, which are as fascinating as those to the west or east across the ocean. Unfortunately, with a continent this huge and a chapter this small, I'm only going to be able to offer a small sample of the area's extremely interesting history and archaeology. I think you'll agree, however, that Asian archaeology is fascinating.

The Indus Valley: Civilization on the Flood Plain

Until the mid-nineteenth century, no one in modern times knew that there was an important ancient society to be found in the midst of the Indus River Valley in what is now Pakistan and northwest India. Fired mud bricks were being quarried from one of

Lost and Found

The Indus Valley script has yet to be convincingly deciphered. The majority of inscriptions are short and appear on square steatite seals. There are no bilingual inscriptions to assist in the decipherment process, and even the language the people were writing in is unknown.

the old cities for use in building a railroad, and along with the bricks were found square seals that provided some of the earliest evidence of this lost civilization. The city is called Harappa and the civilization is known as Harappan, or the Indus Valley civilization.

Apart from the site of Harappa, another large ancient city, called Mohenjodaro, was found. When both were excavated beginning in the 1920s by Indian archaeologists (R. D. Banerji and Rai Sahni, respectively), it became apparent that here was an older civilization of a type hitherto unknown. Since their discoveries, a few other Harappan cities and many other sites have been uncovered over a large region, and it is archaeology that provides us with most everything we know about these people.

Harappan Civilization

The Harappan civilization seems to have begun around 2500 B.C., and it flourished for about 500 years. It possessed the characteristics we have come to expect from a complex society, including monumental architecture, urbanism, elites, craft specialists, and a form of writing.

The architecture of Harappa and Mohenjodaro suggest that centralized planning was involved. Both cities are laid out in a grid-like fashion, with streets and buildings arranged neatly at right angles. Houses and public buildings that have been excavated show a certain sophistication in their design. Many houses contained bathrooms, and a drainage system ran beneath the cities, complete with manholes for maintenance.

The agricultural foundation of the Harappan civilization was based on barley and wheat, and the inhabitants kept cows and a few other domestic animals, including chickens, goats, and pigs. They grew cotton, too—the earliest civilization known to do so.

Diggers

Sir Mortimer Wheeler (1890–1976) could be featured in several different chapters in this book. With a background as a British military officer, he continued the development of precise digging methods. His work on sites in Britain and the Indus Valley is noteworthy. Apart from his field work, Wheeler wrote several books and was a popular public personality, especially as featured on British television.

World-Class Traders

It's clear that the Harappan civilization was heavily involved in trading. Among the products they had to offer were copper, gold, semi-precious stones, and finished goods. There seems to have been some sort of contact with Mesopotamia, either directly or through other peoples. The island of Bahrain in the Persian Gulf, known to the Sumerians as "Dilmun," might have served as an intermediary between the two, and Harappan artifacts have been found in Mesopotamia. In Akkadian, the word "Meluhha" apparently refers to the Indus culture. The Harappans also were engaged in long-distance trade with peoples in places such as Iran, Afghanistan, and Central Asia.

Some scholars have examined Harappan art and suspect that within the culture can be found the roots of the Hindu religion. There are depictions that might represent the early manifestations of various gods, and it's been suggested that there is a major religious component involving water. A large, impressively designed structure at Mohenjodaro has been interpreted as a bath that might have had a ritualistic purpose.

An Ancient Mystery

Where did the people of the Harappan civilization come from? And where did they go? These are both excellent questions with no firm answers. Prior to 2500 B.C., there is little evidence of emerging urbanism, so the civilization must have developed rather quickly. The idea of cultural inspirations from elsewhere has been suggested, as well as the idea that the civilization developed from the indigenous population, for whatever reason. One reason it's a difficult thing for archaeologists to study is because the high water table at some of the Harappan sites makes it difficult to explore their earliest layers.

After 2000 B.C., the big cities of the Indus Valley civilization were essentially abandoned, and the Harappans seem to fade out of the picture. Early ideas attributing this disappearance to catastrophic floods and Aryan invasions no longer appear credible. It's a bit of a mystery. There is certainly a great deal that we don't know about this interesting civilization.

Jargon Unearthed

The name Mohenjodaro means "Mound of the Dead Men." It's not a Harappan name, but one given to the city probably long after it was abandoned.

An example of the yet to be deciphered Indus script. (After Walter A. Fairservis, The Roots of Ancient India [New York: Macmillan, 1971], p. 274, No.4)

Welcome to China

Our second major center of ancient civilization in this chapter is China. The Chinese culture is one of the world's oldest. The area of China was settled by humans early on, perhaps 1.8 million years ago. Many fossils of *Homo erectus* have been found. From this early start, China developed into a huge power in the region and heavily influenced the early civilizations of such neighbors as Japan, Vietnam, and Korea.

Map of China showing some of the sites of archaeological interest.

Real Cave Men

I wasn't going to dwell too much on this caveman stuff, but this example is too interesting to pass up. Between 1928 and 1937, some caves at Zhoukoudian near Peking (a.k.a. Beijing), China, were excavated. The work turned up the remains of about forty examples of *Homo erectus*, which were given the name "Peking Man." Along with the skeletons were found thousands of stone tools, animal bones, and evidence of the use of fire.

During World War II, the bones disappeared, presenting one of the great mysteries from the study of the past. Luckily, we still have casts of the bones that allow us to continue to study these excellent specimens.

During the Neolithic period, China can be roughly divided into two general regions, each featuring a major river. In the north are the fertile plains surrounding the Yellow River, and to the south is the Yangtze. Neolithic societies, beginning around 5000 B.C., grew millet and rice, and animals such as the water buffalo were domesticated. Eventually, a Bronze Age civilization would develop and dominate in the north.

The Early Dynasties

The first line of Chinese rulers is known as the Xia Dynasty (ca. 2000–1500 B.C.). Its existence was only known through tradition until recently, when archaeologists began to find what might be traces of this legendary dynasty.

The Shang Dynasty (ca. 1650–1027 B.C.) followed, and in it we find clear evidence of cultural complexity in its various facets. The Shang is especially known for the superb use of bronze, many wonderful objects of this material being discovered in the tombs of the elites. Warfare was apparently common, and there is plenty of evidence of human sacrifice.

Very importantly, writing also appears in China at this time. Curiously, most of these early examples of writing have survived on "oracle bones," which were used to answer questions magically. Questions were written on animal shoulder bones or on the bottom bits of a turtle shell, and fire was applied. The resulting cracks were then interpreted.

Lost and Found

In 1891, Dutchman Eugene Dubois discovered in Java, Indonesia, the first fossils of *Homo erectus* to be found in that region of southeast Asia. Unfortunately, there were no associated tools or other evidence of lifestyle. The later discovery of the Peking Man fossils helped us to fill in the gaps, but now those bones are missing!

Pitfalls and Pointers

Some of you might think that using burnt bones to tell the future is pretty strange. But when you think about it, it's not that far removed from reading a modern astrological horoscope. Everyone is interested in the future.

215

The Shang Dynasty was replaced by that of the Zhou (1027–221 B.C.). China grew during this time with an increasing population, the expansion of large walled cities, and sophisticated agricultural and irrigation practices.

The Qin Dynasty

The rulers of the early dynasties were not able to control all of China. Various little feudal kingdoms competed with each other during what is called the Warring States period (475–221 B.C.). After centuries of wars and feuds, China was unified under a single empire originating from one of the western states, that of Qin—thus the Qin Dynasty (221–207 B.C.).

The first Qin emperor, Qin Shi Huangdi (r. 221–210 B.C.), enacted unification measures that included the standardization of such things as the Chinese script, coinage, weights and measures, and the law. Roads and canals were built for commerce and control, and a great wall across the frontier was expanded. He also ordered the burning of most books in the year 213 B.C. and persecuted intellectuals.

The terra cotta army of Qin Shi Huangdi. (Courtesy of Superstock)

The Dead March On

In 1974, workers digging a well about a mile from the burial mound of Qin Shi Huangdi near Xi'an, in Shaanxi province, made a truly astounding discovery. Beneath the ground stood a nearly life-size artificial army, complete with soldiers, horses and chariots, and weapons. Made from fired clay, the Terracotta Army, as it is called, has been excavated from huge pits dug in the ground that were once roofed with logs.

Altogether there are over 7,000 figures and, amazingly, each one seems to be different, as if modeled after actual individual living soldiers. There are officers, cavalry men, archers, and hundreds of horses, and the army stands poised as if ready for action. The purpose of the Terracotta Army was to serve the dead emperor. The ceramic soldiers certainly last longer than the real ones.

Another series of vaults were found in 1990 near Xi'an and are associated with the nearby burials of the emperor Liu Qi (188–144 B.C.) and his wife. They also contain an army, but these painted ceramic soldiers are about 20 inches high, hollow, naked, and missing their arms. Perhaps they had originally been clothed and had wooden arms, both of which have rotted away. Once again, amazing individualistic detail is seen in these statues, which are still under excavation. When all are uncovered, it's possible that there might be tens of thousands, if not more.

Lost and Found

The immense burial mound of Qin Shi Huangdi has never been excavated. Legends say that it contains models of the Chinese world and the heavens and is booby-trapped. Perhaps as many as 700,000 laborers worked to build this huge burial site. The artisans who worked within the tomb are said to be sealed within in order to preserve its secrets.

As Seen from Outer Space: The Great Wall

They say that it is the only object of human manufacture visible from the moon. In my opinion, it belongs on an expanded list of the Wonders of the Ancient World: the Great Wall of China. The wall stretches 3,700 miles across the uneven terrain of northern China, serving primarily as a defensive structure.

The earliest parts of the wall were probably built during the time of the Warring States period and joined together during the succeeding Qin Dynasty (221–207 B.C.), and later enhanced during the Ming (1368–1644 A.D.). The wall was built by hundreds of thousands of workers and at a cost of many lives. Along with the wall itself were built numerous watchtowers in view of each other, many gates, and associated structures such as barracks for soldiers.

Pitfalls and Pointers

In China today, construction continues on the Three Gorges Dam. While the dam will ultimately provide flood protection, electricity, and other modern needs, hundreds of valuable archaeological sites will be submerged. Although there have been some salvage efforts, the sheer quantity of sites almost assures that many will be lost.

A section of the Great Wall of China. (Courtesy of Madeleine Lynn)

The Han Dynasty

A power struggle after the death of the first emperor of the Qin dynasty resulted in the establishment of a new dynasty, the Han, which lasted over 400 years (206 B.C.–A.D. 220) and set the stage for the next couple of millennia of Chinese cultural continuity.

Lost and Found

Confucius (551–479 B.C.) was a professional bureaucrat who advocated ethical, fair, and compassionate dealings in both government and in personal lives. His followers compiled collections of his sayings. Confucianism was especially popular during the Han Dynasty and the later Tang Dynasty (A.D. 618–906).

A professional civil service was maintained to sustain a large bureaucracy, and a university was established. Confucianism became the official religion during this period. The highly stratified society of this time included hard-working peasants, merchants, an extensive military, the bureaucrats, and aristocrats whose tombs reflect their wealth and power.

Opening the Imperial Tombs

Chinese rulers were routinely buried in spectacular ways, and the Han Dynasty was no exception. During the last few decades, several royal tombs from this time period have been opened. Let's see what was inside a couple of them.

➤ **The Original Lady Dai.** The Marquis of Dai, along with his wife and son, were buried in three pit tombs excavated by the Chinese in 1972 and

1973 at Mawangdui in Hunan Province. Although the tomb of the Marquis had been robbed, those of his wife and son were quite well preserved and yielded thousands of objects, including silk clothing, books, and lacquered boxes.

The body of Lady Dai is one of the best preserved mummies in the world. Buried in nested coffins and preserved in a solution of mercury salts, the body was virtually intact, with the skin still pliable. An autopsy revealed that she had badly clogged arteries and gallstones, which might have contributed to her death.

➤ **Jade Suits.** The Han tomb of Prince Liu Sheng (died 113 B.C.) and his wife Dou Wan were excavated in Mancheng in 1968. This tomb was carved into rock in the design of a simple palace and featured four chambers containing over 4,000 bronze objects.

Both Liu and Dou were buried in jade suits, each composed of over 2,000 flat jade plaques held together with gold thread. In China, jade was considered to have very special properties, including the ability to prevent the decay of bodies.

Pitfalls and Pointers

The Chinese were the first to make paper, and they can also be credited with a number of other important inventions, including printing with movable type, gunpowder, and the compass.

Writing It Down

You'll probably recall that the ancient Egyptians made a kind of paper out of the papyrus plant. Later on, especially in Europe, writing surfaces called vellum were often made at great expense from animal skins. The Chinese, however, might be credited with the real discovery of paper.

Diggers

Aurel Stein (1862–1943) was an archaeologist whose reputation was made by his exploration of the harsher and more remote areas of East Asia. Following the track of the old Silk Road and other ancient trade routes, Stein made numerous discoveries and retrieved thousands of ancient manuscripts and pieces of art, which he exported to Europe.

As the Chinese script developed and became standardized, strips of bamboo and perhaps occasionally silk became common for writing. The bamboo strips were connected together with strings to complete whole documents. Growing bureaucracies assured that many of the documents were quite unwieldy.

Lost and Found

Lots of frozen bits of the past have turned up in Siberia, including several mammoths from the Pleistocene. A few of these elephants have survived sufficiently intact that scientists can examine their internal anatomy and even determine what they had for their last meals. And as dogs and a few humans have found out, sometimes mammoth meat is still edible after thousands of years.

Paper in China seems to have been invented during the Late Han Dynasty (A.D. 25–200) and was manufactured from the bark of the mulberry tree combined with the pulp from rags and other fibrous substances. Its utility was obvious, and the idea gradually spread. Apparently the technique for manufacturing this paper made its way to the West when some Chinese were captured by Muslims in A.D. 632.

White Folks in the Desert

In the westernmost province of China, Xinjiang, some amazing discoveries are being made. Here in this arid region have been found numerous burials that have produced wonderfully preserved natural human mummies. So what's so amazing? They seem to be white folk, Caucasians, and some are four thousand years old! Some of the mummies have blond or brown hair and sport tattoos, and their clothes, of wool and leather, are likewise in fine shape.

So what's going on here? There doesn't seem to be a mistake. These people are apparently indeed Caucasians related to others out west. Perhaps they were part of a trading network between East and West. It's possible that this discovery could seriously challenge the long-held notion that China developed in isolation. There's certainly a need for a lot more scientific work to sort all of this out!

It's Cold Up There

While we're on the subject of well-preserved tattooed dead people, let's take a brief side excursion to northern Asia, where some extraordinary discoveries have been made. Up north near the border between China and Mongolia lies a grassland area in the Altai mountains of Siberia which was home to nomadic herders. Low mounds have been found which typically contain the frozen burials of their elite, dating to around 400 B.C.

The mounds cover shafts with wooden chambers at their bottom, containing bodies in log coffins along with grave goods such as clothing, textiles, ornaments, and objects of wood and leather. And because they are frozen, just about everything is well preserved. In some cases, up to fourteen horses were buried along with the humans. Some of the textiles suggest some sort of communication with such places as China and Persia.

"Lost" Cities in the Jungle

After the cold and arid regions of the north, it's time to warm up and take a quick look at some great ruins in Southeast Asia! Among the more enduring romantic images from the world of archaeology are the jungle-clad ruins found up the Mekong River in Cambodia. And though they seem like they'd make great fodder for a classic discovery in archaeology, they are neither particularly old nor particularly lost. This huge sprawling complex of architecturally-sophisticated sites includes Angkor Thom and Angkor Wat, one being a palace complex and the other a nearby temple.

The founder of Angkor was the Khmer ruler Jayavarman II (A.D. 802–850). The beautifully ornate stone structures at the site were heavily influenced by both Hindu and Buddhist religious art and architecture. Angkor Thom, a great walled city with five gates and surrounded by a moat, served as the royal Khmer palace. It was abandoned around 1432, after it was threatened by the neighboring Thais.

Although the temple of Angkor Wat continued to be used, both sites fell into great disrepair, and the surrounding jungle encroached. A few reports by Portuguese visitors of a beautiful and mysterious city in the jungle were known in the West, but Angkor never became well-known until the French zoologist Henri Mahout (1826–1861) visited in the late 1850s. Not surprisingly, given the times, many examples of superb statuary and bits and pieces of Angkor ended up in Europe.

Lost and Found

In Thailand, archaeologists have excavated a fascinating, deeply stratified site that reveals 4,000 years of development. The site of Ban Chiang began about 3600 B.C. and was home to rice cultivators. Very controversial is a date which seems to indicate that the people of Ban Chiang were practicing bronze metallurgy in 2000 B.C.: earlier than in China!

Angkor Wat. (From L. Delaporte, Voyage au Cambodge *[Paris: Libraire Ch. Delagrave, 1880])*

Under French supervision, a program of restoration was initiated, and tourists began to flock to the area. Angkor has since been intermittently accessible, depending upon the fluctuating political situation in Cambodia. The immense size and complexity of the structures, however, dictate that maintenance and restoration will be required for decades in order for these incredible monuments to survive.

The Least You Need to Know

➤ Asia has a tremendous variety of important archaeological sites.

➤ The Indus Valley was home to a sophisticated early civilization.

➤ The creative Chinese civilization still continues after 3,000 years.

➤ Recent discoveries in China have revealed the grandeur of royal burials and mysterious mummies on the desert frontier.

➤ The "lost" temples and palaces of Angkor were never really lost, but are nonetheless a stunning reminder of the old Khmer civilization.

Part 5
The New World

What's so new about "the New World"? Not much; it's been around for millions of years, just like the other continents. Nothing new about the people either; humans have lived there for over 12,000 years. In fact, when Northern Europeans were hard at work tilling the soil, great civilizations were beginning to brew in places such as southern Mexico and Peru.

Most of Europe first became aware of North and South America during the time of Columbus, and even so, they initially weren't sure what had been "discovered." They thought they had reached Asia! It finally dawned on them that here were continents of which they were unaware. The name "America" was bestowed upon them after a printer coined the name for a secondary Italian explorer named Amerigo Vespucci (1454–1512) and published maps using the name in 1507.

The explorers of the Americas and the Pacific islands were amazed to find millions of people whose ways they certainly didn't understand, and some of the results were tragic. Archaeologists and historians, however, have set a lot of the record straight, and in the next three chapters, we're going to explore some of the many ancient cultural wonders of the so-called New World.

Chapter 19

Archaeology in Paradise: The South Pacific

In This Chapter

➤ Exploring the giant Pacific

➤ Where did the Polynesians come from?

➤ Polynesian seafaring excellence

➤ The big stone heads on Easter Island

When European explorers ventured out into the Pacific, they were surprised to find people living on nearly every habitable island. Some of these islands were separated by thousands of miles of ocean, yet most of these people spoke similar languages, and their cultures had much in common with each other. In places such as Tahiti, Hawaii, and Tonga, the explorers encountered highly developed societies supporting thousands of people, ruled by great chiefs. It took about 300 years for Europeans to visit most of these many islands in a region of the Pacific called Polynesia.

The Great Ocean

The Pacific Ocean is the largest single geographical feature on the face of this planet—larger than the Atlantic and Indian Oceans combined and greater than all the earth's combined land surfaces. Geographers have divided the islands of the South Pacific into three primary groupings based on geographical, cultural, and human physical factors: Micronesia, Melanesia, and Polynesia.

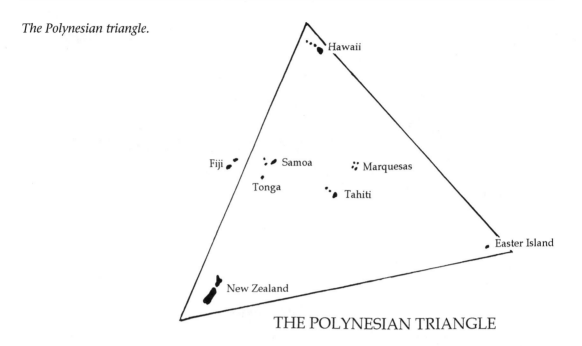

The Polynesian triangle.

THE POLYNESIAN TRIANGLE

Micronesia (literally "the small islands") consists of numerous small islands, including Guam and the Caroline, Marshall, and Gilbert Islands. To the south and just east of the Indonesian area is Melanesia (literally "the black islands"), named for the dark skin of many of its inhabitants.

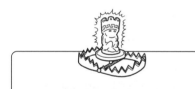

Pitfalls and Pointers

Some modern scholars have criticized the division of the Pacific Islands into three groups, considering it artificial and not completely accurate. At the same time, the terms have been in use for so long that they're probably here to stay.

Melanesia includes New Guinea, the Solomon Islands, New Caledonia, New Hebrides, and the Bismarcks. And to the east, we find the area of our special interest, Polynesia ("many islands"), whose primary cultural borders form a triangle with Easter Island, Hawaii, and New Zealand at the corners.

The Polynesians

It's hard to characterize the Polynesians because the various cultures developed somewhat differently on each island. We can try to make a few generalizations, however. The Polynesians spoke, and still speak, related languages that are part of the greater Austronesian language family. They were obviously great masters of the sea, having reached islands as widely separated as Hawaii, Easter Island, and New Zealand.

Island Bounty

The Polynesians practiced agriculture, growing sweet potatoes, taro, and yams, and on many of the islands pigs, chickens, and dogs were kept and eaten. The sea provided fish and shellfish, and the land offered breadfruit, coconuts, and many other useful plants.

Tools were made from stone, wood, bone, and shell, and many of the Polynesians were masters of their crafts. Images of gods were produced from wood and stone, and great canoes were expertly carved from logs, with sails made from beaten bark cloth.

Canoes and Kings

When Captain James Cook (1728–1779) visited the Hawaiian Islands in 1778, he was greeted by thousands of people and hundreds of canoes. As in Tahiti, he found a culture that we could arguably rank as a complex society but for the absence of writing.

There were chiefs, nobles, warriors, farmers, and artisans in this socially ranked society. Monumental architecture was found in the great stone temple platforms built to serve the gods, and on Easter Island hundreds of immense statues were carved. These were indeed sophisticated cultures.

The Europeans Venture Out

Western knowledge of the Pacific began in 1513, when the Spanish adventurer Vasco Nuñez de Balboa climbed the heights of the Isthmus of Panama and sighted the vast waters of the Great South Sea. To say that Balboa "discovered" the Pacific Ocean would, of course, be inaccurate. Actually, its western Asian border had been known to Europeans for some time. However, its size was unknown, and it would remain for intrepid navigators to explore what might lie between the two continents in the huge expanse of water.

The process began in 1522 with the bold expedition of Ferdinand Magellan, who set out westward from Spain in five ships to circumnavigate the globe in an attempt to find a route to the Spice

Lost and Found

Although Captain Cook is generally credited with being the first European to visit the Hawaiian Islands, there were reports that some of the islanders already had pieces of iron. It has been suggested that a Spanish ship may have visited or been wrecked at a previous time. It's possible. Not every ship that ventured into the Pacific returned!

Lost and Found

The first encounters between the Polynesians and the Europeans were occasionally unpleasant and sometimes ended in violence. On some islands such as Tahiti, the islanders were especially hospitable, and in return, their European visitors gave them the gift of venereal and other diseases, along with metal nails and tools and other trade goods that quickly changed some of their traditional ways.

Islands in the western Pacific. The expedition sailed quickly through Polynesia, passing one of the islands in the Tuamotu archipelago.

Subsequent Spanish expeditions continued to explore the Pacific, and in 1595, the first contact was made between Westerners and Polynesians. During the seventeenth to mid-eighteenth centuries, the Dutch and the English in particular would encounter such places as New Zealand, Tahiti, Easter Island, and Hawaii.

Helmeted Hawaiians in canoes paddle out to greet Captain Cook. (From James Cook and James King, Voyage to the Pacific Ocean *[London, 1784])*

The Original Polynesians

So who were these people spread out all over the eastern Pacific? From where did they come, and how did they get there? Speculation regarding the origins of the Polynesians began early, with various theories during the eighteenth and nineteenth centuries arguing homelands in the west, east, and elsewhere. Here are just a few of the places that were suggested: the East Indian Islands, India, Madagascar, Egypt, the Mediterranean, North Africa, the Americas, and "the lost continent of Mu."

Pitfalls and Pointers

Because of the light skin often found among the Polynesians, some theorists offered bizarre theories about their origins, such as that the Polynesians were "Alpine Caucasians" or part "Aryan."

Let's Start Digging!

As the twentieth century progressed, increasing anthropological and archaeological evidence produced more refined theories. In the 1950s scientific excavations in the Pacific contributed much to the study of early Polynesia.

Prior to this time, the general feeling was that there were few sites of any depth to be found there and that such efforts would be a waste of time. Excavations in such places as Easter Island, Hawaii, New Zealand, and the Marquesas, however, proved quite the opposite. Indeed, their results stimulated a new age of Polynesian archaeology.

In contrast to the earlier confusion of ideas about the origins of the Polynesians, the results of archaeological and other new approaches during the latter half of the twentieth century brought agreement among many scholars. Most now believe that the Polynesians have their origins in the western Pacific from among a group that has been given the name "the Lapita people."

You Will Know Them by Their Pots

The ancient Lapita people became known after the discovery of archaeological sites in the Pacific which contained a distinct decorated pottery style. The pottery was first found in western Melanesia, and later in Tonga and Samoa in western Polynesia. Sites with Lapita potsherds date in various places as far back as 1600 B.C. and continue up to the first century A.D.

Lapita pottery was also found in Fiji, dating to around 1300 B.C., and in Samoa from around 1000 B.C. The location and age of the Lapita sites, from Melanesia into western Polynesia, suggested that there was a colonization of islands by the Lapita people moving from west to east.

In the 1960s, ideas about the Lapita as the source for the Polynesian people grew, along with the continued excavation of archaeological sites. And beginning in the 1970s, there was a growing interest in uncovering the lifestyle of the Lapita people themselves. The Lapita were apparently village-dwelling fishermen and horticulturists, who maintained trade relations by sea with their island neighbors near and far.

In the mid-1960s, a basic framework for the human colonization of Polynesia was proposed, and here's how it went:

➤ Lapita colonists from Melanesia established themselves on Tonga and Samoa around 1000 B.C.

➤ During the next approximately fifteen hundred years, proto-Polynesian society developed on these western islands.

➤ The process of colonizing Eastern Polynesia would began within a century or two on either side of the beginning of the first millennium A.D.

➤ The Marquesas Islands were the first group in Eastern Polynesia to be colonized (ca. A.D. 300) and would serve as a dispersal point to further groups of islands including Hawaii (ca. A.D. 500), Tahiti (ca. A.D. 600), and Easter Island (ca. A.D. 400).

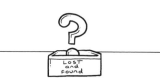

Lost and Found

The use of radiocarbon dating added a new dimension of time to the study of prehistoric Polynesia. Previously, scholars had to rely mostly on local traditions and genealogies, artifact styles, and linguistic speculations to get an idea of age in the islands.

Pitfalls and Pointers

Although pottery with Lapita designs has been found in Western Polynesia in such places as Tonga and Samoa, there is no such pottery to be found in Eastern Polynesia in such places as Hawaii, Easter Island, or New Zealand. So if the early Polynesians were derived from the Lapita, what happened to their pottery skills?

Pitfalls and Pointers

Most scholars dismiss out of hand the idea of a Pacific Northwest origin for the Polynesians, but the fact remains that it has yet to be tested scientifically. In the next few years, it's hoped that DNA and other studies will be conducted in the Pacific Northwest to see if there might be any connection.

➤ The Societies Islands (including Tahiti) in turn would also serve as a dispersal center for further colonization of Hawaii (ca. A.D. 1200) and also of New Zealand (ca. A.D. 800–1000).

After three more decades of study, the original Lapita theory has shown some problems. For starters, there are certain important areas in Polynesia where excavations have yet to be done, so it might still be a bit premature to construct grand scenarios such as the one described above. Moreover, some scholars argue that Polynesia was settled much later than proposed, while others are arguing the opposite. Even the role of the Lapita is being questioned. Could not the islands have even been settled several times from different places?

American Indians in the Pacific?

One of the most controversial ideas around is that the Polynesians may have come from Southeast Asia by way of the Americas. In 1952, the Norwegian scholar and explorer Thor Heyerdahl published a book called *American Indians in the Pacific*, in which he pointed out dramatic similarities between artifacts and cultural practices in the American Pacific Northwest and in Polynesia, especially New Zealand. In both areas are found similar canoes, plank houses, memorial poles, canoes, weapons, and so on.

Heyerdahl's idea is that rather than fighting the usually opposing winds and currents straight across the Pacific from Asia to Polynesia, the people who would be the Polynesians followed the northern Japan current, which whips by the American coast before proceeding out toward Hawaii. After settling in the Northwest, they later migrated into the Pacific and spread out to the islands from there.

Heyerdahl points to two interesting facts to support the possibility of his ideas: Many Asian ships have drifted with the current to the Pacific Northwest, and the Hawaiians are known to have built some of their biggest canoes from Northwest logs washed up on their beaches. If its possible for logs, why not people?

Hey, Sailor

Nearly everyone agrees that the Polynesians were great sailors and navigators. But not everyone agrees on how they managed to get out to all those islands so successfully. Some say that the odds of sailing out into the ocean and finding a remote island like Easter Island are quite small, and that the colonization of Polynesia in general must have involved a great loss of life as canoes full of people sailed into the unknown. Others strongly disagree and argue that the Polynesians were honed navigators who intimately understood the oceans. With such skills, they would be able to determine when an island was near and how to make return voyages.

Sailing Like They Used To

In 1976, an expedition set out to test Polynesian sailing and navigational abilities in a replica of a Hawaiian sailing canoe. The canoe was named the *Hokule'a* and was successful in crossing from Hawaii to Tahiti and back again, a distance of about 3,000 miles each way. The stars, clouds, waves, and other natural phenomena were used to chart their course, and since then, the *Hokule'a* has made additional voyages in the Pacific.

Jargon Unearthed

The highly influential Polynesian scholar Peter Buck referred to the Polynesians as the "Vikings of the Sunrise," in tribute to their great navigational skills.

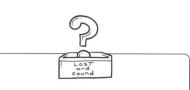

Lost and Found

The voyage of the *Hokule'a* became a symbol of pride for the Hawaiian people, who see it as an affirmation of their ancestors' abilities. The canoe has been celebrated in song, dance, and art.

Island of the Big Heads

We've talked quite a bit about the wheres and hows of the Polynesians in general. Now let's take a look at one of the most unusual islands in the region.

On Easter Day, 1722, the expedition of Dutch navigator Jacob Roggeveen (1659–1779) encountered an island in the Pacific hitherto unknown to Europeans. Easter Island, or "Rapa Nui" as it is called in the native language, was home to one of the most unusual cultures on the planet. Located approximately 2,400 miles from South America and 1,260 miles from the nearest populated island, Rapa Nui has often been described as perhaps the most isolated inhabited place on earth.

During his brief visit, Roggeveen noted hundreds of colossal stone statues, weighing many tons and standing atop impressive stone platforms. These statues, or *moai*, have come to serve as a symbol of Easter Island and its many mysteries: puzzles that have fired the imagination of explorers, travelers, and scholars for over 250 years.

Despite years of study, scholars are still not in agreement concerning many of the island's fascinating questions. Who are the people of Rapa Nui, and where did they come from? Why did they carve the *moai*, and how did they manage to transport these large heavy statues from their quarries to areas miles away? Why did the statue carving cease? What's with the other curious aspects of their culture, and what became of the Rapa Nui civilization? Let's talk about the big heads first.

Diggers

In 1914–1915, the English expedition of Katharine Routledge carried out the first scholarly survey of Easter Island and was followed by a Franco-Belgium project in 1934–1935. The Norwegian Archaeological Expedition in 1955–1956 laid the foundation for international archaeological work that continues to this day.

The Heads

The *moai* are legless stone statues in human form. The typical *moai* is male and has extended ear lobes, pursed lips, and hands with long slender fingers at the base of its rotund belly. Some bear decoration which may represent tattooing or simple clothing.

Jargon Unearthed

Moai is the native name for the famous Easter Island heads.

The majority of the nearly 1,000 *moai* were quarried from an ancient volcano crater called Rana Raraku, probably between the years 1000 and 1500 A.D. Basalt hand axes were used to carve the *moai* in the soft volcanic tuff, and the quarry today still contains statues in many stages of construction. Although superficially identical, the *moai* were produced in many sizes and with a certain degree of variation. The largest statue remains unfinished in the quarry and is 65 feet long.

Jargon Unearthed

An *ahu* is a stone platform upon which a *moai* sits. A *pukao* is a red stone cylinder that sits upon a *moai's* head.

Once completed, the *moai* could be transported to stone platforms found primarily along the island's coast. These platforms, or *ahu*, were apparently special family or clan ceremonial places. Not all *ahu* served as foundations for *moai*, and some contained burials. Many of these platforms are in their own way as impressive as the statues themselves.

Moai might appear alone or in groups as large as fifteen, and were typically erected with their backs to the sea and their eyes inlaid with white coral and red stone. Some of the statues were topped with a heavy cylinder of a red scoria stone derived from a separate quarry. These cylinders, or *pukao*, might represent some sort of headdress or even hair. Most scholars today agree that the *moai* served to commemorate revered ancestors of high status and might have also served as part of their burial monuments.

A half-buried moai on Rapa Nui waits near its quarry to be transported to its ahu. (Courtesy of Dr. Rick Reanier)

Moving the Moai

One of the most fascinating questions regarding the *moai* is how these immense statues were moved for long distances across the island, often on uneven terrain. Island legends explained that the statues had walked to their various locations on their own.

Thor Heyerdahl's expedition in 1955 experimented with moving and erecting *moai*. They found that a statue could be pulled on a sledge by brute strength and then erected on a platform using levers and stones. Other scholars have more recently offered other ideas:

➤ Archaeologist William Mulloy's proposed method involves the *moai* being mounted face down on a sledge. A bipod mast is used for leverage in pulling the statue along the ground.

➤ Archaeologist Jo Anne Van Tilburg has argued that the *moai* could be moved relatively simply by using rollers. She has recently conducted experiments on a replica and found that dragging a statue fixed to a sledge across movable wooden rails works even better.

➤ Czech engineer Pavel Pavel has experimented with the idea that the *moai* could be moved vertically. By swiveling a *moai* with ropes attached to each side of its head, the statue could be made to "walk."

Some of the more imaginative ideas regarding the transportation of the *moai* include extraterrestrial technology and levitation, an aerial tramway from the quarry rim to the platforms near the coast, and volcanic force blasting the *moai* out of the quarry to the vicinity of their present locations.

Pitfalls and Pointers

Although it has been pointed out that some of the characters in the rongo-rongo script bear a superficial resemblance to the Indus Valley script, it should be remembered that the two cultures are separated in time by thousands of years.

Say It in Rongo-Rongo

Rapa Nui is the only Polynesia island that can boast an ancient script. The script, called *rongo-rongo*, was carved on wooden tablets and other wooden objects, fewer than thirty of which survive today. There are a number of theories about the script.

Some say that it's actually writing, while others argue that the characters are pictographs used to jog the memory of someone reciting chants. There have been several claims for the decipherment of the language, but most are unconvincing.

Who Were the Islanders?

Many scholars today accept the idea that the people of Rapa Nui were derived from Polynesian seafarers who colonized the island from the Marquesas or elsewhere, perhaps as early as A.D. 400. A few, however, argue that there was a South American presence on the island that explains many of the culture's unusual features.

Despite the strange nature of the *moai* and other features of the Rapa Nui culture, no scientist accepts the idea that Easter Island and its people are the remnants of a civilization that once thrived on a sunken continent. Furthermore, rumors in the tabloids to the contrary, the notion of extraterrestrial visitors or inhabitants is likewise unsubstantiated.

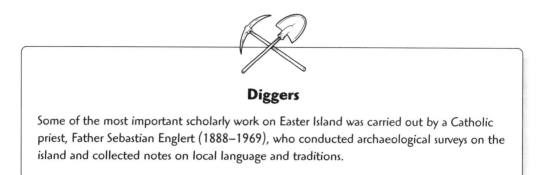

Diggers

Some of the most important scholarly work on Easter Island was carried out by a Catholic priest, Father Sebastian Englert (1888–1969), who conducted archaeological surveys on the island and collected notes on local language and traditions.

What Happened to the Rapa Nui People?

When the Europeans first explored Easter Island, the carving and movement of *moai* had already ceased. The islanders seemed to be living a fairly meager existence, and the land appeared relatively bare. But there must have once been substantial resources available to have managed such huge projects as erecting the moai. What happened?

Environmental Issues

Early explorers noted a profound lack of natural resources such as trees on Easter Island. The place was nearly barren. Growing evidence suggests that the ancient people of Rapa Nui may have initiated an ecological disaster through over-exploitation of the island's limited resources. Botanical evidence in particular shows that trees were once abundant on the island, and their disappearance seems to correspond with an increase in the *moai* building process.

In light of this possible misuse of resources, some scholars have offered the example of Easter Island as a metaphor for our world today. Isolated Easter Island can be viewed as a world unto itself, and the consequences of its environmental abuse might serve as lesson for all of us to heed.

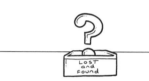

Lost and Found

An interesting Bird-Man cult flourished on Easter Island. One of their rituals involved an annual spring competition during which contestants climbed down a steep cliff to the ocean and swam to a small island in order to collect the egg of a sea bird, the sooty tern. The winner became the "Bird-Man" for the year and was confined and under restriction until his term ended. He retained high status for the rest of his life, however.

War and Europeans

Local legends suggest that there had been periods of inter-tribal warfare which could have led to the decline of the Rapa Nui culture. One famous story tells of a great battle between two groups which led to the virtual extermination of one of them. The early

European explorers noted that some *moai* were still standing in place perched atop their *ahu*. By the latter part of the 1800s, though, not a single statue remained standing; they likely having been pulled down by the islanders themselves.

The coming of Westerners to Easter Island would forever change its character. Peruvian slave traders carried off a couple of thousand islanders in the 1860's and the fifteen survivors who returned to the island brought smallpox. By 1877, the island's population was reduced to a mere 111, and many who knew the old ways had died or had been converted to Catholicism by missionaries.

In 1882 the island was annexed to Chile, and the population has since grown to several thousand people. A visitor to Easter Island today will find the Rapa Nui people to be warm, hospitable, and proud of their native heritage. It's a great place to visit, and there's plenty of *moai* for everyone to see, some of which have been re-erected on their *ahus*.

The Least You Need to Know

➤ Europeans who explored the Pacific were astounded to find people on almost every habitable island.

➤ Archaeologists are still trying to sort out the homeland of the Polynesians and when they might have arrived on the various islands.

➤ Easter Island (Rapa Nui) is one of the most unusual archaeological sites in the world.

➤ The moai of Rapa Nui are amazing creations, and the energy and skill necessary to carve and erect them is impressive.

➤ Controversy still surrounds such issues as non-Polynesian influences on the Rapa Nui culture, how the moai were moved, and the nature of the rongo-rongo script.

Chapter 20

The Ancient Cultural Mosaic of North America

In This Chapter

➤ Humans come to the New World

➤ Hunting bison and building mounds

➤ Making the best of the desert

➤ Living the good life in the Pacific Northwest

North America was and is home to an incredible variety of native cultures. As evidence, it's been estimated that several hundred different languages were spoken throughout the continent. In a land of great environmental diversity, clever humans filled a myriad of ecosystems, whether inland, on the coasts, way up north in the cold, or in arid desert regions. Where there was a niche, ancient Americans usually found a way to make a living there.

There are still a lot of ignorant ideas out there about the American Indians. One is that most were unsophisticated hunters and gathers. That's certainly not so! There were large areas of permanent settlements supported by agriculture, and a few places that you can argue were genuine complex societies, or nearly so. And as for the hunters and gatherers, they definitely knew what they were doing and probably lived a fairly bountiful existence. In this chapter, we're going to look at just a few of the groups of ancient Native Americans and some of the remains they have left.

Peopling the New World: Follow That Mammoth

When did humans first come to the New World, and from where? Who were these ancient immigrants? Many scholars used to think that we had it all figured out. That's no longer necessarily the case. Here's the standard scenario: The earliest Americans arrived from Asia by way of a land bridge connecting Siberia with Alaska during the Ice Age. This land bridge, which has been named *Beringia*, was exposed when sea levels were lower because water was trapped in massive glaciers. Beringia allowed Pleistocene animals to travel between the continents, and some have suggested that perhaps the earliest Americans followed big game such as mammoths across the bridge to the New World.

From Beringia, it would have been necessary to pass through an ice-free corridor between two giant ice sheets in order to enter non-glaciated territories to the south. Once through, the hunters quickly spread out in all directions, moving as far as South America.

The Earliest Immigrants

Some of the earliest sites known belong to groups of hunters known as *Paleoindians*. We, of course, don't know the authentic names of the early human groups in America; consequently, names have been assigned to them, typically after the sites from which they were first described. Both the Clovis and Folsom cultures are named after sites in New Mexico, and are distinguished by the style of their stone artifacts, particularly their projectile points.

The Clovis and Folsom peoples were big-game hunters, and their spear points have been found embedded in the remains of large prehistoric animals, including mammoth and bison. As you might recall from Chapter 5, some scholars have proposed that the entry of humans into the New World may have been the cause, or part of the cause, of the extinction of some of the bigger animals, who were plentiful, naive, and relatively easy to hunt.

Jargon Unearthed

Beringia is the name given to the land bridge in the Bering Straits said to have been exposed during the Ice Age, connecting Asia and North America.

Lost and Found

The camel and several other creatures are thought to have evolved in the Americas, where they later became extinct, although they are still found in Asia and Africa today. Relatives of the old camel are found in South America in such creatures as the llama and the alpaca.

The Age Barrier

The debut of humans in North America may have occurred between 11,000 and 12,000 years ago. Indeed, most of the earliest archaeological sites seem to date to this period. And it's a nice tidy story. It's not that simple, however. There are a number of archaeological sites that appear to be much older than 12,000 years, although there's always been something a little suspicious about them. Questions about the dating, the context of the sites, or the nature of the artifacts are common. Here are a few that shake up everyone:

➤ The Meadowcroft Rockshelter in Pennsylvania has produced an early date of around 14,000 years B.P. There are even older dates, up to about 19,600 years ago. Contamination of the radiocarbon dates has been suggested, but given the care with which the excavation took place, it seems likely that at least the 14,000 B.P. date is probably sound.

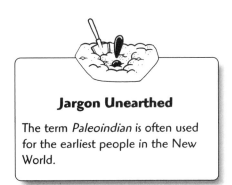

➤ Down in Brazil, the site of Pedra Furada has been dated at more than 40,000 years old. Debates have raged over whether the stone tools are real or merely natural, and whether the charcoal used for dating was produced by humans or nature.

Jargon Unearthed

The term *Paleoindian* is often used for the earliest people in the New World.

➤ At Monte Verde in Chile, an American archaeologist excavated a site found in a peat bog with some amazingly well-preserved items, including wooden artifacts, plant remains, and a human footprint. The site produced a controversial date of around 12,500 B.P. Of course, the date was questioned, but in 1997 a committee of prominent archaeologists visited Monte Verde, and all agreed that the site is indeed competently dated.

Monte Verde is causing a real stir. First, the 12,000 year barrier was broken. Second, why is there a site or sites in South America older than most of those found in the North? There are several possibilities. One is that some of the earliest sites in North America were either destroyed by glaciation or are 300 feet under water on the continental shelf. Perhaps the early hunters followed the coast, which was submerged when the Ice Age glaciers melted.

Another possibility is that they came by boat or kayak along the coast, thus allowing them to make quick progress toward the south. This idea, which was scoffed at twenty years ago, is now making a comeback. Some scholars are claiming that the Bering land bridge theory is defunct, and it's no secret that not everyone was comfortable with the idea of the ice-free corridor. With the Monte Verde breakthrough, the timing of early humans in the Americas is being reconsidered, and perhaps some of the other very early sites will be taken more seriously.

Who Were You?

With the date for the arrival of humans in the New World in question, let's see what we can say about the people themselves. It's generally believed that the New World people had their origins in Asia, as in the scenarios described above.

A study of native languages has suggested that there were three separate migrations, which can account for the diversity of people and languages we find in the Americas. But just as Monte Verde has recently caused a reassessment, the recent discovery of a very old skeleton has caused yet another sensation.

An Odd Skeleton

In 1996, a couple of guys wading along the banks of the Columbia River near Kennewick, Washington, stumbled across a human skull. When more bones were collected and examined by an archaeologist and a coroner, it was claimed that the skeleton belonged to a Caucasoid male in his forties.

A projectile point embedded in his hip suggested that perhaps he was a pioneer who had a run-in with the local population. The style of the projectile point, though, was very early, and when a radiocarbon test was made, everybody was stunned at the results: 8,400 +/– 60 B.P., one of the oldest human skeletons from the New World.

Family Squabbles

Found on federal land, the bones were subject to laws requiring that they be returned to native populations for reburial, and a big problem arose as several tribes filed claims. Even a group practicing an old pagan European religion claimed affiliation.

Archaeologists argued that the bones were probably not related to any known native group and that they were too special to be turned over without some very serious study first. After months of legal wrangling, the bones of "Kennewick Man" are currently being investigated by scientists.

So who is he and where did he come from? Stay tuned! There's bound to be some great stories coming out of all of this!

Diggers

In the United States, archaeology is considered a part of the broader field of anthropology, partly because cultural anthropologists often study the living descendants of the ancient peoples the archaeologists are pursuing. In many cases, these modern people can provide anthropologists with history or legends relating to the cultures and sites of old. Pre-European North America is also uncovered by excavation. Lacking verifiable cases of genuine writing that might provide some ready insights, American archaeologists work carefully at sifting through the most minute of evidence.

Spreading Out on the Great Plains

Whenever the first humans got here, whoever they were, they seem to have spread out as hunters and gathers and adapted to a variety of different environments. The tribes inhabiting the Great Plains are an excellent example. They found themselves in a territory with a huge population of buffalo, or bison, which became the mainstay of their existence; nearly every part of the animal was used for some purpose or another.

Bison are very dangerous animals, and one technique for hunting them was to drive them so as to cause them to run off the edge of a cliff. Several such sites have been found, one of the most famous being the "Head-Smashed-In" Buffalo Jump in Alberta, Canada. A thick deposit of bones along with stones tools was excavated there. The site was used off and on between 5,700 and 200 years ago. After horses and guns were introduced by the white man, the Indians were able to hunt bison in new ways, but much of their culture continued as it had for thousands of years.

Pitfalls and Pointers

It's common to refer to the American bison as a "buffalo," although this is an incorrect term. The bison is related to bovines such as cows, and not to the Cape buffalo of Africa or the Asian water buffalo.

The Mound Builders Pile It Up

If anyone has any doubts about the sophistication of the American Indians, just take a look at some of the incredible monuments found scattered by the thousands in the eastern United States. There, several groups we call "Moundbuilders" built earthworks that were often massive and complex in design, requiring lots of organized labor to move and pile up tons of dirt.

And if the mounds themselves somehow don't impress you, then perhaps their contents will. A good many of them were used for burials, and some contained objects of great artistic refinement, made of precious materials imported from long distances. Archaeologists have identified at least three major groups of Moundbuilder cultures:

➤ Adena: ca. 1000–200 B.C. The Adena were responsible for building thousands of mounds, mostly in the area of modern-day Ohio and Iowa.

➤ Hopewell: ca. 200 B.C.–A.D. 600. Mound sites of the Hopewell tradition are found in a wide area extending approximately from Wisconsin south to Louisiana and as far east as New York.

➤ Mississippian: ca. A.D. 700–1450. The Mississippian Moundbuilders were concentrated primarily in the Mississippi Valley, but extended to parts east and west as well.

It is in the Mississippian sites that we find immense mounds with flat tops that served as

Pitfalls and Pointers

At Effigy Mounds National Park in Iowa, 26 of the nearly 200 mounds found there are in the shape of bears and birds.

platforms for temples or for the residences of the elite. The Mississippian cultures engaged in extensive agriculture, with maize (corn) being the primary crop.

One of the most spectacular Moundbuilder monuments is a huge earthwork in Ohio called Serpent Mound, which is in the form of an undulating snake over 1,300 feet long. Although it was originally attributed to the Adena people, radiocarbon dates of A.D. 1070 suggest that it was built by one of the Mississippian groups.

The great Serpent Mound in Ohio. (From E.G. Squier and E. H. Davis, Ancient Monuments of the Mississippi Valley *[Washington: Smithsonian, 1847])*

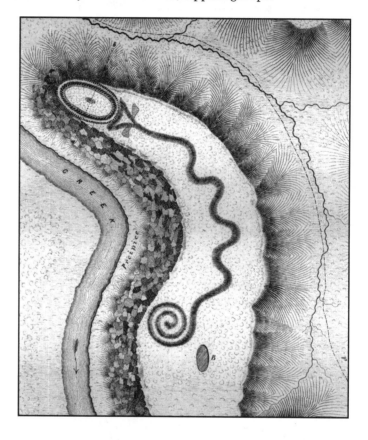

Cahokia: Meet Me Near St. Louis

Mississippian cultures show evidence of what might be a fledgling, or actual, complex society in North America, albeit without writing. Such is the site of Cahokia near St. Louis, Missouri. Cahokia is strategically located not far from where the Missouri and Illinois Rivers join the Mississippi, allowing it to serve as an important exchange center.

The area was used by agriculturists growing maize, beans, and squash between about A.D. 600 and 800, and then the small villages there together developed into the larger community that was Cahokia. At its height, more than 30,000 people lived there.

There are lots of mounds there, including some used for burials and boundary markers and others used as platforms for structures. The largest of this latter kind is called Monks Mound (some monks used to live there in the early nineteenth century) and is considered the largest prehistoric monument in North America. The mound is built up in terraces and was constructed from over 21 million cubit feet of piled-up dirt. The giant complex of mounds and plazas surrounding Monk's Mound was enclosed by a large wall.

Some of the Cahokia burial mounds give ample evidence of a social hierarchy with elaborate grave goods and, in some instances, the practice of sacrificing humans to accompany the deceased. Cahokia began to decline around A.D. 1250, while other large sites such as Moundsville in Alabama seem to take up the Mississippian slack.

Jargon Unearthed

The term *maize* can be a confusing one. Americans refer to this crop as corn, and the term maize is not widely used. In Britain, however, the word "corn" refers to wheat.

Confused Europeans Explain the Natives

Up until around the beginning of the twentieth century, there was a great deal of speculation about the mounds and the people who might have constructed them. The general theme was that the American Indians observed by the encroaching Europeans were basically incapable of producing such mighty works, and therefore some other people must have been involved. Perhaps there was an earlier "race of Moundbuilders" who were responsible, or an ancient group from Europe or the Near East. Anyone but the native Americans.

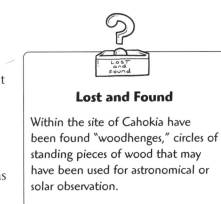

Lost and Found

Within the site of Cahokia have been found "woodhenges," circles of standing pieces of wood that may have been used for astronomical or solar observation.

This attitude of disbelief is unfortunately not an unusual one, and is probably linked to the old notions of the "inferiority" of "savages" in a presumed march toward "civilization." Add to that a big dose of racism, an attitude of cultural superiority, and a genuine sense of amazement. (Recall our discussion in Chapter 17 about the belief that indigenous Africans could not have built Great Zimbabwe.) Archaeological work has clearly demonstrated that neither Egyptians, Phoenicians, nor even people from Atlantis were responsible for the mounds. The industrious indigenous people built those things!

Making a Living in the Desert

Now let's switch our focus from the East to the West. The evidence indicates that Paleoindian hunters and gatherers were living in the American Southwest some 11,000

years ago, and this lifestyle persisted for many millennia. Although maize had been introduced from Mexico around 1000 B.C., it didn't become an important crop until the turn of the following millennium. At that time, small villages were established that were occupied all year round, indicating that agriculture was playing a larger role.

Several cultures developed in the Southwestern desert and thrived ingeniously for hundreds of years. Let's take a look at three of the most famous of them.

The Mogollon: Farmers and Artisans

The Mogollon lived in the eastern part of central Arizona and in the mountains of southeast Arizona and southwest New Mexico between about A.D. 200 to 1000. These people were not only farmers, but artisans as well. They lived in pit house dwellings that were partially excavated in the earth. This clever design produced a home that was warm in winter and cool in the summer. The Mogollon group known as Mimbres produced extraordinary painted pottery featuring fanciful human and animal designs. These pots are highly valued to this day.

The Hohokom: Making the Desert Bloom

The Hohokam lived in southern Arizona and parts of northern Mexico between about A.D. 200 and 1450. Unpredictable rainfall encouraged irrigation for agriculture in this arid terrain, and the desert provided its own special resources.

The site of Snaketown in Arizona is an excellent example of a nicely excavated Hohokam site. Snaketown was located near the Gila River, which provided water for irrigating maize. The site may have accommodated up to 1,000 inhabitants around A.D. 950 and included two courts for a kind of ballgame and some flat-topped mounds.

Two hundred years later, the site was nearly abandoned; by the time the Spaniards arrived a few hundred years after that, the Hohokam were gone. Why? No one knows for sure.

The Anasazi: Real Cliff Hangers

The Anasazi occupied the high plateau of the "Four Corners" area where the modern borders of Arizona, New Mexico, Utah, and Colorado come together. Permanent Anasazi settlements first began to appear around the second century A.D., and their settlements increased in size thereafter. Eventually large communities developed with adobe and masonry structures, some of the most prominent examples being in Chaco Canyon and Mesa Verde.

In Chaco Canyon, New Mexico, the site of Pueblo Bonita (built ca. A.D. 1000) contains a huge multi-story complex of over 800 rooms. It seems to have been a major trade center, especially for turquoise. For reasons unknown, the canyon was mostly abandoned by A.D. 1350. Drought might have played a role, but so might have soil exhaustion or erosion from environmental abuse.

At Mesa Verde in Colorado, the Anasazi built their dwellings in canyons on defensible cliff ledges and caves. They were able to grow crops in the canyon by collecting rainwater. The area was abandoned around A.D. 1300, perhaps because of drought. Over 10,000 sites have been identified in the area of Mesa Verde and some have estimated that the population may have once reached as high as 30,000.

Lost and Found

The dry climate and protective environment of the Anasazi cliff dwellings has allowed for extraordinary preservation of many of their artifacts. Baskets, in particular, have survived very well, as have human bodies, some of which were naturally mummified by the arid conditions.

Anasazi cliff dwellings at Mesa Verde. (Courtesy of Superstock)

Some of the trade goods and customs we find evidence of at these desert sites suggest that there might have been some contact with Mexico. There is little doubt, however, that these remarkable desert cultures were for the most part local adaptations to the environment at hand. Although these cultures are gone, desert life was never abandoned, and several major tribes continue to live in this area.

Diggers

Professional cowboy Richard Wetherill was searching for lost cattle in 1888 when he discovered the ruins of Mesa Verde. Although his initial efforts at retrieving artifacts were quite crude, he became sufficiently educated in the developing archaeological techniques in his day to become a fairly competent amateur archaeologist. He later moved on to Chaco Canyon and began excavations at Pueblo Bonito.

Living in Style in the Pacific Northwest

The Pacific Northwest was home to some truly fascinating cultures wonderfully adapted to a coastal environment. Fish were plentiful, as were marine mammals, shellfish, and seaweed. In the great forests, deer, elk, and other tasty mammals were generally abundant, as were berries and other edible plants. And of course, there were plenty of trees from which planks for homes and canoes could be made, as well as any other thing one might want to carve.

On the coasts of Washington and British Columbia, many groups thrived, and to some extent still do. Tribes such as the Nootka, Kwakiutl, Haida, Bella Coola, and Tsimshian built large lodges and erected ancestral "totem" poles. These people were quite sophisticated, and their hierarchical society included both chiefs and slaves.

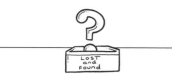

Lost and Found

One of the interesting cultural characteristics of some of the Pacific Northwest cultures is the "potlatch." During a potlatch, the host demonstrated his wealth and generosity by distributing a huge quantity of gifts to the guests. Hosts would try to outdo each other in succeeding potlatches, and the whole operation may have served to redistribute wealth among the people and to reinforce their personal prestige.

Ozette: There Goes the Neighborhood!

On the very northwest tip of Washington State is a coastal site called Ozette, which was discovered in 1970 when a big storm caused part of it to be exposed. Excavations there revealed yet another one of those natural disasters that so often prove a bonanza for archaeologists. Sometime between A.D. 1400 and 1500, a mudslide came down and buried five wooden houses.

The mudslide provided an effective seal from deterioration, and found there were a wealth of artifacts that would typically not survive long in the Northwest environment. Artifacts of wood and fiber products from this important whaling village, such as baskets and ropes, were well preserved.

Ozette is situated on the Makah Indian Reservation, and the Makah people today try to maintain their traditional culture, including the hunting of whales in the ocean in open canoes. The site itself can be reached today by a beautiful hike through forests and marshes and then along the beach. The Makah Cultural and Research Center, located at Neah Bay, houses the artifacts excavated from Ozette.

Diggers

Franz Boas (1858–1942) was one of the most influential anthropologists of all time. Apart from his important theories regarding culture, he conducted many years of fieldwork among the Indians of the Pacific Northwest coast. Boas was keen on recording all that he could of their culture while it lasted, including their language, history, and myths. He trained a whole generation of excellent scholars who followed in his footsteps.

Where'd They Go?

As we saw in the preceding sections, several groups of people have abandoned areas or seemingly disappeared without providing us with a clear explanation. It could have been a single dramatic event or the result of many factors, or we could even be looking at a cultural change rather than an actual disappearance.

It has been estimated that before the Europeans arrived, tens of millions of Indians populated various North American environments. Within a hundred years of Columbus's arrival, a huge number were dead—mostly from introduced European diseases such as smallpox, typhus, and the plague, for which they had little immunity. Some tribes were completely wiped out, while others suffered losses of up to 80 percent.

Lost and Found

Millions of bison roamed the Great Plains until the mid–nineteenth century, when a systematic government campaign was launched to wipe them out and thus deprive the Indian tribes of their livelihood. Millions of tons of meat were left rotting on the plains, and the bones were later collected and shipped east for use in fertilizer. Today the bison, nearly extinct, are making a comeback.

There is also the sad history of what happened to many of the tribes as colonization pushed west. It's not a pretty story, and much of it is not regularly taught. There was a lot of violence on many sides, along with a fair amount of betrayal and coercion.

The end result is that many tribes survive today on lands that in some cases are a mere fraction of their former territory. But on a happier note, many Indian groups continue to teach their languages and traditions, or have recently begun to do so. As interest grows with the younger generation, there's good reason to believe that some of these cultures will live on.

The Least You Need to Know

➤ The old notion that humans first arrived in the New World 12,000 years ago is being revisited. It's possible they were here much earlier.

➤ Native American groups adapted to a wide variety of environments.

➤ The accomplishments of the American Indians were commonly underestimated in the past, but archaeology has demonstrated the ingenuity of these peoples.

➤ Despite the events of the last few hundred years, the cultures of many Native American groups persist today.

Chapter 21

Viva Mexico!

In This Chapter

➤ The mysterious Olmecs

➤ Maya cities and glyphs in the jungle

➤ New World metropoleis

➤ The Aztecs come and go

South of the United States and north of South America is a region called *Mesoamerica*, which was home to several of the world's greatest ancient civilizations. The Olmecs, Maya, and Aztecs developed and declined there, leaving their ruins for archaeologists to ponder today. Great cities flourished in Mesoamerica, some of which were far bigger than most in Europe at the same time. We're going to examine a few of the most famous cultures from this region, and we'll start by taking a brief look at their agricultural foundation.

Civilizations Built on Maize

Agriculture was practiced in Mesoamerica by about 5000 B.C., with beans, squash, and chilies among the most important of many domesticated crops. By far the most significant of them all was maize, or corn. In Chapter 20, I mentioned maize as an important crop in much of North America, particularly in the Southwest and in the Mississipian culture. But maize came to those areas relatively late, after having been cultivated in Mesoamerica for several thousand years.

Map of Mesoamerica.

Jargon Unearthed

Mesoamerica is a term used to designate the area where complex societies were established from central Mexico south to El Salvador.

Jargon Unearthed

Swidden agriculture is a method for growing crops that involves the preparation of fields by first cutting down and then burning the over-growth. It is also know as slash and burn agriculture.

The origin of domesticated maize has long been a hot topic. How did it develop, when and where, and from which wild plant? A good candidate for its ancestor is a wild grass called teosinte. With enough selectivity on the part of humans, a nutritious productive plant might evolve relatively quickly, with numerous varieties that were tolerant of many different environmental conditions.

Once a plant like maize is domesticated, however, it requires a lot of care, and it can't be expected to survive on its own. The need to tend domesticated species probably played a big role in the establishment of permanent villages, many of which were found in Mesoamerica by 2500 B.C.

One of the common techniques used for agriculture in Mesoamerica is what is known as *swidden*, or slash and burn, agriculture. A part of the forest is cleared and burned to produce a field rich in organic substances. Crops are planted, and after a few years, when the soil is becoming exhausted, the process is repeated nearby in patchwork form. The process can be repeated when the earlier fields again become overgrown.

As you might guess, this process can consume a lot of land, especially if there are many people to feed! And with extensive agriculture, the foundation was laid for the development of complex societies, and develop they did.

The Olmecs: Stories in Stone

The earliest known complex society in Mesoamerica was that of the Olmecs, which thrived between 1200 and 400 B.C. The Olmecs lived in the swampy lowlands of the Veracruz area of southern Mexico near the Gulf Coast. Several centers of Olmec civilization have been partially explored, including the important sites of San Lorenzo, La Venta, and Tres Zapotes.

Much is still unknown about these people. Their ceremonial centers and stone carvings have survived, but it's not an ideal environment for the preservation of perishable goods, which, of course, account for most of what people used in daily life.

Pitfalls and Pointers

The name Olmec is actually of Aztec origin and means "people of the rubber country." We have no idea what the Olmecs actually called themselves.

Although a few examples of hieroglyphic writing, which may be a precursor to the later Maya hieroglyphs, have been found, there are not enough to attempt a good decipherment, so we can't even be sure what language they spoke. We do know, however, that they got around quite a bit. Olmec artifacts have been found in far-flung places, and many of the their favored materials, such as jade and obsidian, were imported from elsewhere. Much of what we think we know about the Olmecs has been interpreted from their artifacts, primarily those in stone.

Giant Heads

The Olmecs are probably best known for the giant roundish human heads carved from basalt and found at the principal sites. Seventeen of these heads have been discovered, some of which weigh up to 20 tons. Some were found 60 miles from where they were quarried! We're not sure exactly what these heads are all about, although many think they represent Olmec rulers.

Superficially, they look quite similar to each other, but there is enough difference in them to suggest that they could even be portraits of individual rulers. One scholar has pointed out that many of the heads appear to be recarved altars. It is possible that a king performed rituals at an altar during his lifetime, and that a portrait of him was carved from the monument upon his death.

The heads wear a kind of carved headpiece that has often been described as resembling an early 20th century American football helmet, and have facial characteristics that some have described as African. These characteristics have caused some to wonder if the Olmec civilization could have ties to the African continent, but this suggestion has been regularly dismissed (see Chapter 25). Skeptics will say that one needs only to look at the people living in the old Olmec area today to see a resemblance to the local population.

One of the big stone heads of the Olmec. (Courtesy of Superstock)

Baby Faces

The Olmecs not only carved giant heads, but also built a number of other things out of stone, including carved bench-like structures that may be altars or thrones. There are several known larger statues and lots of small figurines, some of the latter carved from nephrite and serpentine.

Lost and Found

Judging by its popularity as a motif in the Americas, the jaguar must have possessed some real mystique. It's a ferocious, cunning, carnivorous beast which is fast and strong—both feared and respected. Perhaps it was qualities such as these that inspired the awe and mythology surrounding this feline.

The jaguar figures prominently in Olmec art, as it does in the rest of Mesoamerica and South America as well. Apart from its depiction as a fierce cat, it was incorporated into a motif called the "weir-baby," a human baby with a jaguar head. Speaking of babies, the Olmecs also carved human figures in a style described as "baby-faced," with plump cheeks and other infantile features.

In examining what appear to be ceremonial portions of Olmec sites, archaeologists have made some fascinating discoveries. At La Venta, they uncovered an intentionally buried mosaic of a snarling jaguar mask made from large blocks of serpentine. In the same site, they've also uncovered little jade, serpentine, and sandstone human figures arranged as if in a diorama and then buried.

So if the Olmecs were the earliest complex society in Mesoamerica, a region in which several magnificent civilizations would arise, what influence did they have on those to come? This, of course, is a matter of great interest and debate. Some have characterized the Olmec as a "mother culture" which established a foundation for those that followed. On the other hand, perhaps the same factors that inspired the Olmecs in the first place were also at work elsewhere, in which case the ultimate Olmec contribution to later civilizations might have been a limited one.

The Maya: Highly Cultured

Down in southern Mexico, in an area including the Yucatan and extending through Belize and highland Guatemala to Honduras, was one of the largest and most sophisticated civilizations in the Americas: the Maya. Its status as a civilization is on a par with almost anything in the Old World, and its majestic ruins have commanded the fascination of colonists, tourists, and scholars over the last few centuries. The Maya may well be the most studied of all ancient civilizations of the New World. Unlike virtually all other cultures in the region, the Maya left a wealth of genuine written records in the form of hieroglyphic texts.

The Classic Period of Maya civilization extends from about 250 B.C. to around A.D. 900. During this time, large cities arose, led by powerful rulers who enacted religious rites at numerous temples. Maya society was stratified and well organized, with lots of farmers and craft specialists, merchants, and traders along with priests and members of the noble class. The rulers themselves were not only political leaders, but served as intermediaries to the gods and as military commanders. The Maya cities didn't always get along with each other, and violent conflict was not unusual.

Maya ruins as drawn by Frederick Catherwood. (From John L. Stephens, Incidents of Travel in Yucatan *[London, 1843])*

Tikal My Fancy

Many Maya cities still survive—at least the parts built in stone. Quite a few have been swallowed up by the tropical vegetation. Some have been cleared of the overgrowth, while others have barely been visited. The most elaborate, such as Tikal in the Petén region of the Guatemalan jungle, were huge ceremonial centers. There are five tall temples at Tikal along with ceremonial plazas, commemorative stelae, and the domestic remains of the supporting population, all covering an area of over 23 square miles. The stelae contain the names and dates of a long dynasty of rulers.

Pitfalls and Pointers

A kind of ballgame was widely played in Mesoamerica. Many of the larger cities there had long ball courts marked by two parallel walls. The goal was to knock a small rubber ball through stone hoops extending vertically from the walls. The hard part was that you weren't allowed to use your hands. The even harder part: It was not uncommon for the losers to be sacrificed.

The Pyramids of Palenque

In 1949, at the Maya city of Palenque, Mexican archaeologist Alberto Ruz made an extraordinary discovery. While excavating a structure known as the Temple of the Inscriptions, he discovered a hidden rubble-filled stairway leading deep into the interior of the structure. In 1952, the clearance of the stairwell was finally completed. At the bottom were a stone box containing some artifacts and the skeletons of six sacrificial victims. Beyond a sealed door lay a chamber containing a sarcophagus with a large, flat, sculptured lid.

Inside the sarcophagus, Ruz found the body of a Maya ruler. Prior to that time, it was believed that the Maya pyramids had served only as temple platforms and not as burial places. The skeleton wore a jade mosaic mask and had a good collection of jade jewelry and other objects. Hieroglyphs have identified him as the ruler Pacal. According to the glyphs, Pacal died in A.D. 683.

The End of an Era

Like most ancient civilizations, the Maya had their times of prosperity and decline. By around A.D. 900, most of the big cities in the southern Maya area had been abandoned. Several explanations for this, both simple and complex, have been proposed. These involve the usual factors—environmental abuse, overpopulation, warfare, etc. The answer is still not clear, and perhaps we will never know for sure. Some of the areas up in the eastern Yucatan peninsula, especially in Belize and Quintana Roo, seemed to hang on, some even up to the time of the Spanish.

Rediscovering the Maya

By the time the Spanish conquistadors arrived, the classical period of Maya civilization had been over for 600 years. The Spanish were intent on pacifying the various native groups they encountered; through missionaries, they also sought to convert them to Christianity, whether they liked it or not. One of these early missionaries, Diego de Landa (1524–1579), was both a curse and a blessing for future Maya studies.

On the one hand, de Landa is responsible for the burning of Maya books which, had they survived, might have given archaeologists much greater insight into Maya culture. On the other hand, he spent years writing down his observations of Maya lifeways. Most importantly, he recorded information that would later provide the key to understanding the hieroglyphs. His notes, which were eventually published in the nineteenth century, are a vitally important source, coming from someone who saw the last surviving elements of the ancient Maya civilization.

Lost Cities in the Jungle

During the few centuries following Cortes, Maya country had sporadic visits by Europeans; some of them wrote about the ruins, and a few artists attempted to capture the Maya ambiance in sketches and paintings. In 1839, an American travel author named John Lloyd Stephens and English architect Frederick Catherwood set off to visit Maya sites in Mesoamerica.

One of their stops was the old city of Copán in western Honduras, which Stephens purchased for fifty dollars. Stephens took notes on what they saw, while Catherwood made sketches. The book they published in the aftermath of their journey would prove to be a real inspiration to the study of ancient Maya civilization. A second trip by the two beginning in 1841 was equally productive.

Lost and Found

While anchored in the Gulf of Honduras during his fourth voyage to the New World in 1502, Christopher Columbus encountered a Maya canoe carrying native captives. The Indians were welcomed aboard and gifts were exchanged. One can only guess at the incredible stories the returning Maya had to tell of these bearded people on their unusual boats!

Diggers

John Lloyd Stephens (1805–1852) had already published books on his travels in the Near East and Europe before he ventured to Central America. His adventures with Frederick Catherwood (1799–1854) were a crowning achievement and were made public in *Incidents of Travel in Central America, Chiapas, and Yucatan* (1841) and *Incidents of Travel in Yucatan* (1843). Catherwood, too, was quite the traveler, having visited and sketched most notably in Egypt and elsewhere in the Near East.

Many adventurers, tourists, and scholars followed in the wake of Stephens and Catherwood, and in later years some would bring cameras. The archaeological study of the Maya began to develop rapidly in the late nineteenth century with expeditions large and small. The field of Maya studies is alive and well today, with archaeological excavations at several sites and modern methods being applied to the data.

Deciphering the Glyphs

One of most exciting areas of Maya research today is in the decipherment and reading of the Maya glyphs. For a long time, the exact nature of the glyphs was not understood. Was it picture writing, phonetic, or both? The fact that many of the inscriptions contained calendar dates was realized early on, but the glyphs could not be readily read as texts.

Over the last few decades, tremendous breakthroughs have been made in understanding. We can now read some 60 percent of the glyphs, which has lead to the decipherment of many texts. The texts often recount the deeds of rulers, including their births, military exploits, dates of accession, and rituals performed. Many of the more mundane texts, such as those painted on ceramics, merely say, "this is Bob's chocolate pot." Among the most impressive texts are four surviving Mayan books that document the extraordinary astronomical knowledge of the ancient Maya, including the cycles of Venus.

Diggers

Linda Schele (1942–1998) was one of the foremost Maya scholars ever. She was well known for her work with Mayan hieroglyphs and her interpretation of Maya culture and history. Her untimely death is a great loss to ancient studies.

Teotihuacan, Tula, and Toltecs

Twenty five miles north of modern Mexico City stand the remains of one of the largest cities in the ancient New World. Teotihuacan began relatively humbly around 100 B.C., and at its height, around A.D. 600, it accommodated a population of perhaps 200,000 people.

The city was obviously well planned, with its buildings and streets arranged on a grid. One of the largest single structures in the Americas is found there, the huge pyramid known as the Temple of the Sun, accompanied by the smaller but still imposing Temple of the Moon.

Teotihuacan was a complex trade and manufacturing center. It took years for archaeologists just to make a map of the place, with its myriad workshops, apartment buildings, plazas, temples, and administrative centers. After A.D. 600 the site went into decline and around A.D. 750 it was burned to the ground, probably by people from another city, perhaps Cacaxtla. Weakened perhaps by environmental exploitation or ineffective government, the site was a prime target for conquest. Some think that Teotihuacan had a lock on trade and was taxing people too much. The warriors from Cacaxtla appear to have had some affiliation with the merchant class.

While Teotihuacan diminished, another group began to grow in the region. The Toltecs, based in Tula, became a strong and influential power between around A.D. 900 and 1200. Very militaristic, the Toltecs became legendary heroes to the Aztecs, who sought to emulate much of their culture, including the cult of Quetzacoatl, "the Feathered Serpent."

Although they exercised control over a good-sized area in the region of the Valley of Mexico, the Toltecs occasionally reached out to conquer such places as the Maya site of Chichén Itzá in Yucatan, where some of their monuments can still be seen. What happened to the Toltecs? Tula was abandoned around A.D. 1200, probably after being attacked.

Jargon Unearthed

Quetzacoatl was a god widely worshiped as "the plumed serpent." He was a favorite of the Toltecs and Aztecs. To the Maya, he was known as Kukulcan. Aztec ruler Moctezuma apparently thought Cortes might be Quetzacoatl coming back for a visit.

They Came from Atzlan

Along with the Maya, the Aztecs are the best-known civilization from Mesoamerica. And although you might have heard of their mighty empire, it still might surprise you that it existed for less than 100 years before it was wiped out by the Spanish!

The Aztecs had their own stories regarding their history. They claimed to have originated from a mythical place called Aztlan somewhere in northern Mexico. These people spoke a language called Nahuatl and migrated to the Valley of Mexico. According to their legends, one of their gods provided them with a sign telling them where to settle, and they did so, building their city of Tenochtitlan on an island in the middle of Lake Texcoco in A.D. 1325. Much of the city was built on the lake itself, with raised agricultural fields surrounded by canals. The city was massive, and at its height, there were perhaps 200,000 people living there.

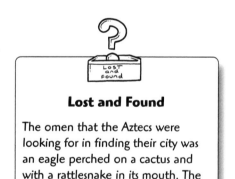

Lost and Found

The omen that the Aztecs were looking for in finding their city was an eagle perched on a cactus and with a rattlesnake in its mouth. The image is prominently featured on the flag of modern Mexico.

The Aztec Empire

A primary god and inspiration of the Aztecs was Huitzilopochtli, a war god. The fierce reputation of the Aztecs developed early as they fought their neighbors. But eventually, a triple alliance between Tenochtitlan and two other major cities was created in A.D. 1426 and formed the foundation of the Aztec empire.

Within less than a hundred years, the Aztecs had conquered much of central and southern Mexico in an area estimated to have included over ten million people. Tribute was demanded from the large variety of conquered people, making cities such as Tenochtitlan incredibly wealthy.

War was a virtue in Aztec society, and the warriors preferred to take their enemies back home alive. In order to sustain Huitzilopochtli, human sacrifices in great numbers were regularly required. It is said that during one particular celebration, over 20,000 people were sacrificed. The procedure was usually quite unpleasant, and often involved having one's heart ripped out while one was still living.

As savage as this might seem, the Aztec civilization had its refined qualities. It maintained a talented class of merchants adept at manufacturing goods from the many materials streaming in from the conquered peoples. There were artisans, and a form of literacy is seen in a kind of folding book made from birchbark paper. Although technically not writing, the books served as pictorial records and as memory joggers. Unfortunately, as would be the case in most parts of Mexico, such priceless records were routinely burned by the early Spanish clergy.

Pitfalls and Pointers

Do you like cocoa? You can thank the Mesoamericans for this popular beverage, which they enjoyed as much as we do today.

The Spaniards Shut Things Down

In 1519, Aztec ruler Moctezuma II (r. 1502–1521) was hearing reports of white bearded men arriving from the east, where the sun rises. He wasn't sure what to make of such a strange thing and couldn't rule out the possibility that this might be the god Quetzacoatl. Unfortunately, it wasn't. It was the Spanish conquistador Hernan Cortes (1485–1547) and several hundred soldiers looking for fortune. They found it when they entered Tenochtitlan, a city whose size and splendor overwhelmed the Europeans.

Cortes met Moctezuma and eventually took him hostage. There were scuffles and massacres, and the Spaniards had to escape from the city in 1520. When Cortes returned in 1521, he attacked Tenochtitlan with a vengeance. The city was blockaded, and tens of thousands died from starvation and a newly introduced disease, smallpox. That was the end of the Aztec empire.

Many people wonder how a relatively small group of Spanish soldiers could conquer the Aztecs. Many variables assisted the process, including better weapons, a confusion about who these strange Spaniards were,

Lost and Found

Both the Spaniards of the conquest and people today are appalled by the violence of the Aztec empire. At the same time, it can be argued that the Spanish conquistadors were not much better. They slaughtered thousands and were responsible for the deaths of hundreds of thousands, if not millions.

the terrifying sight of men on horseback (who were believed at first to be a single creature), and diseases. And the Spaniards were not alone. They were joined by a large number of angry native soldiers recruited from tribes and cities forced to pay tribute to the Aztecs.

Aftermath

The Spanish destroyed many of the Aztec monuments, and modern Mexico City is built on the ruins of Tenochtitlan. In fact, traces of the old city are occasionally found, as happened in 1978 when some utility workers digging a hole accidentally came upon the Great Aztec temple. Several years of digging followed and have provided wonderful information and artifacts from this site of worship and terror.

Although the official language of modern Mexico is Spanish and Roman Catholicism is the dominant religion, many of the ancient ways of life still continue. (Not the human sacrifices, thankfully!) A large portion of the Mexican population is composed of people whose ancestors were part of the great civilizations. There are Maya who still speak their old language, and dishes dating back to the time of the Aztecs are still cooked in small villages.

Today, scholars from many different countries have joined Latin American archaeologists in exploring the region's magnificent past. With entire ancient cities yet unexplored and advances in the decipherment of ancient scripts, we can be confident that there will be many exciting discoveries to come.

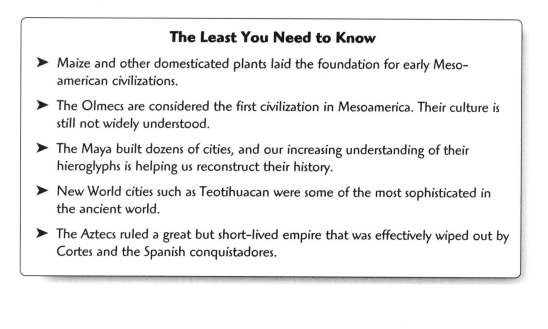

The Least You Need to Know

➤ Maize and other domesticated plants laid the foundation for early Mesoamerican civilizations.

➤ The Olmecs are considered the first civilization in Mesoamerica. Their culture is still not widely understood.

➤ The Maya built dozens of cities, and our increasing understanding of their hieroglyphs is helping us reconstruct their history.

➤ New World cities such as Teotihuacan were some of the most sophisticated in the ancient world.

➤ The Aztecs ruled a great but short-lived empire that was effectively wiped out by Cortes and the Spanish conquistadores.

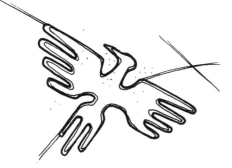

South America: Antiquities in the Andes

Think about ancient South America, and you probably think of the Incas, who maintained a mighty empire and were great builders in stone. You may even have heard of Pizarro, the Spanish conquistador who put an end to it all. The Incas get the majority of the attention, but just like the Aztecs, the Incan empire came and went in a period of about 100 years. And the Incas were real latecomers—civilization in South America had already been flourishing for about 4,000 years before the Incas made their big splash!

South America is host to a great range of environments: Jungles in the Amazon, deserts on the west coast, expansive grasslands, and who could forget the frigid land of Tierra del Fuego? In this chapter, we're going to look at just a few of the early civilizations that grew in the shadow of the Andes, the great mountain range forming a high spine from north to south along the western edge of the South American continent. There, ancient cultures flourished in the fertile highlands and coastal zones in such locations as modern-day Peru, Bolivia, and Ecuador, and in the arid deserts and high mountains.

The West Coast of South America, the land of the Andean civilizations.

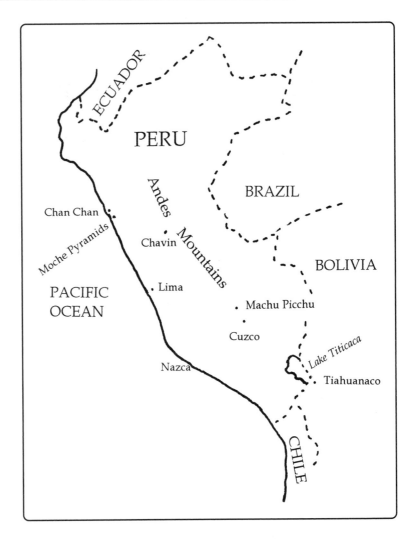

The Early Days

In Chapter 20, I mentioned some exciting discoveries at sites in South America, at least one of which, Monte Verde, has broken the 12,000 year barrier for the earliest human entry into the New World. You might also recall that Monte Verde and other ancient sites might provide additional evidence of far older human occupations.

Finding sites in South America that are much earlier than those in North America could lead us to revise some long-held beliefs about how the Americas were settled. Still, the idea of big-game hunting Paleoindians flowing down from the north holds a lot of currency, although travel by sea might also have played a role in the seemingly quick colonization of the continent.

The classic hunter-gatherer lifestyle seems to have predominated in many areas prior to the development of agriculture. Some new evidence from sites on the coast of Peru suggests that some of the earliest humans there may have been heavily exploiting the marine environment as well.

Adapting to Agriculture

Several features characterize the adaptive genius of the Andean civilizations. The way they developed agriculture is one, along with creative responses to the problem of irrigation in different environments. A number of different crops were domesticated and grown at different elevations, including potatoes, beans, squash, chili peppers, and in some places, maize.

Domesticated cotton was grown, providing the material for another cultural feature that developed to excellence: the art of weaving. Llamas were domesticated and served as sources of meat and beasts of burden; furry alpacas provided wool.

Early Birds

What we refer to as civilization, that is, complex societies, may have started earlier in the Andean region than anywhere else in the New World. At sites such as El Paraiso and Sechin Alto on Peru's desert coast, archaeologists have uncovered evidence of a complex society that predates the Olmec of Mesoamerica by about a thousand years! The sites date to 2500 B.C., and one of the sites, Sechin Alto, became a huge ceremonial center.

Pitfalls and Pointers

Archaeologists have categorized the pre-European Andean cultures with a series of time divisions called periods and horizons. We're not going to go into that much detail here, but it's nice to know that there's a good time framework in place to organize the study of this region.

Lost and Found

Guinea pigs were raised by the Incas as a tasty source of meat.

The Chavin Style

One of the earliest civilizations to develop in the Andean highland region is the Chavin (ca. 850–200 B.C.), named after the site of Chavin de Huantar in Peru. There, in a valley near two rivers, are found the remains of what appears to be a culture whose art, and presumably belief system, were widely influential during its day. The site stands on a route connecting the sea with the mountains, and there is plenty of evidence in Chavin of exchange between both areas.

The great temple at Chavin is U-shaped and features a 15-foot-tall standing stone stele of a "smiling god" that mixes both human and feline characteristics. The jaguar remained a common theme in Andean art. At Chavin there were also representations of other Amazonian jungle creatures that suggest cultural origins or influence from the other side of the Andes.

Diggers

German archaeologist Max Uhle (1856–1944) is considered the founder of South American archaeology. He first visited the continent in 1892 and thereafter conducted digs and studies in Argentina, Bolivia, and Peru. Through his study of pottery and textiles, he was able to establish a pre-Inca chronology for the Andean region.

The Artistic Moche

Many people agree that South American civilization reached its greatest artistic height in the Moche culture. The Moche commanded an area of the north coast of Peru for several centuries, beginning from about the first century A.D. The Moche are known for their massive building projects, outstanding ceramics, and mastery of metallurgy and jewelry-making. Their Huaca del Sol, or Pyramid of the Sun, stood 135 feet tall, and it's estimated that over 140 million adobe bricks were used in its construction.

Moche pots are desired by museums and collectors the world over. Most were formed in molds in a huge variety of shapes. Some pots are in the shape of people or portrait heads, some represent animals, plants, and fanciful creatures. Others feature painted scenes depicting episodes of daily life or mythological or symbolic imagery.

The Moche's work with gold, along with other metals and precious stones, was also highly refined. Unfortunately, the quality of their work has proven to be a disadvantage in the modern age, as both the pots and the jewelry have inspired thousands of tomb looters to plow destructively through Moche pyramids and graves.

Pitfalls and Pointers

The Huaca del Sol pyramid was excavated by early Spanish treasure hunters, who diverted the Moche River in order to hydraulically erode away the pyramid's adobe structure. Although much of the pyramid was destroyed, its internal structure was laid bare, allowing archaeologists to learn that there were eight stages in its construction.

The Lords of Sipan

In 1987, Peruvian archaeologist Walter Alva was asked to examine some artifacts that had recently been confiscated from tomb looters. The objects were of remarkable workmanship and their origin was traced to a site near the village of Sipan.

There, the robbers had discovered the first of several Moche tombs dating from between A.D. 100 and 500.

When Alva excavated these tombs, he found several intact royal burials—in effect, the Tutankhamun's tomb of Peru! The bodies of the rulers were encased in wooden coffins and bedecked in elaborate ornamental clothing, along with jewelry made of gold, beads, and other precious materials—much of it of a kind never seen before.

With the royal burials were found the bodies of both male and female sacrificed human retainers. The royal tombs of Sipan represent another great archaeological discovery, and thanks to them much has been learned about the upper crust of the Moche.

Destroyed by El Niño?

By A.D. 800, the Moche civilization was no more. What happened? Were they conquered? Although it's a convenient idea, the evidence in its favor is not overwhelming. One interesting theory is that the Moche were struck by a series of natural disasters that would probably undermine even the strongest of civilizations.

First came a devastating drought, then some earthquakes, which released sediments that clogged irrigation canals. The massive quantity of sediments traveling down streams and rivers into the ocean provided the material for coastal sand dunes to be created by the wind. And if that wasn't enough, the weather phenomenon known as El Niño occurred, radically disrupting the fishing and causing destructive floods. Ouch!

Chan Chan and the Chimus

Where the Moche once thrived, another talented group, called the Chimus, would develop an empire spreading along over 600 miles of coast. Their sprawling capital, known as Chan Chan, was established around A.D. 850, and was one of the larger urban centers found in the region.

Each Chimu ruler built his own large adobe brick palace and, upon his death, was buried in it. Ten of these palace/mausoleums were found at Chan Chan. The Chimus were one of the many groups conquered by the Incas and were incorporated into their empire around 1470.

Lost and Found

El Niño is a weather phenomenon occurring irregularly during which a southward-flowing warm ocean current displaces the usual northward flowing cold current. The effect can prove disastrous in places like coastal Peru, where fishing is disrupted and heavy rains can cause flooding. El Niño may have significantly influenced events in Andean civilizations, and its effects continue to be felt during modern episodes, most recently in 1998.

Pitfalls and Pointers

In 1953, an archaeological expedition led by Thor Heyerdahl discovered ancient South American pottery in the Galapagos Islands. The evidence suggests that seafarers on rafts or other craft visited the islands, which are located 600 miles from the continent's coast.

The Nazca and Their Lines

Down on the South Coast of Peru, another creative culture, the Nazca, developed at the same time as the Moche. Like their northern counterparts, the Nazca are known for their ceramic expertise and also for their weaving, which often survives well in this dry area. The Nazca were able to exploit the desert by the use of well-planned irrigation systems.

Jargon Unearthed

Geoglyphs are designs constructed in the surface of the earth, some of which are best seen from a distance.

Despite their many artistic achievements, the Nazca are best known for their construction on the desert floor of a vast network of straight lines and designs really best appreciated from the air. Some of the designs are geometrical, while others depict creatures such as a spider, a monkey, birds, and a whale. The Nazca lines and figures were produced by scraping aside the dark desert surface material to reveal the lighter sediments beneath. This kind of art on the earth has been termed *geoglyphs*.

Alien Runways

Given the unusual nature of the "Nazca lines," it's not surprising that many odd theories have arisen to explain them. One silly idea is that the lines served as runways for visiting alien spacecraft (see Chapter 24). Another proposal was that the Nazca possessed hot-air balloon technology, an idea tested by a couple of bold modern aeronauts in their version of such a craft.

Few if any archaeologists consider either of these ideas reasonable. The best explanation for the designs seems to be that these are ceremonial pathways, although recent research has suggested that the lines might actually point to sources of water! Alternatively, the animal figures might have been designed to be viewed by the gods, or as representations of constellations.

One of the giant designs created on the surface of the desert at Nazca. (After Anthony Aveni, ed., The Lines of Nazca *[Philadelphia: American Philosophical Society, 1900], p. 11, fig. 1.4e)*

Going Sailing

There's good evidence that Andean coastal civilizations, and those inland peoples who controlled the coast, were adept at seafaring—at the very least along the coast, if not further out in the ocean. Moche pots and adobe reliefs depict reed boats afloat, and model rafts and wooden steering boards have been recovered from graves.

Our best evidence is actual observation: In the early 1500s the Spanish noted large cargo-carrying rafts with sails. This aspect of ancient South American culture is rarely emphasized, but it's possible that seafaring might have played an important role in short- and long-distance trade and cultural exchange.

Highland Life

Around the time of the Moche, there were a couple of other major cultures up in the highlands. Centered on a high altitude plain not far from Lake Titicaca in Bolivia is the site of Tiwanaku. Tiwanaku seems to have been a major cult and pilgrimage center built over a period of several centuries.

Monumental architecture incorporating superb stonework prevails here. Despite its high altitude, the Tiwanaku area supported perhaps as many as 40,000 people with well-adapted agricultural methods, which included a system of raised fields. This important and influential place maintained its far-reaching trade relations with the help of llama caravans.

Around the same time, in the Peruvian central highlands, a small empire known as Huari flourished from around A.D. 750 to 1000. The Huari dominated much of the highlands of Peru and were experts at high-altitude irrigation and agriculture. They were particularly adept at growing maize. They kept their little empire together by a series of roads that the later Incas were more than happy to expropriate.

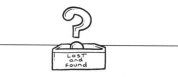

Lost and Found

Roads have always been important to civilizations trying to control large territories. Both the Persians and the Romans were famous for their long-distance highways, and some of the South American civilizations also produced excellent trails and roads. The Incas, in particular, were masterful, and along with their stone-paved roads, they built amazing rope bridges to overcome deep ravines and canyons.

Here Come the Incas!

In the fifteenth century A.D., the Incas lived in an area centered around their town of Cuzco, one of several groups that lived in the region and often didn't get along with one another. The Incas, though, started to achieve some success in conquering their immediate neighbors.

The Inca ruler Pachakuti (r. 1438–1471) was instrumental in this and he, along with his successors, rapidly built an immense empire. Ultimately, the territory under Inca control spanned about 2,600 miles from north to south, from the southern border of Columbia down to central Chile, including parts of northwest Argentina and Bolivia.

All Roads Lead to Cuzco

The ruler of the Incas was called "the Inca." He was considered a descendant of the sun and was treated accordingly. The empire was divided up into four quarters, with the center running through Cuzco. An elaborate hierarchy of governors and bureaucrats was put in place to manage these expansive territories. The Incas were known for their great building projects. An incredible system of very well-constructed roads extending through the empire assured that supplies, tribute, and soldiers could travel as needed. Professional runners called *chasquis* were employed to relay messages along the routes. Inca architecture is famous for its use of dressed giant stones fit together so finely that you can't shove a sheet of paper (or a knifeblade, take your pick, they're both clichés) between the blocks.

Although the Incas had no writing system, they were able to keep economic and census records on a complex series of knotted and colored strings called *quipus*. The quipus could be examined and read by specialists trained in such matters. Inca history and tradition was transmitted orally, and much of this was recorded by the Spanish during and after their conquest. The Inca language, Quechua, was imposed as the language of the Inca empire, and even today it is widely spoken by native populations in the old Inca territories.

Jargon Unearthed

Chasquis were professional relay runners who could shuttle messages along the great roads spanning the Inca empire. Messages could travel up to 150 miles a day with this method. The messages might be memorized or recorded on a *quipu*, a complex series of knotted strings.

Lost and Found

Over the last several decades, mountain climbers in the Andes of Peru, Chile, and Argentina have made some remarkable discoveries. Near the summits of high peaks, they found the naturally mummified remains of young people, apparently hit on the head and left to freeze as religious offerings. Because of the cold, dry conditions, the bodies are splendidly preserved.

There Go the Incas!

Francisco Pizarro (ca. 1475–1541) was a Spanish adventurer who came to the New World in search of gold, power, and adventure. While in Panama, he heard tales of a golden kingdom far south down the Pacific coast. Eventually he succeeded in reaching the Inca Empire, and in 1532, he and his 168 men began the relatively easy conquest of Peru. Apart from their scary weapons and horses, there were other factors that assisted the conquistadors:

➤ The Inca Empire was probably overextended by the time the Spanish arrived.

➤ There had been civil strife. After the death of the Inca Huayna Capuc (1493–1525), a power struggle broke out between the rightful heir,

Huascar, and his brother Atahualpa. The latter won the conflict just as the Spanish were arriving.

➤ Smallpox was having its effect on the population. (It's said that Huayna Capuc died of the disease.)

Pizarro and his men deviously captured Atahualpa and demanded a huge ransom in gold and silver. After the demands were met, they killed Atahualpa anyway, and it wouldn't be very long before most of the Inca Empire was under Spanish domination.

The Lost City of Machu Picchu

In 1911, American explorer Hiram Bingham went in search of a lost city said to have been the refuge of the last Inca ruler after the Spanish conquered the capital of Cuzco. Local people told him of ancient ruins high up on a mountain. With a guide, Bingham made the arduous jungle climb out of a deep river canyon to the top of a ridge between two peaks. What greeted him was the spectacular remains of a royal Inca estate called Machu Picchu.

The lost ruins of Machu Picchu. (Courtesy Madeleine Lynn)

The site was abandoned except for a few farmers living amid the ruins. A major expedition was launched to clear the site of vegetation and to map, record, and study the ruins. The dramatic beauty of its location and its superb Inca stone architecture have established Machu Picchu as among the most admired archaeological sites in the world. The estate was built by the Inca ruler Pachacuti, who ruled from around A.D. 1438 to 1471, and was probably abandoned not long after the Spanish conquest.

As was typical of Inca royal estates, there were quarters for the ruler and his family, and housing and farmland for resident workers. There were also places for the devotional activities of the king and those who would care for his mummy following his death.

269

Diggers

American Hiram Bingham (1875–1956) is credited with the discovery of the lost city of Machu Picchu in 1911. His explorations in South America began several years earlier with treks in different parts of the continent. His varied and distinguished career included missionary work, a Ph.D. from Harvard, and service as a military officer and U.S. Senator.

By now, you've probably got the idea that the ancient civilizations of South America were truly impressive. In this chapter, I've emphasized the dramatic civilizations found on the west side of the Andes, but I assure you that the rest of the continent is likewise rich in interesting history and archaeology.

I'm quite amazed that apart from Machu Picchu, and occasionally Tiwanaku, the archaeology of this wonderful continent seems to be relatively unknown to the public-at-large. That's a shame. Explorers are still finding ruins in the mountains and jungles, and will continue to do so for some time. And there are enough sites to keep archaeologists busy for generations. Spread the word: South American archaeology is awesome.

The Least You Need to Know

➤ The civilizations that developed in the Andean region were cleverly adapted to their environments, especially in their agriculture and irrigation systems.

➤ Civilizations such as the Moche built huge pyramids of adobe, while others demonstrated a mastery of construction in stone.

➤ Coastal seafaring and road networks show that these people could get around.

➤ The famous Incas were real latecomers, but they built the largest empire in the New World before their approximately 100 years of regional domination came to an end with the Spanish conquistadors.

Part 6
Controversial Issues

The study of ancient civilizations is certainly fascinating, with all of the excavations, discoveries and puzzles to sort out. But it certainly has its serious and wild sides as well!

In the next few chapters, we're going to take a look at some issues that aren't always discussed and a few topics that tend to fall to the wayside. In Chapter 23, we're going to talk about some of the ethical issues behind what we're doing when we're dealing with the remains of the past. In the following chapter, we'll enter the wild and woolly world of "fringe archaeology," with its curious theories about aliens, lost continents, pyramid power, and mummy curses.

In Chapter 25, we'll discuss a very controversial and important subject: the possible impact of ancient civilizations on other cultures across the oceans prior to Columbus. Finally, we'll end with some frank talk about the world of archaeology and where you might fit in.

Chapter 23

We Need to Talk

In This Chapter

➤ Serious questions and ethical dilemmas

➤ Who owns the past?

➤ Should we be digging up dead people?

➤ Frauds and scams

➤ Saving the past

So far, we've looked at a lot of interesting people and places in this book, along with many great discoveries and fascinating questions. If only all of archaeology was like that! But apart from the quest to uncover and interpret the past, archaeology has some serious problems to consider, both abstract and tangible, and we need to have a little chat about them.

Socrates reportedly said "the unexamined life is not worth living," and perhaps the same could be said for archaeology, or any other human pursuit. ("The unexamined archaeological site is not worth digging?"...no, that one doesn't work.) What is it that we archaeologists are trying to do, and is it worth doing? Is what we are doing a good thing? How does it affect other people or life in general? Do I sound like a philosophy professor yet?

We've already answered the first question early on in this book. We are trying to explain the past, and there is some value to this in terms of lessons learned, cultural enrichment, and occasionally practical information. As for the other questions, there's lots of room for discussion, and often no clear-cut answers.

Who Owns the Past?

Who owns the past? Such a profound question! There are major museums all over the world (particularly in North America and Europe) full of antiquities from other parts of the globe. Fragments of the marble frieze from ancient Athens' beautiful Parthenon (the "Elgin Marbles") are in London, the stele with the Law Code of Hammurabi is in Paris, and museums in New York, Boston, and elsewhere in America are loaded with Egyptian antiquities.

On many occasions I have heard off-the-cuff remarks by people regarding all of the stuff from Egypt in the British Museum or elsewhere "stolen" by the likes of Belzoni and others. Shouldn't these objects be returned to Egypt? A serious question indeed. Are they not part of the Egyptian ancient cultural heritage? Does Egypt care?

Yes, there have been occasional calls to give artifacts back. On the other hand, you might be surprised to learn that the overwhelming majority of the stuff you see in museums is not technically stolen. Most of the treasures of the British Museum were obtained at a time when it was permitted to do so. Belzoni had permission from the government in charge during his era to remove what he liked from Egypt, as did his rivals. So did Lord Elgin in Greece.

One Man's Trash...

Certainly in Egypt during much of the nineteenth century, there was not much national interest in a long distant past among a generally poor population that was by this late date overwhelmingly Islamic. It probably came as quite a surprise when enterprising Egyptians living near sites of antiquities learned that visiting Europeans were interested in this old debris and were willing to pay for it!

Lost and Found

One of the most popular museum exhibitions ever was a collection of objects from the Tomb of Tutankhamun which toured Britain and the United States in the 1970s. The exhibit attracted millions at venues such as New York's Metropolitan Museum of Art and London's British Museum.

The freestyle digging and export of Egyptian antiquities was somewhat curtailed with the establishment of a regulatory antiquities service in the 1850s, and a national museum was founded. Thereafter, the rules required that excavators split their finds 50/50 with Egypt, thus rewarding foreign museums for their efforts. And until just a couple of decades ago, there were government-licensed antiquities dealers in Egypt who were allowed to sell unremarkable run-of-the-mill objects.

Bring It on Home

You can be sure of one thing—Egypt isn't letting such things happen now. The days of the 50/50 split are long gone. Now archaeologists are no longer allowed to remove antiquities from Egypt—not even small samples for analysis—unless very special permission is granted by an antiquities committee. And the antiquities shops no longer operate. After the 1952 revolution, the Egyptians were fully in charge of governing their country. Schools now teach about the grandeur of ancient Egypt and promote a national pride in the past.

Others argue that Egyptian artifacts permanently housed in foreign museums are the best advertising there is for tourism, which plays a large role in Egypt's economy. Not only do museum-goers leave with an appreciation of the ancient culture, but many of them are inspired to visit Egypt to see the antiquities in-situ. And few dispute that the objects in such museums are well-cared for. Moreover, from a practical point of view, museums fear that to return objects would establish a precedent that could result in the shrinking of their collections.

There are now in place international treaties and conventions that provide rules for the return of various objects in certain circumstances. Many objects have been returned to their country of origin on a case-by-case basis. Certainly, objects that were actually stolen are covered by these agreements, and there are now organizations that circulate information about recent thefts in order to alert museums and collectors.

Grave Robbers?

Here's a question that makes some people uncomfortable. Are archaeologists merely another kind of grave robber, but with a more sophisticated philosophy and more refined excavation methods? Who are we to be digging up someone's ancient relatives? A fair question, I think.

Pitfalls and Pointers

In some recent incidents, Egypt has curtailed even traveling exhibits of their antiquities, fearing that they might be damaged. They would also like to encourage foreigners to come to Egypt if they want to see some of this stuff.

Jargon Unearthed

What's the difference between a grave robber and an archaeologist? A grave robber plunders tombs for few other reasons than personal profit. An archaeologist strives to document, study and preserve the past.

Let's drift back in time a few thousand years. King Tut, the boy king, has just met his untimely demise by a means not clearly understood. His wife and family are probably terribly upset. The body is carefully mummified, and a procession to the Valley of the Kings carries tons of gold- gilded objects to a small tomb. The jewelry-clad mummy of Tut, with its exquisite gold mask, encased in three splendid coffins, is placed in its sarcophagus; the tomb is sealed.

It's nearly miraculous that greedy robbers didn't effectively loot the tomb, and archaeologist Howard Carter finds it in 1922. Ooooh! Aaaah! says everyone when the news comes out and Tut becomes a celebrity! The mummy is removed from its coffin and examined, and the objects from his tomb make their way to Cairo for exhibition. So what's the big deal? Keep reading.

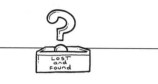

Lost and Found

King Tut's mummy really took a beating! Many of his body parts were snapped off in the process of removing jewelry, and his head became detached from his body. He's even missing a part of his anatomy that I don't want to talk about. It was there when they found him...

A poor farmer in Peru goes out at night with a shovel to find an ancient grave. He's successful in uncovering several beautiful Moche pots that he sells to enhance his meager income. Are both cases not in some ways similar, although different in the matter of scale, sophistication, and intent? Isn't the end result essentially the same: A grave is disrupted and its contents dispersed?

Bones of Contention

Do we have any right to excavate the remains of ancient people, many of them lovingly interred in their final resting places by grieving friends and relatives? Should they be dug up and measured and their bones and their grave possessions put on display, or stored in boxes or shelves in a museum storeroom? Have we no respect?

Or do we say: Who cares, because they're dead anyway and nobody alive knows them? Should the dead be used to satisfy the curiosity of the living? You can bet that King Tut or any other of the great pharaohs never expected that their bodies would be put on public display and their sacred tombs would be visited by millions of tourists.

Digging up Granny

Pitfalls and Pointers

In Israel, excavating human remains is a touchy subject. If there's any chance whatsoever that the bones might be those of Jewish individuals, then ultra-orthodox religious groups don't want them tampered with. When such bones are found, it's not unusual for large protests to take place, causing digs to shut down.

I'm really curious about your heritage. May I dig up your grandmother? What? Too recent? How about your great great grandmother? Is that okay? I want to measure her teeth! You get the picture, and if you're looking to me for an answer, I don't have one. But I hope the questions and scenarios above give you something to ponder.

A number of American museums have large collections of Indian skeletons and grave goods. Many were excavated professionally and serve as important reference materials for physical anthropologists and others. Some native people want the bones back for reburial, and their requests are taken very seriously.

In 1990, the Native American Graves Protection and Repatriation Act (NAGPRA) was enacted in the United States. NAGPRA sets rules for the protection and return of American Indian bones and funerary and sacred artifacts found on federal lands or housed in museums that receive federal funds.

Museums are required to make an inventory and identify the objects and bones in their collections, which can then be requested for return by tribal organizations. Remember the Kennewick Man we met in Chapter 20? The big controversy over who gets to keep him is governed by NAGPRA, and the judicial system had a difficult time deciding what to do with these unusual bones.

National Treasure or World Heritage?

So back to the question of who owns the past. There are Maya temples in the jungle that are slowly deteriorating. In Asia, heads are being removed from ancient statues of the Buddha for sale on the art market. Some extremists in Egypt have expressed a desire to blow up pharaonic antiquities which are the remains of an undesirable pagan past and an attraction to pagan Westerners.

Should we care? Is it any of our darn business what goes on with the antiquities within the borders of another nation? Are we in any way personally related or connected to these things that belong to other cultures in other lands?

There are some who argue that although they themselves might not be Iraqi or Sudanese, they are nonetheless tied to the Sumerians or Nubians as fellow members of the human race. Are we all not ultimately genetically connected? And although our histories are dispersed, does not the human cultural heritage belong to us all of us? That's something to think about.

A Little Something for Me?

How about owning antiquities yourself? There are numerous private collectors in this world. Some people collect Roman coins while others might specialize in classical Greek vases or Mexican ceramic figurines. Is there anything wrong with this? Some archaeologists think so. They contend that the existence of antiquities dealers and the private ownership of antiquities encourage the looting of archaeological sites.

On the other hand, collectors will argue that owning a piece of the past develops a sincere appreciation for it. Should everything belong in a museum, since only a fraction of a museum's collection is on display, while the rest is warehoused and not immediately accessible to the public at large?

Why should museums be the only ones to have old objects, especially when there are millions of Native American projectile points lying around? Should farmers wait for archaeologists to show up every time an arrowhead is found in a plowed field? Why can't they give it to their children as a lesson in ancient life?

Finding the Greater Good

Then again, if something is really different, unique, or exquisite, shouldn't the public be able to enjoy it as well? And just one last point, based on personal experience, to throw into the mix. I have several pottery sherds from a Middle Eastern country where it is not illegal to obtain such things. (In fact, untold millions of broken pottery sherds have to be carted away from sites after archaeologists have deemed that they are nothing special).

When I have given talks about archaeology to school children, I have passed these little pieces around, and the kids are utterly amazed to be touching something so old, and they are full of questions. It's great advertising for archaeology and inspires an interest in the past.

How Old Is Old?

So, is owning a few things here and there okay, or should we employ teams of builders to construct massive warehouses for all the world's little potsherds? Should we employ big crews of archaeologists to reconstruct every pot ever broken in human history and then give them to a museum for display or storage? Should we just leave stuff lying around?

Another question: When does something become "old"? Does something need to be 500 years old to be an antique? Loads of antique shops all over the world will sell you things only 50 years old at a formidable price. Some of those silly toys, lunch boxes, and other little things we used to use, wear out, or break when I was a kid (not all that long ago) are commanding real collector's prices.

Phony Baloney!

Since we've been talking about the ownership of antiquities, both privately and by museums, there's a fascinating subject that's related: What's authentic and what's fake. There are many examples of fake antiquities, some of which are obviously fraudulent, and others it took years to expose. A lot of money has been spent on these things, which wouldn't otherwise be worth much more than the material they are made from.

Lost and Found

Assigning ownership of native bones or artifacts can be quite complicated, especially when the remains are many thousands of years old. Native groups presently living in the area where the material is found may stake their claim because their myths, legends or religion might explain that their people have always lived there since the time of creation. It is a difficult argument to dispute.

Pitfalls and Pointers

In at least one Middle Eastern country where the illicit traffic in antiquities was once rampant, it is now illegal to own anything over 100 years old. The results have been mixed. While antiquity trading has decreased, people who find something accidentally tend to hide or destroy it rather than come under scrutiny. And what about heirlooms that have been in the family for centuries?

There have been fake manuscripts, fake coins, fake fossils, and even fake people! Let's take a look at some of these curious cases.

The Monkey Man

In Chapter 4, I mentioned the famous case of the Piltdown Man, in which the jawbone of an orangutan was found in the vicinity of a human cranium in an English gravel pit. Scientists were convinced that they had found the fossilized missing link between apes and humans!

Although the fossils were originally found in the early twentieth century, it wasn't until 1953 that the hoax was revealed, when a dating method demonstrated that the jaw and cranium did not belong together and had been artificially "aged" to look old. Meanwhile, Mr. Piltdown appeared in many a textbook and scientific study. The suspects in this old case are several, and include some prominent scientists.

Stone Cold Giant

While Piltdown Man was sufficiently clever to fool scientists, another famous hoax made a lot of money for the schemers involved. In 1869, some workers digging a well on the farm of Stub Newell near Cardiff, New York, hit something hard. Further excavation revealed what appeared to be the petrified body of an ancient man ten feet tall! The news of the discovery of the "Cardiff Giant" brought many thousands of visitors who paid to have a look.

Most scientists who viewed the body were immediately unimpressed, but that didn't stop the tourists and the money from rolling in! After only a couple of months of Giant-Mania, a relative of Stubs named George Hull confessed. The giant was a statue carved from gypsum; with the cooperation of Stubs, it had been buried on the farm for a year before the unsuspecting well diggers were brought in.

Lost and Found

The great showman P. T. Barnum tried to purchase the Cardiff Giant, but his offer was refused. So he made his own and put it on display.

Dr. Beringer's Fossils

One of the most pitiable stories of fakes is the story of Dr. Beringer (1667–1740), a physician and natural historian with the University of Wurzburg in Germany. Interested in fossils, he sent students out to a nearby mountain where fossils could be collected, and they returned with some marvelous stones.

Some were inscribed with the amazing likenesses of insects, a salamander, worms, a spider catching a fly, frogs mating, and many other curious themes. More fantastic were the engraved designs of such things as comets, stars, and Hebrew letters, including some spelling the name of God.

Beringer was impressed and published a book on the supposed fossils, in which he even considered and dismissed the possibility that they were fake. Legend has it that Beringer only learned of the hoax when he discovered a stone bearing his own name.

Pitfalls and Pointers

P. T. Barnum provided the credo for frauds of all kinds when he stated that "a sucker is born every minute." This attitude was amplified by Edward Albee in a line made famous by W. C. Fields: "Never give a sucker an even break."

Though often reported as a prank pulled upon the professor by some of his bored and mischievous students, the deed was apparently intentionally designed to embarrass Beringer by at least a couple of mean-spirited academic colleagues at the University of Wurzburg. His book was widely circulated, and it is said that the professor spent much money and energy in an attempt to lessen the spread of his humiliation by purchasing all available copies.

Unfortunately, Dr. Beringer is usually remembered today as a sucker. His tale appears both amusing and tragic, but as stupid as it all seems, we shouldn't forget that the whole incident took place during a time when the true nature of fossils as the remains of past life was not well understood.

It Sounded Good when I Read It!

Fake bones, bodies, and fossils aren't the only things that get passed around. Some of the most interesting forgeries are those of manuscripts. While it might take a clever craftsman to churn out some old Roman coins, it takes a real master to produce documents, which require old writing materials plus a good knowledge of the history, handwriting, spelling, and word usage of the day.

Many frauds there have been, including the lost diaries of Hitler and some unknown plays of Shakespeare, but clever analyses or the confession of perpetrators has often resulted in exposure. Take a look at a couple of examples.

A Bad Scam Gone Worse

In the 1980s one of the most bizarre cases of the forgery of historic documents was uncovered. A dealer in documents dating from the early history of Mormonism (nineteenth century) apparently was running out of material to sell. So he started making some of his own "historical" documents. He tore blank pages out of old books from the early nineteenth century and used the mix of ink appropriate for that time. His handwriting skills were outstanding, and he was even able to duplicate perfectly the signatures of some of the important historical figures of the time.

One of his most famous forgeries was a potentially embarrassing letter purportedly written by the founder of the Church in which the Mormon prophet communicates with a talking white salamander. This particular letter, although appearing to be authentically old, was nonetheless suspect due to its contents. The whole charade came to an end when the forger started planting bombs and killing people. During his confession, he provided a fascinating account of a master forger at work.

Real, Fake, Real

In 1965, Yale University published a remarkable manuscript that included an old map of Europe dating to about 1450. What makes this particular map so special is that off to the edge west of Iceland and Greenland is depicted an island labeled "the island of Vinland." The map apparently shows a knowledge of the New World decades before the voyage of Columbus! This "Vinland Map" was examined by experts and declared authentic.

In 1972, the map was sent to a laboratory for examination, and scientists there concluded that there were elements present in the ink that weren't used until the 1920s; as a result, they declared the map a fake. Subsequent examinations by another lab with much experience in studying medieval documents claimed that there was nothing unusual about the ink and that the "suspicious" elements occurred naturally in other documents of similar age. So some have declared the map to be genuine once again, while several of the skeptics continue to hold their ground.

Pitfalls and Pointers

Any tourist who has been to Egypt has no doubt been approached by dozens of men and boys selling "antikas". Although often presented as the genuine artifacts, most are obvious fakes. Besides, it's illegal to sell or buy antiquities in Egypt. Some visitors, however, enjoy collecting these amusing items including postcards laminated to potsherds and crudely carved miniature alabaster mummy cases containing even cruder little alabaster mummies.

Sorting It Out

The tools of scientists can be put to work in many instances to uncover a fraud. Chemical analysis of inks and pigments, X-rays, and dating techniques can all contribute to exposing the phony artifact. Good scholarly detective work to track the history of an object might also point to the dubious origins of this or that object.

Why would anyone do these sorts of deceitful things? I think you know the most obvious answer: financial gain! Sell or display something phony and make a bunch of money. This was certainly the case with the Cardiff Giant and the Mormon manuscripts, but there are other reasons as well.

Fakes and hoaxes can be driven by scholarly vanity. A scholar with a dull career or envious of the success of another might fabricate a new and exciting discovery. Others, as in the case of Dr. Beringer's nemeses, might be motivated by a desire to humiliate or embarrass experts. A couple of forgers have also taken great personal pride in being able to produce work of high quality.

So how do you protect yourself against this sort of abuse? First of all, you should consider the arguments above and decide if you are even interested in owning or collecting antiquities. If you are, then you should seek reputable dealers who can guarantee both authenticity and origin so you don't end up with something stolen or fake.

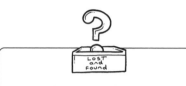

Lost and Found

Some archaeological magazines refuse to allow advertising from antiquities dealers, while others have weighed the morality and in the interest of freedom have permitted the ads. There is even at least one archaeological magazine that is produced by a dealer and contains legitimate scholarly articles and news. Many archaeologists, however, avoid contributing so as not to be associated with or endorse such enterprises.

Pitfalls and Pointers

I once proposed a solution to the problem of protecting some of the smaller, rarely visited tombs in Egypt's Valley of the Kings and elsewhere: rebury them! It's difficult for flood water, wind, bats and humans to damage tombs that are inaccessible. The extraordinary preservation of tombs such as that of Tutankhamun attest to the benefits of a well-sealed sepulcher.

Also, if you choose to own a piece of the past, now's the time to learn as much as you can about whatever it is that you own. Many museums keep a collection of fakes, which provide great comparative material when questionable objects are brought in. They also are good for teaching how to tell the real from the bogus, and serve as a lesson in how fakes are produced.

Saving the Past

While we're dealing with all of these philosophical dilemmas and archaeological quandaries, let's save a really important subject for last. Should we save the past at all, and if so, what and how much? How can it be done?

I've already mentioned that there are lots of rules on the books in various countries to protect antiquities. Still, at what point should the past give way to the present and the future? Building dams to protect living people and provide power for modern homes and industry has often resulted in the flooding and destruction of archaeological sites. What should take priority?

The Past Meets the Present

In places such as Egypt, which is practically one big archaeological site, housing construction can barely keep up with a rapidly expanding population. Should everything come to a halt to protect the remains of ancient people? How should decisions be made regarding what is significant and what should be saved, salvaged, or discarded? The great international rush to save archaeological sites from the rising waters behind Egypt's Aswan Dam is a famous example of emergency salvage.

On the other hand, some archaeological sites are being "loved to death." In Egypt's Valley of the Kings, for example, millions of tourist have tramped through these relatively fragile tombs. Some people touch the painted walls, some leave graffiti and garbage, and some take flash photos, even though all of these things are forbidden.

Even their breathing is harmful, as gallons of moisture from respiration are deposited in the tombs daily. Other tombs nearby are badly affected by bats, wind erosion, and even the rare flash flood. Although protective measures against all of these factors are being taken, it's a big project and very expensive!

Faking It in a Good Cause

You may recall the solution at Lascaux, in which the actual cave was closed and visitors redirected to a wonderful replica. Some Swiss Egyptologists have proposed a similar thing for the tombs in the Valley of the Kings, and I have suggested that the royal mummies currently on display in Cairo be placed back in their tombs and the doors shut. After all, it's a royal cemetery!

The tombs could first be intensely studied and documented by archaeologists and the tourists sent to visit representative full-scale models of the tombs in their pristine condition. I was surprised by the response of many aficionados of Egyptology to these ideas. They want to visit the actual tombs, rather than replicas, as if it is their right to do so.

An International Interest

Both public and private organizations have taken a lead in protecting the world's precious archaeological heritage. The aim of the United Nations World Heritage Convention is to "protect natural and cultural properties of outstanding universal value against the threat of damage in a rapidly developing world." Sites that meet these descriptions are listed, and assistance is given for their protection.

A similar, though private, organization is the World Monuments Fund, which has provided much-needed assistance for the conservation of fragile or threatened sites in many countries. At least something is being done, but the problems and questions persist. How we deal with the past is a question for all of us to consider.

The Least You Need to Know

➤ Archaeology is not immune to discussions of ethics.

➤ Questions such as who owns the past and the rights of the deceased are very controversial.

➤ How to balance the needs of the present and future with our appreciation of the past is a difficult dilemma.

➤ In the case of antiquities, not everything is always as it appears to be, and occasionally fakes and scams can fool us.

Chapter 24

Lost Continents and Ancient Astronauts

In This Chapter

➤ A walk on the wild side

➤ The lost continent of Atlantis

➤ Ancient astronauts

➤ The curse of the mummy!

Archaeology generally likes to portray itself as a scientific endeavor. It borrows from the best of various disciplines in order to achieve reasonable perspectives about the human past. Archaeologists like to deal with materials that can be measured, and if they speculate they usually (or at least should) qualify it with words such as "perhaps," "maybe," and "it seems."

There are others, though, who deal with the past in unusual and interesting ways, playing by a different set of rules. They tend to have wide followings based on superficially credible theories. Archaeologists are often annoyed by these sorts of theories and their proponents and followers, because typically their claims are outlandishly attractive and detract from mainstream archaeology.

In fact, mainstream archaeologists are often painted as the bad guys in all this—they're too stuck up to consider what's presented as the hidden "real truth," or they're part of the great conspiracy to cover it up. In this chapter, we'll take a look at some of the more popular fringe ideas, things like lost continents, ancient astronauts, and mummy curses.

"Way Down, Beneath the Ocean..."

One of the most popular targets of odd speculation has been the idea that there are lost continents submerged beneath the oceans, continents that were once home to highly advanced civilizations dating to a time well before the ancient civilizations we recognize today.

Catastrophes occurred, so the story goes, which caused these land masses to sink, effectively extinguishing their cultures. The most popular continent of this sort is called Atlantis, and there is a great range of speculation about it.

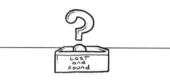

Lost and Found

Atlantis has been a favorite subject of authors and songwriters alike. The sunken ruins of the lost continent were visited by Capt. Nemo in Jules Verne's *Twenty Thousand Leagues under the Sea*, among many other novels of varying quality. Atlantis has been immortalized in a popular song by Donovan Leitch and even gets a mention by Frank Zappa.

Pitfalls and Pointers

Apart from the places mentioned above, Atlantis has also been located by various writers in such places as Ceylon, Palestine, Malta, Tunisia, Morocco, Central France, Nigeria, Brazil, the Arctic, South Africa, Greenland, Central America, Sweden, and Iran, among others.

Blame It on Plato

So where did this idea of a lost continent come from? The story of Atlantis is actually found in the writings of the great Greek philosopher Plato (ca. 429–347 B.C.). Plato often presented his ideas in the form of dialogues between Socrates or himself and students or other philosophers. In two such dialogues (the *Critias* and *Timaeus*), a student named Critias shares what he knows about a long-gone ancient society. The information about Atlantis is presented as at least third-hand information, with the source being the Greek politician, poet, and traveler Solon (ca. 600 B.C.). Solon is said to have gotten his information from an Egyptian priest.

Atlantis is described as a huge island outside "the gates of Hercules," bigger than the area of Asia and Libya together. The gates of Hercules are generally thought to be in the area of Gibraltar, where the Mediterranean meets the Atlantic Ocean. Atlantis, therefore, would lie somewhere in the Atlantic.

As the story goes, Atlantis was a beautiful place to live and at one time controlled parts of lands bordering the Mediterranean. Originally a wise and noble people, the Atlanteans had become evil and were fighting with the Athenians and Egyptians. As a result, the gods destroyed Atlantis in a terrible catastrophic earthquake 9,000 years before Solon received the story, which would make it around 9600 B.C.

It's Over Here, It's Over There

Those who feel that Atlantis is an actual place have promoted several different sites for its location. Here are a few:

➤ The Azores or Canary Islands in the east Atlantic Ocean. In this view, these volcanic islands are really the mountain tops of the sunken continents, perhaps destroyed by cataclysmic volcanic eruptions.

➤ The Caribbean, where it is claimed that columns and stone blocks from Atlantis have been discovered underwater.

➤ Antarctica, where there was supposedly a hospitable climate long ago.

➤ The South China Sea. So what does that have to do with the Atlantic Ocean? According to the advocates of this theory, the Greek worldview depicted the earth as a land mass surrounded by water and would not have allowed for the existence of more than one ocean. Atlantis, in this view, was submerged by the sea-level rise that occurred as the Ice Age ended.

➤ Western Turkey. Atlantis sunk into a lake during an earthquake.

➤ Atlantis was actually an exploding planet.

The Real Atlantis?

There are some people who take a moderate standpoint and try to link the Atlantis story to known history and geology. In one of the more popular theories, the explosive eruption of the volcano Thera in the Mediterranean in 1628 destroyed Atlantis, which was located on the island, now called Santorini. You may recall Thera. It's been linked to the destruction on Crete during Minoan times, and Bible theorists try to connect its eruption to the story of the Hebrew exodus.

Turn Back Time

A few things have to be modified in the descriptions in Plato to keep that idea intact. First of all, the location of Atlantis would need to be changed, because Santorini certainly isn't outside the gates of Hercules, unless these gates were located in some other place than Gibraltar. Secondly, there has to be a major modification in the date if Atlantis was destroyed around 9600 B.C. and Thera blew up around 1650 to 1400 B.C.

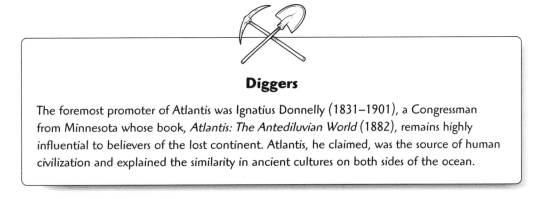

Diggers

The foremost promoter of Atlantis was Ignatius Donnelly (1831–1901), a Congressman from Minnesota whose book, *Atlantis: The Antediluvian World* (1882), remains highly influential to believers of the lost continent. Atlantis, he claimed, was the source of human civilization and explained the similarity in ancient cultures on both sides of the ocean.

Also, it's highly unlikely that Atlanteans would be fighting with Egyptians or Athenians at such an early date, as the Egyptians were hunting and gathering, and there was neither an Athens nor any Athenians at that time. Advocates have suggested that the dating makes more sense if we believe that an extra zero has been accidentally added to the date, so that Atlantis disappeared 900 years before Solon, thus making the date 1500 B.C. and putting it within Thera range.

Making Sense of It All

Most of the theories presented about Atlantis are either geologically unfeasible or severely lacking in physical evidence. So how about the drowned cities people claim to have seen underwater? Some people like to point out examples like the city of Port Royal (see Chapter 8), parts of which disappeared into the water after an earthquake. But Port Royal wasn't a whole continent, just a town built on an unfortunate piece of land. And the columns and roads? These have been investigated and have proven to be naturally symmetrical geological phenomena, some of which can be seen on dry land as well.

Pitfalls and Pointers

Nature occasionally produces things that look like those of human manufacture. Basalt, for example, is volcanically formed and can fracture in columns with a uniform geometrical profile that looks like it was precisely cut.

We have pretty good general maps of the ocean floors, including that of the Atlantic. Sorry to say, no lost continent has turned up yet. It's altogether possible that after the millions of words written about Atlantis, and the endless hours of speculation, it might be just a story, a literary device of Mr. Plato trying to explain something that's apparently not coming through too clearly.

The Atlanteans Speak Up

The lack of credible archaeological evidence hasn't stopped the Atlanteans themselves from trying to communicate with us and share their history and wisdom. There are those who claim to have been in direct contact with the source. Let's see what they have to offer.

Edgar Cayce Tells It Like It Was

Edgar Cayce (1877–1945) was known as "the sleeping prophet." Edgar would drop into a trance and talk about many different things, including Atlantis. Among his claims was that an ancient archive can be found under the feet of the Great Sphinx of Giza. This has yet to be located.

Perhaps more important to our discussion, Cayce predicted that Atlantis would rise from the ocean in the 1960s. Well, the 1960s came and went, and where is it? If this is an example of his prophetic abilities, I now lack confidence in the rest of his predictions.

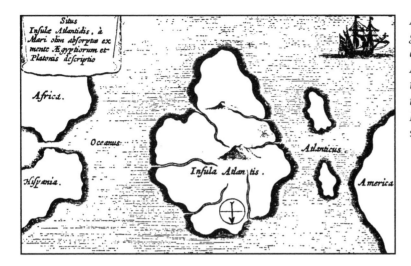

A map showing a suggested location for Atlantis as proposed in 1644 by Athanasius Kircher. Note that the map is drawn upside down. (From Kircher, Mundus subterraneus)

Words of the Wise Warrior?

Since 1972, J. Z. Knight of Yelm, Washington, has had quite a life. J. Z. claims to be able to "channel" the spirit of a 35,000-year-old male warrior from Atlantis. "Channeling" involves going into a trance and then allowing a spirit to take over one's body for the purpose of communication—an unusual concept even without Atlantis thrown in. The name of J. Z.'s warrior friend is Ramtha.

When Ramtha manifests himself in J. Z., she goes into a trance, strikes a sturdy manly pose, and speaks with a curious accent. Ramtha dispenses timeless Atlantean wisdom and has a large following. Thousands have paid large sums to be enlightened by the channeled warrior, and J. Z. owns a huge, beautifully developed ranch where her seminars are held.

Lemuria: Monkey-faced Ancestors of the Atlanteans

A couple of other lost continents get attention once in a while. One is Lemuria, which is believed by some to have predated Atlantis. According to one theorist, the Lemurians were an evolving race, and in their classic stage they were tall, had extra-big feet, three eyes, including one looking back, a protruding muzzle, and brown skin. A few people think that refugees from Lemuria live in the vicinity of Mt. Shasta in northern California.

Lost and Found

Ever hear of the lost sunken continent of Mu? It's supposed to be out in the central Pacific. Easter Island is a surviving mountaintop of Mu, or so it has been said. It seems to be a spin-off of Lemuria.

Lemuria has an even weaker pedigree than Atlantis. The idea of such a continent apparently had its origin in nineteenth century speculation about the distribution of animal life. To explain why lemurs are found in Africa and also in India, it was proposed that the two areas were once connected by a land mass, and the name given to this hypothetical land was Lemuria.

They Came from Outer Space

We archaeologists got it all wrong, according to some. If we want to know how civilizations were created and how our ancestors accomplished their amazing engineering feats, we need to look to the sky. According to this view, aliens have visited our planet in the past and have taught us sophisticated things like stone carving and pyramid building. Perhaps they are even responsible for the human race itself, having mated with simple-minded hominids. Maybe Jesus, Moses, Mohammed, and the Buddha were all extraterrestrial messengers from outer space!

According to Erich von Daniken, the godfather of this sort of speculation, evidence of alien mentors is everywhere. Illustrations and descriptions of these beings can be seen in everything from drawings in caves to intricately carved Maya art to ancient myths and the Bible.

And how else can you explain the big heads of Easter Island or the complex engineering that appears in ancient Egypt and elsewhere? And superior beings would explain how civilizations appear seemingly out of nowhere. Von Daniken's best-selling book, *Chariots of the Gods?*, was first published in 1968, and was followed by many sequels.

Pitfalls and Pointers

A popular idea among some of the ancient UFO crowd is that anatomically modern humans are a result of genetic manipulation by, or actual breeding with, alien beings. This, they say, would explain the intelligence found in *Homo sapiens* and why we don't look quite like *Homo erectus* or Neanderthals. My opinion? It's an unnecessary and highly unlikely scenario.

Who's Driving the Chariot?

It doesn't take a professional archaeologist to find a myriad of holes in such books as *Chariots of the Gods*. I first read the book when I was fourteen years old, and it was clear to me even then that something was quite wrong. We can narrow von Daniken's approach down to a few things:

➤ He starts with a conclusion and finds evidence for it everywhere he looks. One scholar compared it to the old psychologist's ink blot test. One person sees a spider and someone else sees the Statue of Liberty. Von Daniken sees ancient astronauts.

➤ It is assumed that ancient humans were neither particularly bright nor creative. Knowing what we know about the intelligence and mobility of early people, why call on strange and otherworldly forces to account for human achievements?

➤ Only information that fits the idea is used. Contrary information is ignored or discarded as silly or irrelevant.

Besides all this skewing of information, the ancient astronauts theory lacks something at its core. Without getting into the UFO debate, I can say that it has never been positively proven or publicly acknowledged that superior beings have visited the earth from other planets.

Many scientists will concede that life elsewhere in the universe is possible, if not probable. But even so, there is no guarantee that other life forms are necessarily multi-celled, nor can we expect that the random course of evolution would produce anything that resembles primates on earth. And then there's the matter of time and distance. Needless to say, I'm not convinced. As I've noted elsewhere in this book, I believe that ancient people were both smart and creative, and I don't see any need to call on aliens to explain their achievements.

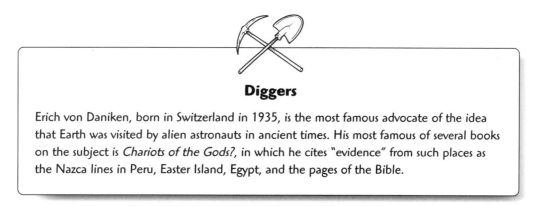

Diggers

Erich von Daniken, born in Switzerland in 1935, is the most famous advocate of the idea that Earth was visited by alien astronauts in ancient times. His most famous of several books on the subject is *Chariots of the Gods?*, in which he cites "evidence" from such places as the Nazca lines in Peru, Easter Island, Egypt, and the pages of the Bible.

Extraterrestrial Archaeology

What? Not satisfied with the evidence for aliens visiting the Earth and making us build big stone things? Perhaps you would be more convinced of life on other planets if you saw the ruins of alien civilization! According to a couple of investigators, the remains of an ancient civilization can be seen in photographs of the surface of Mars taken in 1976 by the Viking mission. The most famous shows what appears to be an immense simian-like face peering out at us. And in the immediate vicinity are other features that appear to be manu-factured structures, the remains of ancient Martian civilization.

Pitfalls and Pointers

Scientists humorously point out other land formations on Mars. One resembles a smiling "happy face" and another looks like Kermit the Frog. What does that say about the Martians?

The face on Mars created quite a sensation and has appeared on the cover of tabloid newspapers and as the subject of entire books. So what's this all about? A government conspiracy? Hardly. First of all, the pictures are readily obtainable from the government.

Secondly, most space scientists I have met would eagerly welcome any credible evidence of life outside our planet. As for our monkey-faced Martian monument, other photos taken from different angles, with different shadows, expose it for what it is: a big rock formation.

If you aren't convinced that there's life on Mars, how about the moon? Yes, someone is actually promoting the idea that on the moon there are ancient monuments, perhaps a billion years old—crystal towers and such. I guess Mars was getting boring.

The "face on Mars" photographed in different lighting conditions, demonstrating that the "face" is merely a product of shadows. (Courtesy of NASA/Malin Space Science Systems)

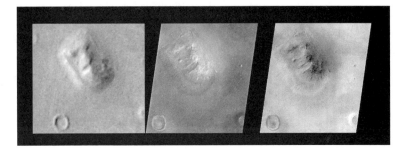

Egypt: A Veritable Magnet for Odd Theories

There's no need to travel to outer space to conjure up odd theories. There are plenty right here on planet Earth! Do you like crystals, reincarnation, dowsing, prophesy, and loads of mystical wisdom? Then ancient Egypt is just the place for you.

Pyramid Power

In the 1970s, there was quite a fad going around dealing with pyramids and the alleged power of that shape. Pyramidal structures oriented to the cardinal directions were said to perform such feats as keeping fruits and flowers fresh and sharpening dull razor blades. And as an added bonus, of course, the pyramid shape contributes to the preservation of Egyptian mummies.

Some people constructed pyramids over their beds or made special pyramid-shaped solariums in their homes, providing places to experience these mysterious curative and rejuvenating powers. If it really works, then the pyramids must shut themselves down on occasion, because scientific experiments have not been able to show any extraordinary effects.

The Sphinx-People

Recently, there have been arguments that the Great Sphinx at Giza was carved between 5000 and 7000 B.C., several millennia earlier than Egyptologists generally believe. The idea was put forth by a promoter of ancient Egyptian mysticism backed up by a geologist from an American university. The geologist claimed that the area around the Sphinx was far more eroded than the surrounding monuments known to date to the Old Kingdom (2575–2134 B.C.).

The Sphinx belongs to an earlier age, so goes the claim, and was created by an early advanced civilization. The head of the Sphinx was probably originally that of a lion, and during the Old Kingdom it was recarved to the likeness of King Chephren, with whose pyramid the statue is traditionally associated. Other geologists are not convinced, and archaeologists point to the fact that there are no related artifacts or other physical evidence of this so-called advanced civilization.

The Mummy's Curse

And while we're at it, we might as well talk about the so-called mummy's curse. This is the idea that there are ancient curses placed on Egyptian tombs that will lead to death or misfortune for anyone who violates them, tomb robbers and Egyptologists alike.

The most famous curse story surrounds the tomb of Tutankhamun, discovered in November 1922. It was reported that a tablet or inscription was found saying "death will come on swift wings" to whomever violated the tomb. In April 1923, Lord Carnarvon, the sponsor of the Tut excavation, died in Cairo, and several visitors to the tomb likewise died in short order.

Let's look at the facts. No written curse was ever found. The story was apparently the fabrication of bored newspaper reporters posted at the tomb and looking for an angle. Lord Carnarvon died of blood poisoning derived from an infected mosquito bite in the days before effective antibiotics.

Howard Carter, on the other hand, who discovered the tomb and spent ten years working there, died in 1939 of Hodgkin's disease, almost 17 years after

Pitfalls and Pointers

I have met a good number of people who claim to be reincarnated ancient Egyptians. Most assert that they are royalty or other famous individuals and I have yet to meet a "reincarnated" farmer, pot-maker or palace floor-scrubber. There are also duplicate Nefertiti's and King Tut's. No wonder I'm skeptical!

Pitfalls and Pointers

The curse story has also been perpetuated by the wonderfully fun mummy movies put out by Universal Studios. The first picture, *The Mummy* (1932), starring Boris Karloff, features a plot in which a tomb is discovered by Egyptologists and a mummy is reanimated.

the discovery. Dr. Douglas Derry (1874–1961), who performed the autopsy on the mummy in 1925, lived to a ripe old age. And so did many others involved with the excavation.

Some have suggested that the ancient Egyptians might have intentionally placed poison in some of the tombs to thwart robbers. If so, it was completely ineffective, as the overwhelming majority of royal Egyptian tombs were robbed. If curses or poisons are to be effective deterrents, they have to work before the fact. If someone dies a year later—well, the tomb has already been robbed!

There may be some basis in fact for the idea of a mummy's curse, though. It's possible that some people may have died from contracting infections from mold, dust, or other material naturally produced in tombs. For instance, I became seriously ill on a couple of occasions while sifting fine-particled tomb dust that was mixed with bat guano.

Fulfilling a Need

I could go on and on. Examples of fringe archaeology are seemingly endless. There are the catastrophists, who believe that cataclysmic planetary events such as comet collisions and other space events, giant floods, or earthquakes have radically shaped our history. Although some of the suggestions are theoretically possible, others don't conform to known laws of nature or to geological or archaeological evidence.

Others find solace and inspiration in "power places," such as the pyramids, Stonehenge, or astronomically-oriented ancient sites. And you can throw the extreme diffusionists in there as well; we'll be talking about them in the next chapter.

Why do people believe in this sort of stuff? There are several possible reasons:

➤ Belief in supernatural phenomena provides a psychologically satisfying explanation for things that are not readily explainable.

➤ Calling on outside superior forces reinforces our belief that no one before us could have been as intelligent as we are.

➤ People have a lack of trust in, or suspicion of, authority.

➤ It's fun!

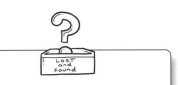

Lost and Found

Skeptics who examine unusual phenomena have a saying: Extraordinary claims require extraordinary proof. It is rarely forthcoming.

The stranger aspects of this pseudo-archaeology can be classified with UFO's, Bigfoot, and other such speculation. As an exercise with students, I have asked how many believe in UFO's. Many will raise their hands. I then ask how many believe in fairies, and very few if any hands go up. I then go on to show them that the evidence for the two is similar. There are credible eyewitnesses and photographs of fairies, but few choose to believe in them, although they were quite popular in the last century, prior to aviation.

Dealing with This Funny Business

The way I look at it, there are basically two kinds of people involved in promoting these offbeat ideas: true believers and frauds. True believers are those with a sincere belief in a given idea who usually want to share it with others. Frauds are those who knowingly promote false information in order to make a buck from the public, or by exploiting the true believers. Unfortunately, it is very difficult to tell the two groups apart. You should be very careful before calling anyone a fraud, but anyone knowingly taking advantage of others in such a way should be held accountable.

Although I remain thoroughly unconvinced by most of the views above, I don't condemn those who choose to believe this stuff. They are entitled to their beliefs, and berating them and calling them names (as many archeologists do) certainly doesn't help. In fact, it often hardens their opinions and adds fuel to the idea that scientists are closed-minded or conspiratorial. As a rule, an insult greatly lessens the chance that they will listen to and consider scientific perspectives on their subjects.

Pitfalls and Pointers

More modern published editions of the ancient Egyptian *Book of the Dead* are probably bought by individuals seeking mystical wisdom than by Egyptologists. Readers looking for cosmic truth might be disappointed to find that it is a guidebook to assist the deceased in safely traversing the underworld and surviving judgement. Removed from its cultural environment, the book has little practical meaning, but if someone today can somehow find something inspirational in it, what the heck!

An Open Mind

I have read some of what archaeologists consider to be fringe literature. Why? I want to be exposed to the range of ideas floating around, and I want to have a polite and informed response when people ask me about this or that. Not only that, but once in a while these people, in their great enthusiasm, dig up something (usually in a library or museum) or point out something that is genuinely valuable for mainstream investigation.

That having been said, read the curious theories and read the response by archaeologists and other experts. Then think for yourself, and if the odd theory still convinces you, then at least you have considered the alternatives. There are a lot of archaeologists who could benefit from doing the same.

The Least You Need to Know

➤ The evidence for lost continents such as Atlantis is not particularly strong.

➤ There is no scientifically convincing evidence of visits to Earth by ancient astronauts, nor is there evidence of alien civilizations on other planets.

➤ The curse of the mummy is a silly belief, but a pretty good movie.

➤ Being open-minded but skeptical is a good approach to dealing with controversial subjects.

Chapter 25

You Mean Columbus Wasn't Here First?

In This Chapter

➤ Were there Old World visitors to the New World prior to Columbus?

➤ Were the oceans highways or barriers to ancient people?

➤ Why is this a controversial topic?

➤ The archaeological evidence

One of the basic "facts" of history routinely taught in schools was that in 1492, Christopher Columbus "discovered" America. Such a statement, however, is quite incorrect. There were millions of people living in a land first colonized by humans over 10,000 years before he arrived. And it certainly wasn't called America.

We can give credit to Columbus for being a great and bold explorer from the Europe of his day. Willing to venture where few would go, his real accomplishment was demonstrating that an ocean could be crossed and land would be met on the other side, even if it wasn't the land he thought it was. But perhaps his most important accomplishment was to open the door, a Pandora's box of sorts, to the European colonization of what they would call "The New World."

But was Columbus the first? Did the American continents remain isolated from the rest of the world but for a handful of Ice Age migrations from Asia? Did it take the "sophisticated" technology of Columbus and his three wooden boats to finally break thousands of years of isolation? We'll take a look at those questions in this chapter.

The Taboo Topic

In Mexico, great civilizations appeared that in many ways resemble those in Asia or the Old World. Is this mere coincidence, or was there ancient contact across the oceans?

In the New World, a number of artifacts and inscriptions suggest that there were other visitors, if not colonists, prior to Columbus. Are these genuine, fake, or merely misinterpreted? The subject is one of the most controversial in archaeology. Archaeologist Dr. Alice Kehoe calls it "the taboo topic."

There are several reasons why this topic is shunned, especially in American archaeology. First of all, it has been abused. Using foreign migrations to explain the beginnings of a civilization or a change in a culture was once over-done, especially in the nineteenth century. For example, the scholar G. Elliot Smith (1871–1937) proposed that all civilization originated from Egypt no matter where it was found in the world.

Pitfalls and Pointers

Anthropologist Jeffrey Goodman surprised everyone with his novel theory of origins. In his 1981 book, *American Genesis*, Goodman proposed that humans ultimately evolved in California and then spread from the North American continent. Needless to say, this is contrary to all that we seem to know and the idea has few, if any, scientific supporters.

The Diffusion Conspiracy

The subject has also been given a bad reputation by many well-meaning, over-enthusiastic amateurs who regularly make dramatic claims, most of which do not stand up to scientific scrutiny. And then, like the boy who cried wolf, when their claims really merit our attention, no one wants to listen. The archaeologists are then thought of as part of the "vast conspiracy" that wants to keep the public from "knowing the truth."

Perhaps the greatest force opposing the idea of Pre-Columbian transoceanic contact is the notion that it deprives the indigenous people of their own creativity, especially when it comes to the matter of civilizations. Anthropologists like to think of human societies as having an equal chance of developing in any which way.

Outside Influences

Some argue that to insinuate that the Olmecs or Maya or any other New World civilization must be the result of outside intervention is a slap in the face to the local people. And it doesn't help that, as we have seen more than once in this book, there is a long history of Europeans speculating that every artistic or engineering achievement by ancient Americans could only have been the result of culturally superior outsiders.

Jargon Unearthed

Diffusion is the transfer of ideas between people.

The idea of the transfer of ideas between peoples is called *diffusion*. The idea itself isn't so radical, is it? In American society, you can drive down the street in nearly any good-sized town and see a Mexican restaurant, a sushi bar, and a place that will repair your Volkswagen. Well, we have boats and airplanes, you might say, so it's easy for people today to get around and share their artifacts and ideas. Good point. Let's take a closer look.

The Oceans: Scary Waters of Doom or Super-Highways?

A big point of contention in the diffusion debate is the nature of the oceans. Were they dangerous barriers preventing interaction between the continents prior to 1492? Or were they veritable highways people could successfully traverse almost at will?

In the two centuries following Columbus, droves of European ships crossed the Atlantic to the New World, and as shipbuilding improved, even more arrived. Today the oceans are routinely crossed in great safety. A large part of the contribution Columbus made was psychological: He proved that yes, there was something out there, and you could survive the trip out and back.

The Terrifying Atlantic

So how dangerous and impenetrable are the oceans? Here are a few recent clues:

➤ Just in the last 30 years, the Atlantic has been crossed by at least three boats under six feet long, the smallest being 5 feet 4 inches.

➤ Two Frenchmen crossed the Atlantic on a sailboard in 39 days. A similar stunt was accomplished in $24^{1}/_{2}$ days.

➤ It took a man in a pedal boat 74 days to make the crossing.

➤ The Atlantic has also been crossed in a rubber life raft, a dugout canoe, kayaks, and an amphibious Jeep.

➤ In 1970, Norwegian Thor Heyerdahl successfully crossed the Atlantic on a boat with an ancient design made of papyrus.

Pitfalls and Pointers

Although experimental voyages or ocean crossings in odd ways do demonstrate that it is possible to readily traverse the seas, it doesn't prove that it actually happened in ancient times. Archaeological information will have to provide the actual evidence.

The Impenetrable Pacific

If the evidence above seems to indicate that the Atlantic Ocean poses no huge obstacles in its crossing, how about the mighty Pacific? A few examples below provide some insight.

➤ In 1947, Thor Heyerdahl and his crew left Peru on a balsa raft—the *Kon-Tiki*—designed after those in use by early South Americans. After 101 days, they made landfall in Polynesia.

➤ After the voyage of the *Kon-Tiki*, many log rafts have continued to successfully cross the Pacific to Polynesia or Australia from east to west following the natural winds and currents.

➤ A similar voyage has been made in a reed boat.

➤ In the early twentieth century, a converted Indian dugout canoe was sailed from British Columbia across the Pacific and nearly around the world.

➤ A good number of disabled drifting Asian ships have been known to make their way to North America by way of the currents. And these are just the ones that have been noted during historic times.

➤ The old Polynesians themselves were great voyagers and navigators and traveled great distances across open water.

So what do you think of the oceans now? Thor Heyerdahl, who would know, finds the oceans a genuinely hospitable place, especially in a smaller, buoyant vessel that can survive the waves. Being near the coast is the most dangerous part, he says. And if your boat is disabled or you are lost, the currents might just take you to a new place.

Diffusion or Isolation?

Those who advocate the possibility of the sharing of ideas between separated people in ancient times are called diffusionists. Diffusionists come in all varieties, from the stubbornly cautious to the absolutely reckless. On the opposite end of the spectrum are the isolationists, who argue that ancient people are perfectly capable of developing on their own, and the likelihood of significant cultural diffusion across the oceans in ancient times is minimal. Would you like to see a cat-fight? Put a few of each of these folks in a room together and get ready to turn on the hose when things get out of hand!

Jargon Unearthed

Diffusionists believe in the possibility of cultural contact and influence across the oceans in ancient times. *Isolationists* are very skeptical about this idea and argue for the independent development of ancient civilizations.

Finding the Old World in the New

There are a number of similarities between Old and New World civilizations. Here's a sample of some of the resemblances: sun-worship, writing systems, pyramids, stonecutting and transport technology, mummification, trepanation, circumcision, similarities in metallurgy and specialized ceramic art, depictions of mythical birds, felines, and serpents, sophisticated knowledge of mathematics and calendrics, and similarities in irrigation. And the list goes on.

African Olmecs

Some of the most provocative parallels are found in Central America. As I pointed out in Chapter 17, some people regard the giant carved stone heads in the Olmec culture as African in appearance. At the same time, there are groups of jade figures that look utterly Asian. And one Chinese scholar has claimed that there are readable Shang dynasty characters on some of the Olmec artifacts.

In the same region, diffusionists have also drawn interesting parallels between Maya temples and other architectural and artistic features with those in Asia. Isolationists counter that "the African look" is part of the normal range of physical variation among the local people and "the Asian look" is stylistic. The native peoples of the New World were originally from Asia, right? And as for the Shang writing? Not everyone is convinced by that claim.

Many interesting objects that have turned up from the fields of local farmers or elsewhere unfortunately lack archaeologically credible assurance of their provenience. And when something rare does turn up, alternative explanations are regularly given. In 1933, for example, while excavating an ancient site in Mexico, an archaeologist uncovered what appears to be a small Roman statue head dating to around A.D. 200 in a sealed layer. How it got there is a matter for conjecture.

Lost and Found

Lots of Roman and Greek coins have been found in North America. Unfortunately, coins are all too portable, and most of the discoveries have been random. Many old Chinese coins have been found in the Pacific Northwest, but then again, the Chinese were involved in the fur trade in historic times.

Tales of Bearded Gods

Along with the physical resemblances between things, a variety of myths are often pointed to that bear on the question of diffusion. Among them are the tales of bearded gods or travelers noted by the early Spanish explorers in both Central and South America.

Advocates of Old World visitors often see this as suggestive of earlier contact with outsiders. Some believe that such stories assisted conquistadors such as Cortes and Pizarro in their relatively easy conquest of the great Aztec and Inca civilizations. Skeptics might question their validity as filtered and perhaps distorted through the minds of the Spanish chroniclers.

Show Me Some Proof!

Trying to prove transoceanic cultural contact and influence, of course, is a very difficult task. Ideas themselves, for example, do not leave a mark in the archaeological record. Let's say some potential borrowers admire a potential donor's pottery style.

The borrower might incorporate that idea into the local pottery in a slightly altered way, filtered through the borrower's own cultural traditions. The evidence might be there, but it has been transformed. The same can be true of technology.

Setting Standards

In order to build an argument that diffusion has taken place across the oceans, there need to be some minimum standards of evidence. Here are a few:

➤ The traits suspected of being diffused must be chronologically appropriate. For example, it's difficult to build a case for transoceanic diffusion of the Egyptian step-pyramid to the Maya. They're separated in time by 3,000 years!

➤ The borrowed trait should have a history of development in the area of origin and appear without such a history in the borrower's area.

➤ A large number of such traits builds a better argument than just one or a few.

➤ And then there is the question of the actual means of contact. Did either of the peoples have worthy seacraft?

Pitfalls and Pointers

Critics will often suggest that diffusionists should not only consider the similarities between cultures, but they should examine the numerous differences as well.

An argument is strengthened if the trait in question is a matter of style rather than function. Widely separated people might make a spoon in essentially the same way because that's the shape that works best. But if it's got big mouse ears on it and little eels carved on the back, it's provocative if the same thing occurs on the other side of the ocean at the same time.

Bird Toes and Sweet Potatoes

Some of the best evidence is and will be biological: Old World plants or animals in the New World, and vice-versa. Diffusionists cite several such cases, but most can be explained away by the skeptics, who will often suggest that the plants were introduced by seeds stuck between the toes of birds, arrived inside floating gourds, or were carried along on drifting logs. The diffusionists might counter with the point that if logs and gourds can float, why can't people in a boat or a canoe float as well?

The most solid evidence of transoceanic contact is the case of the delicious sweet potato found all over Polynesia. The plant is indigenous to South America and can only be perpetuated by transplanting its tubers. The sweet potato provides definite evidence of contact between South America and the Pacific islands, but was it brought to the islands by South Americans or picked up on the continent by Polynesians? The subject is debated, of course. In the future, DNA evidence should provide new evidence that addresses all of these issues: the movement of plants, animals, and people.

Diggers

In a strange and very controversial discovery, traces of nicotine, cocaine, and hashish have been detected in the soft tissues of several ancient Egyptian mummies. All three of these substances are known as New World plants. Could there have been transoceanic trade in these materials? Is there something wrong with the laboratory testing methods? Could these or similar plants have also grown in the Old World? A satisfactory answer to this bizarre puzzle has yet to be found.

Vikings in America

Despite the loads of speculation, there is only one site in the New World that has been well-accepted by archaeologists as proof of contact between the Old and New World prior to Columbus. Old Norse sagas talked of a land called Vinland that lay to the west of Iceland and Greenland. The Norwegian Helge Ingstad studied the descriptions in the sagas, and in 1960 identified a genuine Norse site at L'Anse aux Meadow on the north coast of Newfoundland.

Eight turf structures, including three houses, were excavated, along with over twenty-five hundred artifacts. It's estimated that the little settlement probably held no more than 100 people, and it wasn't occupied for very long. Norse legends suggest that the settlers were run off by the local Indians. The site dates to about 1000 A.D., 500 years before Columbus.

Although there have been many claims of additional evidence for a Norse presence in the New World, the only other artifact that seems to have gained acceptance is a Norse coin found in Maine in a credibly dated archaeological context.

The Kensington Rune Stone

While we're on the subject, though, there have been many advocates for Viking settlement not only on the eastern coast of America, but far inland as well. Artifacts such as Viking hatchets and swords have appeared, although most have proven of dubious provenience or of recent manufacture. The most famous example is the Kensington Rune Stone. In 1898, Norwegian farmer Olaf Ohman was pulling up tree stumps on his Minnesota farm near Kensington when he discovered a large stone three feet high and sixteen inches wide.

The Kensington Rune Stone. (Courtesy of the Runestone Museum, Alexandria, Minnesota)

The stone was carved with a large runic inscription. When translated, it told the sorry tale of "eight Goths and twenty-two Norwegians" who traveled on an exploratory journey from Vinland. A group went fishing and returned home to find ten of their men dead. The date 1362 is given. After intensive study, the stone has been both hailed as a great discovery and condemned as a miserable fake. Most, but certainly not all, scholars today support the latter option.

Lost and Found

At the Makah Indian site of Ozette on the coast of Washington State, several iron blades have been found predating the time of European contact. It's been suggested that they may have been retrieved from wrecked Asian ships.

Controversial Claims

Is it a fake? Skeptics cite the use of words not compatible with the date, including the English word "dead," and the fact that the stone appears relatively unweathered. Apart from that, what are Norse sea explorers doing in inland Minnesota?

Defenders of the stone's authenticity point out that it was found within a tree's roots and that the discoverer had no economic stake in the matter, selling the stone for a few dollars. Also, they'll point to discrepancies in the writing as proof. A forger would have done better.

The Stone still remains controversial, when scholars even remember to consider it. Other Nordic runes found in

North America in places such as Oklahoma are even less convincing. Skeptics are quick to point out that the majority of the alleged discoveries are in areas where Norwegians have settled in the last couple of hundred years, like Minnesota, so ethnic pride, or at least a suitable knowledge of runes, might have inspired a forger.

Inscriptions Everywhere!

A number of people claim not only that Vikings visited America, but also just about anyone in the Old World who ever owned a boat, including the Egyptians, Carthaginians, Phoenicians, Irish, Africans, Romans, and Palestinian Jews. Although these advocates may be sincere in their efforts, their enthusiasm often gets the better of them, so that it takes very little for a few scratches on a rock wall to become a Semitic inscription written in Germanic runes.

Pitfalls and Pointers

Many people are impressed by individuals with titles—a Ph.D., for example—and put a lot of faith in such credentials. In the case of Barry Fell, his degree was in zoology, not ancient languages. On the other hand, we can't automatically dismiss scholars with expertise in several unrelated fields, even in this day of super-specialists.

Many books on this topic have been sold, and the king of this approach was Harvard professor Dr. Barry Fell. In his books, he and his loyal followers turn up inscriptions everywhere, and Fell translates them. If his findings are correct, then he's the greatest decipherer of ancient texts of all times. Unfortunately, there are numerous holes in the work, and that serves to scare away professional scholars who don't want to be tarnished by an interesting subject tainted with a dubious reputation.

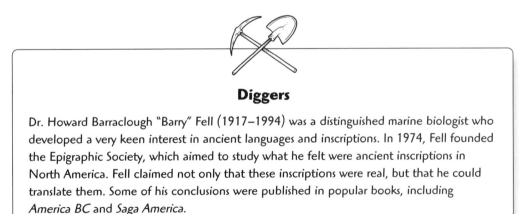

Diggers

Dr. Howard Barraclough "Barry" Fell (1917–1994) was a distinguished marine biologist who developed a very keen interest in ancient languages and inscriptions. In 1974, Fell founded the Epigraphic Society, which aimed to study what he felt were ancient inscriptions in North America. Fell claimed not only that these inscriptions were real, but that he could translate them. Some of his conclusions were published in popular books, including *America BC* and *Saga America*.

Part of the problem involved in all of this is the dependency on the expertise of others to provide the truth for you: an understandable situation when you have your own life to lead and don't have personal command of a dozen ancient languages. I, for example, am not an expert on Celtic runes, so it's difficult for me to analyze those kinds of inscriptions with any authority. On the other hand, I do know ancient Egyptian and Hebrew, and most of the discoveries involving those kinds of texts look really dubious.

The Strange Case of the Bat Creek Stone

Although I am skeptical of many of the claims for Old World inscriptions in North America, there's one that I kind of like because it's so weird. In 1889, an old undisturbed Indian mound at Bat Creek in Tennessee was excavated as part of the Smithsonian's Mound Survey Project. The project was under the direction of professional archaeologist Cyrus Thomas, although the actual work was carried out by one of Thomas's assistants, John W. Emmert. Emmert uncovered nine skeletons in the mound, one of which was laid out in the opposite direction from the other eight. Under its head was found a stone with strange scratches on it.

Lost and Found

There have been other discoveries of "Jewish artifacts" in America, including a petroglyph of the Ten Commandments on a boulder in New Mexico, several inscribed stones from mounds in Ohio (some of which are conclusively fake), and a mound in Ohio shaped like a menorah.

Thomas published his findings about the stone and identified the scratches as Cherokee script. In the 1960s some scholars looking at a picture of the stone upside down noted a strange resemblance to paleo-Hebrew. This of course made things exciting, especially when one of the country's most senior scholars of Semitic languages and writing, Professor Cyrus Gordon, gave his endorsement. Read as first or second century paleo-Hebrew, the signs can be read as something to the effect of "for Judah."

The controversial inscription of the Bat Creek Stone. (After Cyrus Thomas, "Report on the Mound Explorations." In Twelfth Annual Report of the Bureau of Ethnology *[Washington: Smithsonian, 1894], p. 394, fig. 273)*

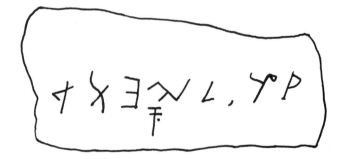

Advocates of the stone's authenticity point to the Roman persecution at that time as a historical incentive for Jews to appear in the New World. They also point to Roman-like brass bracelets found with the skeleton and fragments of wooden earspools, which have been dated with a 95 percent confidence level between the years 32 and 769 A.D.

Critics have attacked the Bat Creek Stone from all sides, and many are convinced that it is a hoax, probably involving John Emmert. It's a great scholarly debate, but if it weren't for the fact that it was part of an official Smithsonian project, it would not have received the attention it has.

A Meeting of Minds?

Although there are still many hunters and believers looking for the lost secrets that we scholars "want to cover up," there have been some refreshing changes. Since Barry Fell's death in 1994, a few of his followers have taken a good hard look at their mentor's work and have taken note of both his strengths and weaknesses.

Some have even gone so far as to try to understand why mainstream scholars will have nothing to do with them and what can be done to change that situation. I find this refreshingly positive, and a partnership between enthusiastic amateurs and scholars with a willing expertise might produce some truly exciting results.

Diggers

Some of the best work on the subject of pre-Columbian transoceanic contact is conducted by scholars of the Mormon Church (Church of Jesus Christ of Latter-Day Saints). Although their research is driven by their spiritual beliefs, their work is beneficial to anyone interested in the field. Most notable is the Foundation for Ancient Research and Mormon Studies, located in Provo, Utah.

What's It Going to Take?

We know that North America received foreign visitors at least once before Columbus, but might there have been dozens of visits involving a variety of different people? Some scholars reluctantly admit that a few Old World folk might have managed to get there, but in the big picture, it's the impact of such visitors that is most important. And most scholars will firmly assert that there was little or no impact.

What it will take is the discovery of other sites like L'Anse aux Meadow that are excavated carefully by archaeologists. Unfortunately, this amounts to finding a very small needle in an immense haystack, especially in environments that are not always conducive to the survival of the evidence that is needed.

Pitfalls and Pointers

I read a lot of the so-called fringe literature because among some of the ridiculous claims and speculations are occasionally found real gems that lead to good information. And just because one thing is fake doesn't mean that its neighbor is. In short, be careful about throwing out the baby with the bath water.

It will also take a major shift in the attitude of scholars, though, to set aside their biases and take a serious look at a provocative subject. There is hope. In Chapter 9 I mentioned the recent discoveries indicating very early seafaring in East Asia and Australia and perhaps by some of the first immigrants to America. Once the blinders are off, we very well might find that human history is far more interesting and complex than we ever imagined.

The Least You Need to Know

➤ Old World contact with New World cultures prior to the time of Columbus is a very controversial topic.

➤ Diffusionists and isolationists maintain opposite views regarding how New World civilizations might have developed.

➤ Exaggerated claims and questionable artifacts plague the discussion of this topic.

➤ So far, there is only one bona fide pre-Columbian European site in the New World—the Viking settlement of L'Anse aux Meadow in Newfoundland.

Chapter 26

The Real Dirt on Archaeology

In This Chapter

➤ What it takes to become a professional archaeologist

➤ The jobs available to archaeologists

➤ How to get a piece of the action

➤ A few parting words

If I had a nickel for everyone who's ever told me that they wanted to be an archaeologist…well, I'd have enough money to keep me in fresh trowels for a good long time. Yes, archaeology is one of those professions that seems almost too good to be true. To the typical member of the public, it all sounds like travel, glamour, and adventure. Archaeology has long had that reputation, and our fantasy friend Indiana Jones certainly enhanced it. In this chapter, we're going to explore the notion of being an archaeologist—what it entails and what the opportunities are.

So You Want to Be an Archaeologist?

Perhaps another name for this chapter could be "Reality Check." I don't want to be discouraging nor overly cynical, but since you were kind enough to buy this book, I'm going to be direct with you. And if, after you hear the "this" and the "that," the good and the bad, you still want to be an archaeologist, *go for it!* At least you'll have some idea about what might be in store.

The Temple of Gloom

First of all, as I mentioned in the first chapter, it's not all fun and games. Much of archaeology is tedious work. Digging itself can be tough and strenuous, and depending upon where the site is located, it can be brutally hot, cold and rainy, muggy, or have mosquitoes the size of crows. Given the necessity of careful recording, the work needs to be done very meticulously and requires a great deal of patience. If it's a big site and lots of dirt needs to be moved, then there are usually heavy buckets and wheelbarrows involved, and that means hard manual labor.

And if you think that sounds like fun, the excavation itself is only the tip of the iceberg. Some digs conduct their analyses in a field laboratory, while others study samples and artifacts at a facility elsewhere. The lab work can involve months of sorting bones, scrutinizing little flakes of stone, drawing maps, entering data into a computer, and numerous other tedious jobs.

Once the information is all compiled, it needs to be studied and conclusions drawn. This usually involves the preparation of scientific articles, conference papers, and a formal publication presenting the findings of the field work.

Pitfalls and Pointers

Many excavations in the Middle East take place in the summer. In Egypt's Valley of the Kings, to give you an example, temperatures can soar past 125 degrees Fahrenheit in the afternoon. Not surprisingly, many excavators begin their day's work at dawn in hopes of being finished before the heat becomes unbearable.

Nice Work If You Can Get It

So, if you have the idea of fun in the sun, hiking around and finding lost temples and such...well this can be had, but it's only a small part of the experience. Take a look at Indiana Jones. Do you see him scrutinizing pollen grains under a microscope? No. You usually see him getting into life-and-death situations and then running off with objects taken out of their context. Do you ever see him using surveying instruments or even a camera to map and record his work before the giant ball chases him out of the booby-trapped tomb? Nope.

Diggers

Just prior to World War I, several British archaeologists were involved in digging where they could not only conduct useful scientific excavations, but also spy on the activities of the enemy. The British excavation at Carchemish in northern Syria is a classic example during which David Hogarth (soon to be a senior intelligence officer during the war), T. E. Lawrence (later known as Lawrence of Arabia), and others were able to observe the activities of the Turks, who were in cahoots with the Germans.

I think we're very fortunate that life is usually not like that. I can be perfectly happy all day long without saboteurs, terrorists, and spies interfering with my archaeological work.

The fact of the matter is, there aren't a lot of jobs to be had in archaeology. It's one of those fun fields that sounds great but has fairly dismal employment opportunities. Sort of like being a ski instructor all year round.

Although archaeology is a great and interesting subject of significant worth, it only occasionally produces anything of practical economic value (see Chapter 1). It doesn't regularly produce cures for diseases or invent new products for improving the comfort or efficiency of modern life. So let's ask the basic questions: Who hires these people anyway, and what's it take to get a job in this field?

Professing: Passing the Torch

One of the few areas where archaeologists are hired is on a university faculty. What do they do? Generally speaking, they teach archaeology to produce more archaeologists, or they teach archaeology as enrichment or specialty courses for students at large, and they conduct research. In the United States, that would typically be in a Department of Anthropology. The usual minimum requirement for being hired by a University is a Ph.D. in an appropriate field.

Getting the Basics

The very first step to a Ph.D. is to achieve the basic, typically four-year, Bachelor's Degree. The process of achieving this is referred to as "undergraduate education" (as opposed to "graduate"). If you're on the archaeology track from the very beginning, you might choose a school that has an archaeology program, or that at least offers a few classes in anthropology or ancient history.

If you're interested in a particular area, ancient Egypt, for example, then you might want to enroll in Beginning Hieroglyphs or other Egyptology courses. If possible, the budding archaeologist should participate in one of the many field schools that are offered all over the country (and the world, too) to learn how to excavate while gaining college credit.

Jargon Unearthed

Ph.D. means *Doctor of Philosophy* and usually involves demonstrating comprehensive knowledge in a given field and doing original research. A Ph.D. allows you to bear the title "Dr." but is different from the kind that makes a lot of money and saves lives. Those people have an M.D., the Doctor of Medicine degree.

Grad School

Graduate school is really where it happens, though. Some can be very competitive, while others will let in anyone who has a pulse and a Bachelor's degree. The first stage of graduate work is a Master's degree, which usually takes about two years to obtain. This typically involves more advanced coursework specifically in archaeology and the writing of a research paper or thesis. To get to the next stage, a Ph.D. program, a student usually has to pass a rigorous written and sometimes oral exam.

After that, there might be more coursework and a major original research project called a dissertation. It can take anywhere from two to ten years or more to finish a dissertation, depending upon the topic, your level of motivation, and your life circumstances. Many graduate students in big universities receive stipends to do research or teach undergraduate classes, and the money provides enough for them to live on. (So, given the miserable job prospects after they graduate, quite a few take their time.)

Lost and Found

There are lots of specialists out there who know the intimate details of one little area of knowledge. There is so much information available these days that many scholars are afraid to generalize for fear of not knowing everything and getting something wrong. On the other hand, we need generalists who can put the pieces together to show us a bigger picture.

Pitfalls and Pointers

This advice has often been given to people pursuing graduate work in such arcane studies as Egyptology and Sumerology: You should either be independently wealthy or not care about money, because there is no guarantee of any sort of employment afterwards.

Get a Job

After the dissertation is approved by a committee (which can be a tricky political game), you've earned your Ph.D. Hooray! Good job, fancy pants! Now what? Maybe you're thirty-five years old and you know two things really well: You're the world's foremost expert on the cognitive aspects of the middle Bronze Age anachronistic microlithic burin cult of Lower Slovenia, and, you know how to teach Archaeology 101. Let's find some work!

There aren't a lot of job openings in the academic world. If you scrutinize the trade papers, you might find one of the few advertisements. It's a one-year replacement position at Obscure University for an archaeologist who specializes in the archaeology of Southeast Minnesota with a side interest in pre-Incan Peruvian ceramics! It sounds like an inside candidate, someone they already intend to hire, yet the university is legally obliged to go through a national search process. Even so, they get a hundred applications.

On the Tenure Track

Yes, it's hard to get a position in the academic world. One of the reasons is a thing called tenure, which guarantees that there won't be a lot of job turnover. Tenured faculty essentially have a job for life. Here is how it works. After you're initially hired, there's usually a four- to six-year probation period during which you are scrutinized for productivity, effectiveness, and a pleasing personality. If you pass, you get tenure, and if you don't, few others will want to hire you, because you were passed up.

Let's say you get a job as a faculty member. Depending on the University, you might teach anywhere from one to three classes per quarter or semester. Some schools demand that their professors emphasize research, assisted by graduate students who also teach some of the undergraduate courses. It can be a really easy life, or it can be a miserable drudge—but either way, you're employed in archaeology.

I've met a few professors who check in about twice a week, teach an hour at a time, disappear to who knows where, and make a tremendous salary. Others can be found working faithfully in their office all day long at least six days a week. Many professors work hard at writing grants to provide the funds for their research projects. With a limited amount of money available, the competition can be tight, and often it happens that when the grant isn't won, the work doesn't get done.

Community Work

Community colleges typically require only a Master's degree for their faculty, although more are hiring from a growing pool of under-employed Ph.D.'s. Many depend on part-time faculty who might teach one course every quarter to supplement their income. The teaching load is pretty heavy for a full-timer and ordinarily involves introductory classes, but there is usually no demand for research.

I taught at community colleges for a few years, and they had me teaching not only archaeology, but cultural anthropology, physical anthropology, geography, ancient history, and history of the Middle East as well. So it helps to be flexible, especially if you've got a degree in Hittitology!

Museums: Minding the Warehouse

Another source of employment is in museums. Again, not so many jobs, but they often have technical or secondary curator jobs that don't require a Ph.D. Such work might involve the study of the museum's collection, care and restoration of artifacts, dealing with the public, and all sorts of other things.

Museums can be wonderful places to work. If you don't mind staying indoors working with databases and old objects, and if libraries are your thing, then a museum might be for you. If you're artistically inclined, there's work designing new exhibits, and if you have a knack for public relations, doing promotional work for the museum might prove fun and challenging.

Museums come in all sizes, from massive institutions like the Metropolitan Museum of Art in New York City or the Smithsonian in Washington, D.C., to local historical societies in small towns. There are even a few universities that offer courses or

Pitfalls and Pointers

I recommend to my students that if they choose to pursue archaeology or some other kind of ancient studies, they should also develop a practical skill that will keep them employed while they are looking for an archaeological job. Certification for teaching is a good option, as are other widely useful occupations.

degrees in "museology," the study of all aspects of museum work, including general administration, collections management, and exhibitions.

Preceding the Bulldozers

While jobs in universities and museums are relatively scarce, yet another option often appears in the private sector: contract archaeology. Some companies specialize in doing archaeological surveys, usually in areas that are about to be developed in one way or another. Perhaps a housing project is being proposed, or a highway is being extended, or property is being considered for preservation. Whatever the reason, contract archaeologists are hired to see if there are any archaeological sites that might be affected, and if so, to develop a recommendation or plan of action to deal with them.

Cultural Resource Management

Another term for this sort of work is C.R.M., or "cultural resource management." In the U.S., there are all manner of laws on the books requiring investigation of "cultural resources"—which often means archaeological sites, especially if federal funds are being used or if work is taking place on federal lands. The simplest of surveys might involve walking a stretch of land, digging a few test holes here and there, and filing a report. If nothing is found, then the project can proceed without worrying about destroying cultural resources. If something is found, though, things might get complicated.

Finding an archaeological site in the way of a big construction project can cause incredible delays and cost lots of money. In this sense, contract archaeologists have a lot of power and need to maintain a strong sense of professional ethics. Archaeologists need to decide such questions as how significant the site is. If it's just like the 30,000 other ancient campfires or tool scatters found in the region, they might decide to remove it quickly and let the project proceed. On the other hand, if the material discovered is deemed important, then an excavation might be required, and professional archaeologists may be called in to excavate.

In some cases, the archaeologist might argue that the site is too special and that the construction project must be altered in some way to preserve all, or a portion of, the site. Occasionally archaeological sites are discovered accidentally in the midst of a work project. In that case, people from a local university or museum are sometimes called in, or a contract archaeologist might be hired.

Lost and Found

The northwest "Kona" coast of Hawaii has been a favorite place for resort developers, and CRM (cultural resource management) archaeologists have spent lots of time in the lava beds looking for archaeological sites. Consequently, ancient Hawaiian petroglyphs and trails can now be seen preserved in the midst of world-class golf courses and condos.

Salvage Archaeology

The building of dams usually provides a lot of work for contract archaeologists. Since a big dam produces a large lake behind it, the area to be flooded must be thoroughly investigated, and excavated if necessary, before it is submerged beneath the rising waters.

Contract archaeologists were also called in after the ship *Exxon Valdez* spilled 11.2 million gallons of oil into Alaskan waters in 1989. Archaeologists spent months traveling the oil-stained beaches assessing the possible damage to cultural resources there.

Some CRM firms will hire archaeologists with a Bachelor's degree or even less if the individual is competent and experienced in field work. And some government agencies have their own archaeologists on staff who do the same sort of work. Not all of the effort is out in the field, of course. A lot of time is spent doing analysis, writing reports, and putting together proposals to bid against other companies for specific jobs.

Before you write a check to help out your local under-employed archaeologist, keep in mind that Ph.D.'s in all fields are often hired by the government or private sector for their intellectual skills and research and writing abilities. If that doesn't work, they are just as qualified as the next person to flip a few burgers, join the Army, or get a regular job.

Jargon Unearthed

CRM, or Cultural Resource Management, involves the location, identification, assessment, and possible excavation or conservation of cultural resources, including archaeological remains, both historic and prehistoric.

"May I take your order please?" The author serving it up at "Glyph-Burger." Achieving a degree in archaeology by no means guarantees employment in that field. (Courtesy of Josh Miller)

Getting a Piece of the Action Anyway

Did I scare you with the above? Good. It's better to be informed with a little jolt of reality than to stumble blindly and idealistically into the dark well of disappointment. I've met a good number of Ph.D.'s, some approaching retirement age, who have never been able to achieve a full career in archaeology or ancient studies, and a few are disappointed and bitter.

On the other hand, far be it from me to be a dream-squelcher! If you're willing to accept the negative employment possibilities, then by all means *go for it*. Just know what you might be getting into. If it works out, great. And if it doesn't, don't worry about it. Be prepared and make the best of it.

Given the limited employment opportunities, you might be able to argue that it's even better to be an amateur archaeologist than a professional. That way you can participate to the extent that you like, without having to deal with the economic uncertainties and much of the politics.

Volunteering Your Services

Do you want to go on a dig? There are numerous opportunities for that! Apart from the many field schools that are offered by universities, there are volunteer programs that usually accept applicants of all ages and walks of life. Such programs can be found at a number of sites in North America, Europe, and elsewhere in the world.

Israel is well-known for its use of volunteers on dozens of digs each summer. The digs there, in fact, depend on hundreds of volunteers who pay their own expenses to work in an exciting environment. The volunteers are well supervised by professionals or graduate students, and often an educational program is provided, including field trips. Some amateur archaeologists have become sufficiently competent that they are allowed to supervise some of the field work, and sometimes they are promoted to bona fide staff members.

Diggers

One of the more experienced archaeologists in Israel is neither a full-time professional nor an Israeli, but an American man named Gary Lindstrom but known to all as "Termite." Termite began his archaeological career as a volunteer over twenty-five years ago, and his abilities are now so highly respected that he is sought after to serve on digs. When he's not digging during the summer, he runs a termite extermination business in California.

Participating on a dig is also a great way to learn a lot about yourself. For some it might be a first opportunity to do serious manual labor, deal with unfamiliar places and living arrangements, or tolerate others in close quarters. Believe me when I tell you that not everyone is suited for field work. Here are a just a few desirable traits. You should be:

➤ Tolerant of grungy working conditions and able to get along with whomever.

➤ Willing to work hard, sleep in weird places, and eat what food is given to you.

➤ Sincerely interested in the local people and environment and able to demonstrate cultural sensitivity.

➤ Able to take orders cheerfully and carry out instructions carefully.

➤ Able to maintain a good sense of humor.

➤ Willing to listen and learn.

Some countries do not like amateurs or volunteers on archaeological projects. They want professionals dealing with their cultural treasures. And some archaeologists have limited funds or can't otherwise accommodate the flood of requests from the public wishing to participate on their projects.

Here's a big tip. If you can develop a special skill that is very useful on an archaeological dig, you might become needed, and even sought after. Such skills include surveying, the ability to make accurate drawings of artifacts, photography, and conservation. If you're good enough, you might get your expenses paid or even a small salary, which then makes you, in fact, a professional.

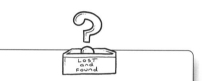

Lost and Found

A friend of mine was an attorney in Los Angeles specializing in immigration cases. His real love, though, is archaeology. In his forties, he decided to pursue his dream and went to London for a year to study artifact conservation. Now he's having the time of his life and is in demand as a paid professional on a variety of digs.

Have Some Fun

Here are some things you can do to enjoy archaeology as a non-professional. (See Appendix C for some more details.)

➤ Read archaeology books and buy archaeology books. Thank you for buying this one.

➤ Subscribe to an appropriate magazine.

➤ Attend lectures and museum exhibits.

➤ Keep an eye out for archaeological and historical programs found on educational television channels.

➤ Join local or national archaeological societies or museum associations.

➤ Participate in an archaeological field school or volunteer program.

317

➤ Offer your abilities to your local archaeologist as a volunteer assistant. They might say no, but then again, they might appreciate your help.

➤ Support your favorite projects with your money, assistance, or good wishes.

➤ Get on out there. Travel and visit the many archaeological sites and museums worldwide. There's nothing like seeing the real thing!

Happy archaeologists and volunteers on a dig in the Canary Islands.

See You Later

In closing, I hope you have enjoyed learning a little about lost civilizations and archaeology. As I explained in the introduction, we can only scratch the surface in a book such as this. In fact, whole books have been written about some of the things we had to cover in a paragraph. If anything here caught your interest, check out Appendix B for some suggestions for further reading, and Appendix C for even more resources.

I hope you had as much fun reading this book as I had writing it. The study of ancient civilizations is interesting whether you're a professional or an amateur. It's fun whether there's ancient dirt under your fingernails or you have your face buried in an archaeology magazine.

And do you know what? It's going to get even more interesting in the future, as we find more ways to make sense of the evidence. And for all of you deadbeats who think it's all been found, keep thinking that way, because guys like me and a lot of other adventurous folk will be more than happy to keep on looking where you won't! Good luck to all of you as you dig through life!

The Least You Need to Know

➤ Professional archaeologists are typically employed at universities, museums, contract firms, or government agencies.

➤ The job prospects in all of these areas are not great.

➤ There are many excellent resources and opportunities for the non-professional to enjoy and participate in archaeology.

➤ Whether you're an amateur or professional, the study of lost civilizations and archaeology is still one of the most interesting things around!

Technical Talk

A.D. *Anno Domini*, "the year of our Lord." The number of years since the birth of Jesus.

absolute dating Dating methods that attempt to obtain dates in calendar years.

Afrocentrism A perspective on a given subject from an African point of view, as opposed to Eurocentrism, which is a perspective from a European point of view.

alphabet A system of writing in which (ideally) a single symbol stands for a single sound. The word is derived from the names of the first two letters of the Greek alphabet, "alpha" and "beta."

anthropology The study of humans. In the United States, at least, it is divided into four sub-disciplines. Cultural anthropology studies all cultural aspects of living or recently living peoples, while archaeology addresses the human past. Physical anthropologists study the physical nature of human beings, including differences and similarities within and among different groups. They also study primates and human evolution. Linguistics is the study of human languages.

archaeoastronomy The study of how people in the past understood and utilized astronomy.

archaeological record The physical remains of the past are in general referred to as the archaeological record.

archaeological site Anywhere that artifacts or other traces of human activity have been found.

archaeology The interdisciplinary study of the human past. It attempts to reconstruct and explain past human behavior primarily by means of the careful analysis of surviving material remains.

archaeometry The scientific analysis of archaeological materials.

artifact   Anything used, manufactured, or modified by human beings.

assemblage   A group of artifacts found together.

Assyriology   The study of ancient Mesopotamia as practiced by Assyriologists.

B.C.   "Before Christ"—refers to the number of years before the birth of Jesus. B.C.E., or "Before the Common Era," refers to the same time period as B.C.

B.P.   "Before Present"—the number of years prior to the present. Essentially, it means "years ago."

Beringia   The land bridge connecting Asia and North America exposed during the Ice Age.

Bronze Age   A time period in a given culture during which bronze is used.

C.E.   "Common Era"—the equivalent of A.D., the number of years since the birth of Jesus.

Chalcolithic   A time in a culture's history when copper has become part of the "stone age" technological ensemble.

characterization   The science of identifying unique characteristics within artifacts that allow them to be traced to their original source of material.

circa   "around that time." Usually abbreviated "ca." or "c."

city-state   An independent political entity with a city as its core.

civilization   A historically complicated term used to describe a state of cultural complexity. Usually used today to describe a "complex society."

classics   The study of the civilizations of ancient Greece and Rome is called "classics" and its practitioners are "classicists."

complex society   A human society characterized by such features as class, wealth, and status differences, political, economic, and religious elites, craft specialists, relatively large populations, monumental architecture, and writing.

context   The complete situation in which an artifact is found. Where? In what? With what?

coprolites   Surviving examples of old dung.

cultural resource management ("CRM")   The professional location, identification, assessment, and possible excavation or conservation of cultural resources, including archaeological remains, both historic and prehistoric.

cuneiform   Wedged-shaped scripts, typically impressed into clay, which were used to write such languages as Sumerian, Akkadian, Elamite, and Old Persian.

dendrochronology   An absolute dating method based on the study of annual rings formed in trees.

diffusion   The transfer of ideas between people.

diffusionists   Those who believe in the possibility of cultural contact and influence across the oceans in ancient times.

DNA (deoxyribonucleic acid)   The chemical genetic code housed in our chromosomes.

Egyptology   The study of ancient Egypt as practiced by Egyptologists.

environment of deposition   The location and physical conditions in which the physical remains of human behavior are deposited.

experimental archaeology   Attempts to understand the past by replicating or recreating ancient technology and events.

feature   A non-portable artifact.

flintknapping   The art of creating stone tools.

geoarchaeologists   Archaeologists who concern themselves with the soils and sediments found in the archaeological record and what it all might mean.

geoglyphs   Designs constructed on the surface of the earth.

Hellenistic   An adjective meaning "Greek," from the word *Hellas,* meaning "Greece" in Greek.

hieroglyphs   A kind of writing that uses pictures for its symbols, such as those used in Egypt and by the Maya.

historic period   A time period in a given culture in which written documents are available.

history   What happened in the past, or a written description of the same.

Hittitology   The study of the Hittites as studied by Hittitologists.

Holocene   Our present geological epoch, beginning 10,000 years ago; the latter part of the Quaternary period.

Homo erectus   The biological term assigned to a pre-modern species of *Homo* that spread out of Africa ca. 1.8 million years ago.

Homo sapiens neanderthalensis   "Neanderthals." A burly sub-species of *Homo sapiens* that went extinct 30,000 years ago.

Homo sapiens sapiens   The biological term assigned to the present living human species.

Indo-European languages   A language family that includes Sanskrit, Greek, Latin, English, Persian, Turkish, German, and Spanish among others.

in situ   The term used to describe artifacts in the place in which they were found.

323

Iron Age   A time period in a given culture during which iron is used, typically following the use of bronze.

isolationists   Those who argue for the independent development of ancient civilizations. They are typically skeptical of diffusionists.

lithics   Stone tools.

maize   A plant that Americans call corn.

maritime or **nautical archaeology**   The study of all aspects of the sea and ancient seafaring.

megalithic   Refers to ancient constructions involving the use of large stones.

Mesolithic   A period in certain cultures where there was an extensive period between the end of the Ice Age and the adoption of agriculture. During this period, groups adapted to the new environments in novel and creative ways.

monotheism   A belief in one god, as opposed to polytheism, a belief in many gods.

mtDNA   A type of DNA inherited unmixed from one's maternal line that can provide evidence of long-term inheritance.

Neolithic   A period in a given culture when the hunting and gathering lifestyle has given way to permanent settlements and the tending of plants and animals. Stone tools are still widely used, and pottery and other new kinds of tools reflect the new way of life.

New World   The continents of North and South America.

Old World   The inhabited continents known to Europeans prior to the time of Columbus: Europe, Africa, and Asia.

osteology   The study of bones.

ostraca (singular "**ostracon**")   Pieces of pottery or flakes of limestone that were used as writing surfaces.

Paleoindian   A term often used for the earliest people in the New World.

Paleolithic, or "**Stone Age**"   As a lifestyle, it is characterized by the use of stone tools and hunting and gathering. As a time period, it spans from about 2 million years to 10,000 years ago, roughly corresponding to the Pleistocene epoch.

palynology   The study of pollen, practiced by palynologists.

papyri (sing. "**papyrus**")   Documents written on papyrus paper. A papyrologist is someone who studies such documents.

Ph.D.   Doctor of Philosophy, an advanced academic degree.

Pleistocene   A geologic period also known as the Ice Age, beginning around 2.4 million years ago and lasting until about 10,000 years ago. Part of the Quaternary Period.

polis (pl. "**poleis**")   A Greek city-state.

potassium-argon dating   A method for dating that uses volcanic rocks or tuffs as its subject material. Good for dates on materials older than 50,000 years.

Precolumbian   In the New World, the time prior to the year A.D. 1492, when the first voyage of Columbus opened the way for European exploration and colonization of North and South America.

prehistory   A time period in a given culture prior to the occurrence of writing.

provenience   The specific archaeological context in which an object is found. A variation of this same word is "provenance."

Quaternary   Our present geologic period. The Quaternary began around 2.4 million years ago and is divided into two epochs: the Pleistocene and the Holocene.

radiocarbon dating   An absolute dating technique based on the radioactive decay of carbon-14 absorbed by living organisms. Used primarily on materials between 400 and 50,000 years old.

relative dating   Dating methods that can determine that one thing is older than another, but not specifically how much older.

remote-sensing   Techniques used for the location and study of buried archaeological material; these techniques leave sub-surface remains undisturbed.

runologist   Someone who studies runes.

sampling   Examining only portions of an archaeological site in order to gain a representative view of its whole.

scientific method   A research method that involves formulating an idea to explain a given phenomena (a "hypothesis") and then using deduction to test the validity of the idea.

sediments   Dirt.

Semitic languages   A language family that includes Akkadian, Arabic, Aramaic, Hebrew, and Phoenician.

seriation   The dating of associated groups of objects based on changing styles.

site-formation processes   Processes that create the physical nature of the archaeological site. These can be of both natural and human origin.

soils   The uppermost life-supporting layers of sediments.

stele (pl. "**stelae**")   A standing stone slab, often with carved decorations and/or an inscription.

stratigraphy   The study of layers or "strata" (sing. "**stratum**") in the earth.

structure   A term referring to buildings.

Sumerologist   A specialist who studies ancient Sumer.

swidden agriculture   A method for growing crops that involves the preparation of fields by first cutting down and then burning the overgrowth. It is also know as "slash and burn."

taphonomy   The study of what happens to the remains of living things after death.

tell   A mound that is the accumulated debris of human occupation. Tells are commonly found as archaeological sites throughout the Near East.

thermoluminescence   A dating technique that determines age by measuring the light intensity of accumulated released electrons. Especially useful for dating pottery, this method is ideal for artifacts ranging in date from just a few hundred years to several hundred thousand years, its range being far greater than that of carbon-14.

trepanation   The surgical removal of a piece of bone from the cranium.

typology   The organization of artifacts based on their similarity.

underwater archaeology   Any archaeology that takes place underwater.

zooarchaeologist, **archaeozoologist**, or **faunal analyst**   A specialist who studies the remains of animals, typically bones, found in archaeological sites.

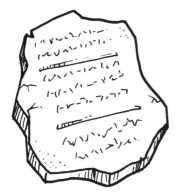

Exploring on Your Own: A Select Bibliography

Much of the study of lost civilizations is pursued in the world of books, so I hope you like to read. The story of the past is built piece by piece by assembling the work of lots of scholars. Below is a list of books I think are quite good that will provide a nice foundation for your further education on the subject.

General

Ashmore, Wendy and Robert J. Sharer. *Discovering Our Past: A Brief Introduction to Archaeology*. Mountain View: Mayfield, 1995.

Fagan, Brian, ed. *The Oxford Companion to Archaeology*. New York: Oxford Univ. Press, 1996.

———. *In the Beginning: An Introduction to Archaeology*. New York: Harper Collins, 1993.

Hester, Thomas R., Harry J. Shafer, and Kenneth L. Feder. *Field Methods in Archaeology*. Mountain View: Mayfield, 1997.

Renfrew, Colin and Paul Bahn. *Archaeology: Theory, Methods and Practice*. New York: Thames and Hudson, 1996.

Webster, David L., Susan T. Evans, and William T. Sanders. *Out of the Past: An Introduction to Archaeology*. Mountain View: Mayfield, 1993.

Humans: The Early Days

Bahn, Paul. *Journey Through the Ice Age*. Berkeley: Univ. of California Press, 1997.

Fagan, Brian. *People of the Earth: An Introduction to World Prehistory*. New York: Harper Collins, 1995.

Feder, Kenneth L. *The Past in Perspective: An Introduction to Human Prehistory*. Mountain View: Mayfield, 1996.

Lewin, Roger. *Bones of Contention: Controversies in the Search for Human Origins.* New York: Simon and Schuster, 1987.

Wenke, Robert J. *Patterns in Prehistory.* New York: Oxford Univ., 1999.

History of Archaeology and Great Discoveries

Bahn, Paul G., ed. *The Cambridge Illustrated History of Archaeology.* Cambridge: Cambridge Univ. Press, 1996.

Ceram, C. *Gods, Graves, and Scholars: The Story of Archaeology.* New York: Alfred Knopf, 1952.

Daniel, Glyn. *A Short History of Archaeology.* Thames and Hudson, 1981.

Fagan. Brian, ed. *Eyewitness to Discovery.* New York: Oxford Univ. Press. 1996

Stiebing, William H., Jr. *Uncovering the Past: A History of Archaeology.* New York, Oxford Univ. Press, 1993.

The Ancient Near East

Aldred, Cyril. *The Egyptians,* rev. ed. London: Thames and Hudson, 1984

Baines, John and Jaromir Malek. *Atlas of Ancient Egypt.* New York: Facts on File, 1980.

Crawford, Harriet. *Sumer and the Sumerians.* Cambridge: Cambridge Univ. Press, 1991.

Finegan, Jack. *The Archaeology of the New Testament.* Princeton: Princeton Univ. Press, 1992.

Fritz, Volmar. *An Introduction to Biblical Archaeology.* Sheffield: Sheffield Academic Press, 1994.

Lloyd, Seton. *The Archaeology of Mesopotamia: From the Old Stone Age to the Persian Conquest,* rev. ed. London: Thames and Hudson, 1984.

MacQueen, J. G. *The Hittites.* New York: Thames and Hudson, 1986.

Oates, Joan. *Babylon.* New York: Thames and Hudson, 1986.

Quirke, Stephen and Jeffrey Spencer, eds. *The British Museum Book of Ancient Egypt.* London: British Museum, 1992.

Reeves, C. N. and Richard Wilkinson. *The Complete Valley of the Kings.* New York: Thames and Hudson, 1996.

Reeves, C. N. *The Complete Tutankhamun: The King, the Tomb, the Royal Treasure.* New York: Thames and Hudson, 1990.

Roaf, Michael. *Cultural Atlas of Mesopotamia and the Ancient Near East.* New York: Facts On File, 1990.

Rogerson, J. W. *Atlas of the Bible.* New York: Facts on File, 1985.

Europe and the Mediterranean

Biers, William R. *The Archaeology of Greece: An Introduction*. Ithaca: Cornell Univ. Press, 1996.

Boardman, John, Jasper Griffin, and Oswyn Murray. *The Oxford History of the Classical World*. New York: Oxford Univ. Press, 1986.

Chadwick, John. *The World of the Mycenaeans*. Cambridge: Cambridge Univ. Press, 1976.

Chippendale, Christopher. *Stonehenge Complete*. Ithaca: Cornell Univ. Press, 1987.

Cornell, Tim and John Matthews. *Atlas of the Roman World*. New York: Facts on File, 1982.

Graham-Campbell, James, ed. *Cultural Atlas of the Viking World*. New York: Facts on File, 1994.

Grant, Michael. *The Visible Past: Recent Archaeological Discoveries of Greek and Roman History*. New York: Scribners, 1990.

Kitto, H. D. F. *The Greeks*. New York: Penguin, 1991.

Levi, Peter. *Atlas of the Greek World*. New York: Facts on File, 1981.

Powell, T. G. *The Celts*. New York: Thames and Hudson, 1983.

Scarre, Chris. *Chronicle of the Roman Emperors*. New York: Thames and Hudson, 1995.

Africa, Asia, and the Pacific

Barnes, Gina Lee. *China, Korea, and Japan: The Rise of Civilization in East Asia*. London: Thames and Hudson, 1993.

Bellwood, Peter. *The Polynesians: Prehistory of an Island People,* rev. ed. London: Thames and Hudson, 1987.

Connab, Graham. *African Civilizations: Precolonial Cities and States in Tropical Africa: An Archaeological Perspective*. New York: Cambridge Univ. Press, 1987.

Fairservis, Walter A. *The Roots of Ancient India*. New York, Macmillan, 1971.

Finney, Ben. et al. *Voyage of Rediscovery: A Cultural Odyssey through Polynesia*. Berkeley, Univ. of California, 1994.

Heyerdahl, Thor. *Easter Island: The Mystery Solved*. New York: Random House, 1989.

Oliver, Roland. *The African Experience*. New York: Harper Collins, 1992.

Phillipson, David W. *African Archaeology,* 2d ed. Cambridge: Cambridge Univ. Press, 1993.

Van Tilburg, Jo Anne. *Easter Island: Archaeology, Ecology and Culture*. London: British Museum, 1994.

Welsby, Derek A. *The Kingdom of Kush: The Napatan and Meroitic Empires*. London: British Museum Press, 1996.

New World

Coe, Michael. *Mexico: From the Olmecs to the Aztecs*. New York: Thames and Hudson, 1994.

———. *The Maya*. New York: Thames and Hudson, 1999.

Coe, Michael, D. Snow, and E. Benson. *Atlas of Ancient America*. New York: Facts on File, 1980.

Fagan, Brian. *Ancient North America*. New York: Thames and Hudson, 1995.

———. *Kingdoms of Gold, Kingdoms of Jade: The Americas Before Columbus*. New York: Thames and Hudson, 1991.

Folsom, Franklin and Mary Folsom. *America's Ancient Treasures*. Univ. of New Mexico Press, 1993.

Jennings, Jesse D. *Prehistory of North America*. Mountain View: Mayfield, 1989.

Moseley, Michael E. *The Inca and Their Ancestors: The Archaeology of Peru*. New York: Thames and Hudson, 1992.

Schele, Linda and David A. Freidel. *A Forest of Kings: The Untold Story of the Ancient Maya*. New York: William Morrow, 1990.

Controversial Subjects

Feder, Kenneth L. *Frauds, Myths, and Mysteries: Science and Pseudoscience in Archaeology*. Toronto: Mayfield, 1996.

Fingerhut, Eugene R. *Explorers of Pre-Columbian America?* Claremont: Regina, 1994.

Greenfield, Jeanette. *The Return of Cultural Treasures*. Cambridge: Cambridge Univ. Press, 1995.

Heyerdahl, Thor. *Early Man and the Ocean*. Garden City: Doubleday, 1979.

Williams, Stephen. *Fantastic Archaeology: The Wild Side of North American Prehistory*. Philadelphia: Univ. of Pennsylvania, 1991.

Ancient Writing

Gaur, Albertine. *A History of Writing*. London: British Library, 1984.

Deuel, Leo. *Testaments of Time: The Search for Lost Manuscripts and Records*. New York: Alfred Knopf, 1965.

Robinson, Andrew. *The Story of Writing*. London: Thames and Hudson, 1995.

Schmandt-Besserat, Denise. *How Writing Came About*. Austin: Univ. of Texas, 1997.

I also recommend the following volumes in the *Reading the Past* series published by the British Museum Press and Univ. of California Press:

Bonfante, Larissa. *Etruscan*. 1990

Chadwick, John. *Linear B and Related Scripts*. 1987

Cook, B. F. *Greek Inscriptions*. 1987

Davies, W. V. *Egyptian Hieroglyphs*. 1987

Dilke, O. A. W. *Mathematics and Measurement*. 1987

Healey, John F. *The Early Alphabet*. 1990

Houston, S. D. *Maya Glyphs*. 1989

Page, R. I. *Runes*. 1987

Walker, C. B. F. *Cuneiform*. 1987

A collection of the above is found in one volume under the title *Ancient Writing from Cuneiform to the Alphabet*, 1991.

Special Topics

Brothwell, Don. *Digging Up Bones*. Ithaca: Cornell Univ. Press, 1981.

———. *The Bogman and the Archaeology of People*. Cambridge: Harvard Univ. Press, 1987.

Cole, John. *Experimental Archaeology*. New York: Academic Press, 1979.

Delgado, James P. *Encyclopedia of Underwater Archaeology*. New Haven: Yale Univ. Press, 1997.

Lambert, Joseph B. *Traces of the Past: Unravelling the Secrets of Archaeology Through Chemistry*. Reading: Perseus, 1997.

The British Museum and University of California presses have published an excellent series of little books on specific archaeological topics under the theme *Interpreting the Past*:

Bowman, Sheridan. *Radiocarbon Dating*. 1990.

Burnett, Andrew. *Coins*. 1991.

Chamberlain, Andrew. *Human Remains*. 1994.

Collon, Dominique. *Near Eastern Seals*. 1990.

Greene, Kevin. *Roman Pottery*. 1992.

Ogden, Jack. *Ancient Jewelry*. 1992.

Rackham, James. *Animal Bones*. 1994.

For some lovely fictional archaeological entertainment, I highly recommend the books by mystery novelist "Elizabeth Peters," who writes a series of books featuring the character Amelia Peabody, a Victorian-era Egyptologist. In real life, Elizabeth Peters is Barbara Mertz, a respected scholar with a Ph.D. in Egyptology. She has also written two superb introductory books about ancient Egypt called *Red Land, Black Land* and *Temples, Tombs and Hieroglyphs*.

For true adventure, the exciting and inspirational expedition books of Thor Heyerdahl are hard to beat. These include *Kon-Tiki*, *Aku-Aku*, *The Ra Expeditions*, and *The Tigris Expedition*.

Resources for Further Exploration

Below are listed a number of other resources, besides books, that can help you pursue your interest in lost civilizations. These include specialty magazines and Internet websites, along with information on opportunities for participating. A word of caution about the Internet sites: Web sites come and go in the anarchist world of the Information Highway. Sometimes they change addresses or disappear altogether. The Web site addresses listed below were current as of early January 1999.

Magazines

Archaeology Magazine is published by the Archaeological Institute of America. *Archaeology* provides well-illustrated articles and news on archaeological sites and subjects worldwide and is highly recommended.

Contact:
Archaeology, Subscription Service
P.O. Box 469025
Escondido, CA 92046-9659 USA
Tel. (877) 275-9782

For a location where *Archaeology* is sold in your area, call:

(800) 221-3148 (from within the U.S.)

American Archaeology is published by The Archaeological Conservancy, a fine organization that operates with the goal of preserving archaeological sites. The magazine comes out four times a year and covers interesting subjects throughout the Americas.

Contact:
American Archaeology
The Archaeological Conservancy
5301 Central Avenue N.E., Suite 1218
Albuquerque, NM 87108-9899
Tel. (505) 266-1540

Current Archaeology deals mostly with the fascinating world of British archaeology.

Contact:
Current Archaeology
9 Nassington Road, London NW3 2TX U.K.
Tel. 44-171-435-7517
Web site: **www.compulink.co.uk/~archaeology/**

DIG is a new magazine designed for children aged 8 to 13 and is produced by the Archaeological Institute of America, publishers of *Archaeology Magazine.*

Contact:
DIG
P.O. Box 469039
Escondido, CA 92046-9607

Discovering Archaeology Magazine has recently appeared and covers topics from around the globe.

Contact:
Discovering Archaeology Magazine
1205 N. Oregon St.
El Paso, TX 79902
Web site: **www.discoveringarchaeology.com**

Near Eastern Archaeology (formerly *Biblical Archaeologist*) is produced by the American School for Oriental Research. As the title suggests, it deals with the Near East, land of the Bible. They often have theme issues.

Contact:
Membership/Subscriber Services
P.O. Box 15399
Atlanta, GA 30333-0399
Web site: **www.asor.org/BA/BAHP.html**

Biblical Archaeology Review deals with the rarely boring world of Biblical archaeology. Along with the latest news and great articles by important scholars, it regularly contains sassy commentary on a variety of controversial issues and occasionally takes an activist stance.

Contact:
Biblical Archaeology Review
c/o Biblical Archaeology Society
4710 41st Street NW
Washington, D.C. 20016
Phone: (800) 221-4644

KMT: A Modern Journal of Ancient Egypt. Is Ancient Egypt your thing? Then KMT will give you your fix four times a year, with loads of news and great articles written by scholars.

Contact:
KMT Communications
1531 Golden Gate Avenue
San Francisco, CA 94115
Web site: **www.egyptology.com/kmt/**

Minerva is a magazine produced in Britain. Its coverage of archaeological subjects is broad, and it contains a lot of information from the world of antiquities dealers.

Contact:
Minerva Magazine
14 Old Bond Street
London W1X 4JL, U.K.

From the people who bring you *Biblical Archaeology Review* comes *Archaeology Odyssey*, which covers the Mediterranean world, including Greece, Rome, and the Near East.

Contact:
Archaeology Odyssey
P.O. Box 7654
Red Oak, IA 51591-2654

National Geographic has always been an excellent source of beautifully illustrated articles on archaeological discoveries.

Contact:
National Geographic Society
P. O. Box 98012
Washington, D.C. 20077-9762
Web site: **www.nationalgeographic.com**

Societies

There are many archaeological and historical societies of all sizes. Check with your local archaeologist or museum for further information. Some can be found listed on the following Internet Web site:

"Directory of Archaeological Societies and Newsletters"
Web site: **www.serv.net/~mallard/hr/archsoc.html**

Here are some of the larger organizations:

Archaeological Institute of America
656 Beacon Street
Boston, MA 02215-2010
Web site: **www.archaeological.org**

The Archaeological Conservancy
5301 Central Avenue N.E., Suite 1218
Albuquerque, NM 87108-9899

Egypt Exploration Society
3 Doughty Mews
London WC1N 2PG U.K.
Tel: 44-171-142-1880
Web site: **britac3.britac.ac.uk/institutes/egypt/index.html**

Society for American Archaeology
900 Second St. NE, Suite 12
Washington, D.C. 20002
Web site: **www.saa.org**

American Research Center in Egypt
30 East 20 Street, Suite 401
New York, NY 10003
Web site: **www.arce.org**

Opportunities to Participate

Do you want a piece of the action? Take a look at these resources:

The Archaeological Institute of America produces an annual *Archaeological Fieldwork Opportunities Bulletin* that is available for purchase. It lists field schools and volunteer opportunities along with other useful information.

Order your copy from:

AIA Order Department
For telephone orders: (800) 228-0810 or (319) 589-1000
Web site: **www.archaeological.org/publications/index.html**

The University of California, Los Angeles, maintains an Internet Web site that lists "Archaeological Fieldwork Opportunities." Check it out:

Web site: **sscnet.ucla.edu/ioa/afs/testpit.html**

Also, in their January/February issue, the magazine *Biblical Archaeology Review* usually publishes a list of excavations soliciting summer volunteers to work in Israel and sometimes Jordan. These excavations are a great way to learn how to dig under supervision in an exciting region of the world. See the information above for the magazine.

Both *Earthwatch International* and the *University of California Research Expeditions* are non-profit organizations which advertise volunteer programs that help support scientific research in a variety of fields, including archaeology. Here's how to contact them:

Earthwatch International
680 Mt. Auburn St.
P.O. Box 9104
Watertown, MA 02272
Tel: (800) 776-0188
Web site: **gaia.earthwatch.org**

University of California Research Expeditions Program
University Research Expeditions Program
University of California
One Shields Avenue
Davis, CA 95616
Tel: (530) 752-0692
Web site: **urep.ucdavis.edu**

The *Crow Canyon Archaeological Center* in Cortez, Colorado, and the *Center for American Archaeology* in Kampsville, Illinois, offer an excellent variety of archaeological educational programs, including excavations. To find out more:

Crow Canyon Archaeological Center
23390 Road K
Cortez, CO 81321 USA
Tel: (800) 422-8975, or (970) 565-8975
Web site: **www.crowcanyon.org**

Center for American Archaeology
Box 366
Kampsville, IL 62053 USA
Tel: (618) 653-4316
Web site: **www.caa-archeology.org**

The National Park Service in the United States has a program called *Passport in Time*, which provides opportunities to work on historic preservation and archaeological projects. A bulletin listing these opportunities, the *PIT Traveler*, is published twice a year.

Contact:
Passport in Time Clearing House
P.O. Box 31315
Tuscon, AZ 85751-1315
Tel: (520) 722-2716
Web site: **www.swanet.org/pit99.html**

Internet Web Sites

Here are a few of the many Web sites to be found on the Internet. There are far too many to list here, so I've selected a few of the more general sites with lots of links to others, along with a small sample of some sites that address specific interests. Go surfing; follow some links and hopefully they'll take you to some good and fascinating places.

General Sites

WWWorld of Archaeology
www.archaeology.org/wwwarky/wwwarky.html

Ancient World Web
www.julen.net/aw/

Ancient World Cultures
eawc.evansville.edu/index.htm

Anthropology in the News
www.tamu.edu/anthropology/news.html

Archaeology on the Net
www.serve.com/archaeology/

ArchNet
archnet.uconn.edu

Variety Show!

Ancient Mesoamerican Civilizations
www.angelfire.com/ca/humanorigins/index.html

Archaeological Resource Guide for Europe
odur.let.rug.nl/arge/

Ancient Scripts
alumni.eecs.berkeley.edu/~lorentz/Ancient_Scripts/

Archaeological Parks in the U.S.
www.uark.edu/misc/aras/

Archaeology in Fiction Bibliography
www.tamu.edu/anthropology/fiction.html

The Atrium
web.idirect.com/~atrium/

BA Guide to U.K. Archaeology on the Internet
www.britarch.ac.uk/info/uklinks.html

Classics and Mediterranean Archaeology
rome.classics.lsa.umich.edu/welcome.html

Easter Island Home Page
www.netaxs.com/~trance/rapanui.html

Egyptology Resources—Cambridge
www.newton.cam.ac.uk/egypt/index.html

Exploring Ancient World Cultures
eawc.evansville.edu

A Guide to Underwater Archaeology Resources on the Internet
www.pophaus.com/underwater/

Jennifer's Archaeology Website
arch.hutchey.com

LINKS to the Past (National Park Service)
www.nps.gov/crweb1/

The Lithics Site
wings.buffalo.edu/anthropology/lithics.html

NativeTech: Native American Technology and Art
www.nativeweb.org/NativeTech

Prehistory of Alaska
www.nps.gov/akso/akarc/

Rabbit in the Moon (Maya language and other resources)
www.halfmoon.org

Reeder's Egypt Page
www.egyptology.com/reeder/

Southwestern Archaeology
www.swanet.org

Unconventional Archaeology
artalpha.anu.edu.au/web/arc/resources/cult/cult1.htm

The *author*'s own Web site can be found at:
www.plu.edu/~ryandp/

Index